Career English for Nurses

Career English for Nurses

Fourth Edition

Selva Rose
formerly, Reader
College of Nursing
Christian Medical College, Vellore

Orient BlackSwan

CAREER ENGLISH FOR NURSES, FOURTH EDITION

ORIENT BLACKSWAN PRIVATE LIMITED

Registered Office
3-6-752 Himayatnagar, Hyderabad 500 029, Telangana, India
Email: centraloffice@orientblackswan.com

Other Offices
Bengaluru, Bhopal, Chennai, Guwahati, Hyderabad, Jaipur, Kolkata, Lucknow, Mumbai, New Delhi, Noida, Patna, Visakhapatnam

First published 1996
Reprinted 1997, 2004
Second edition 2006
Reprinted 2006, 2009, 2010, 2011, 2012, 2013
Third edition 2015
Fourth edition 2016
Reprinted 2016, 2017, 2019 (twice)

031008

Cover and book design

ISBN 978 81 250 6385 8

Illustrated by
Mithila Maniketh and Aparna Gopalakrishnan

Typeset in Life BT 10.5/13 *by* OSDATA, Hyderabad 500 029

Printed at
The Print Park
Chennai

Published by
Orient Blackswan Private Limited
3-6-752 Himayatnagar, Hyderabad 500 029, Telangana, India
Email: info@orientblackswan.com

To the memory of my parents,
Donnilet and Richard

Author's Acknowledgements

I would like to thank my teachers Dr Anita Pincas, Dr Henry Widdowson, Dr Peter Skehan and Dr Paul Roberts of the University of London, and Rev. Sr Casillda of Holy Cross College for highlighting the different dimensions of language pedagogy.

Dr Anand Rose, Dr Dolly Daniel, Dr Jeyanth Rose, Mrs Violet Jeyachandran and Mrs Mary Johnson for their invaluable help in reviewing and clarifying the medical content in the book; Ms Padmaja Anant, Vice President (Humanities), Orient Blackswan, for her constructive and valuable guidance in developing the current (fourth) edition; late Dr Devi Gopalakrishnan, former Associate Publisher, Orient Blackswan, for her expertise, commitment and creative suggestions in shaping the previous editions; Ms Usha Aroor, former Director (Schools and ELT), Orient Blackswan, for her contribution to the initial shaping of the book.

Contents

LANGUAGE SYLLABUS

Unit	Reading comprehension	Pronunciation and vocabulary	Grammar	Speaking	Writing	Poetry appreciation	Page
1.	'The Story of My Life' by Helen Keller	letters and sounds, minimal pairs, using a dictionary, medical terminology	correction of errors in usage	fixed expressions used in routine interactions, group discussion, soft skills	descriptive paragraphs	'When I Set Out for Lyonnesse' by Thomas Hardy	1
2.	'Deliverance' by Gunjan Sharma	word stress, stress shift, building vocabulary, BrE–AmE spellings, using the thesaurus	subject–verb agreement, interrogatives, tag questions	non-verbal communication, interview	expressing views	'Warblers' by Hortense Wood	36
3.	'Jimmy Valentine' by O. Henry	sentence stress and rhythm, weak forms, intonation, homonyms, homophones, homographs, medical terms	parts of speech, linking words, cohesion and coherence	discussions and debates	essays and emails	'All the World's a Stage' by William Shakespeare	68
4.	'Bird Song In Your Drawing Room' by S.Theodore Baskaran	silent letters, word formation: prefixes and suffixes, and compound words, medical terms, abbreviations	irregular verb forms: active and passive voice	psychosocial aspects of communication, role play on facilitation and barriers to communication, group discussion, debate	note taking and note making, transferring information from a diagram/graph to a paragraph	'The Diaphragm' by Benjamin Midler	100

Publisher's Acknowledgements

Gunjan Sharma, 'Deliverance,' cover story, *Health Supplement, The Week*, 12 January 2014. Reproduced with permission of *The Week*.

Hortense Wood, 'Warblers.' Reprinted from *Character Lines*, in *Geriatric Nursing*, volume 15, issue 5, 1994, p. 290. © Elsevier 1994. Reproduced with permission of Elsevier.

S. Theodore Baskaran, 'Bird Song in your Drawing Room,' *The Hindu*, 9 April 1995. Reproduced with permission of the author.

Swagata Yadavar, 'Down and Out …Standing!' cover story, *Health Supplement, The Week*, 22 June 2014. Reproduced with permission of *The Week*.

Ranjit Lal, 'Plumage Paintbox', from *Young World* section, *The Hindu*, 15 April 2005. Reprinted with permission of the author.

Hugh and Coleen Gantzer, 'Wetland-wise', *The Hindu*, 17 April 2005. Reproduced with permission of the authors.

Bertrand Russell, excerpt from 'Prologue: What I Have Lived For' from *The Autobiography of Bertrand Russell*, 2nd edition, by Bertrand Russell, published by Routledge, p. 9. © The Bertrand Russell Peace Foundation Ltd. 1996. Reproduced by arrangement with Taylor & Francis Books UK.

Veena Bharathi, 'Holding a torch', *The New Indian Express*, Bangalore edition, 22 February 2005. Reprinted with permission of the author.

Howard G Kirkman, 'Laughter' from *Veterans' Voices*. Reproduced with permission of the Veterans' Voices Writing Project.

Ranjana Srivastava, 'My Friend Mike'. First published in *Fairfax Media*. Reproduced with permission of the author.

Joshua Kalapati, 'Human Brain: Leftist or Rightist?' *The Hindu*, 23 June 1996. Reproduced with permission of *The Hindu*.

Kathleen M Blong, '*The Circle of* Life', Reflections on Women's Health, *AWHONN Lifelines*, volume 7, issue 6, December 2003, pp. 574–76. © Elsevier 2003. Reproduced with permission of Elsevier.

Harindranath Chattopadhyaya, 'Shaper Shaped' from *The Divine Vagabond* by Harindranath Chattopadhyaya, published by Theosophical Publishing House, 1950. Reproduced by permission of the publisher.

Gunjan Sharma, 'Young at Heart', cover story, *Health Supplement*, *The Week*, 28 February 2016. Reproduced with permission of *The Week*.

Mallika Tiruvadanan, 'Palliative Care for Cancer Patients' from the *Cancer Care: Is it enough? The Hindu*, 7 September 2003. Reproduced by permission of the author on behalf of 'Lakshmi Pain and Palliative Care Trust', www.lakshmitrust.org

Every effort has been made to trace copyright holders and to obtain their permission for the use of copyright material. The publisher apologises for any errors or omissions, and would be grateful if notified of any corrections that should be incorporated in future reprints or editions of this book.

Introduction

Career English for Nurses, first published in 1996, is specially designed to help students of the BSc Nursing programme communicate intelligibly and fluently in academic, clinical and social settings. It is intended to bridge the gap between the students' existing level of proficiency in English and the standard expected of them at the tertiary level, and to develop their communication skill repertoire so that they will be able to use the language to perform different functions across a wide range of situations.

The revised edition focuses on enabling mastery of communication skills, consisting of the four language skills—speaking, listening, reading and writing—combined with soft skills leading to the appropriate use of the English language in different settings and situations. It includes activities designed to orient learners towards important sub-skills and is aimed at giving them practice in linguistic decoding and production. The methodology is a blend of communicative activities and traditional exercises, which contributes to the development of both fluency and accuracy in language use. The book offers effective remedial measures to improve language proficiency and, further, exercises that are meant for the development of valuable study skills (such as using the dictionary, thesaurus and note making) and the enhancement of reading speed and practice in common English usage. Due attention is given in the book to enabling mastery of medical terminology, which would be of great help when students start their practical training in hospital wards. Stimulating opportunities are provided for language use through quizzes, language games, debates, discussions as well as group and pair work activities. Telephone etiquette, using the computer, CV writing, interview techniques and the underlying principles of nursing documentation are discussed and explained with practice activities.

The book comprises ten units, each focusing on different aspects of pronunciation, vocabulary of high surrender value, and grammatical and idiomatic usage with exercises aimed at reinforcing available language skills as well as internalising additional communicative aspects that will enhance the learner's linguistic competence. Also included are tasks that provide comprehensive practice in speaking, listening, reading and writing. Apart from providing a variety of standard expressions that can be readily used in different situations, tips are given on how to improve pronunciation, build vocabulary, prepare for public speaking and write essays. This will help students not only in academic and social settings but also when taking competitive exams and attending interviews and in their career development.

All the reading passages are based on real-life experiences and have been taken from newspapers, magazines, journals or biographies. Most of them have a medical slant and illustrate nursing ethics as well as other values of intrinsic worth. The poems at the end of each unit are meant to sensitise nursing students to literary elegance and add to their enjoyment of learning English.

A teacher's book with a note on the rationale for the choice of the materials and approach used as well as a key to the exercises is available for the teacher's reference. The medical content in the lessons may, in some cases, lose validity because of new developments, which occur constantly and at a fast pace in the medical field. However, it is to be noted that the answers to the comprehension questions are to be based entirely on the given texts.

The primary concern of the book is not only the mastery of linguistic skills but also the understanding of the psychosocial dimensions of communication, for these contribute in equal measure towards building of good interpersonal skills. Based on the humanistic approach to learning, the activities and organisational patterns in the book have been planned so as to nurture self-confidence, creativity, motivation and cooperation among students who are training to be nurses.

It is hoped that the learner-centred language practice activities in the book will stimulate interest and encourage student involvement, which in turn will facilitate the acquisition of the desired level of communication skills in English.

July 2016

Selva Rose
selvarosevir@yahoo.com

UNIT 1

The Story of My Life

> Whatever you can do or dream you can, begin it.
> Boldness has genius, power and magic in it.
>
> —*Goethe*

Read the following passage for a glimpse of Helen Keller's childhood.

1. Up to the time of the illness that took away my sight and hearing, I lived with my father and mother in a tiny house. It had one large square room and another smaller one in which the servant slept. The house was completely covered with roses and other climbing plants, the favourite home of birds and bees.
2. The big Keller house, where the family lived, was a few steps from our little place with its lovely garden, so dear to me in childhood. Even in the days before my teacher came, I used to feel along the square, still bushes, and guided by the sense of smell, would find the first spring flowers.
3. What joy it was to lose myself in that garden of flowers and wander happily from place to place, until coming suddenly upon a beautiful creeper, I recognised it by its leaves and blossoms and knew that I had reached the old summer house at the bottom of the garden.
4. The beginning of my life was simple and much the same as every other little life. I came, I saw, I conquered, as the first

baby in the family always does. There was the usual amount of talk about a name for me. At last my mother's choice was accepted, and I was called Helen.

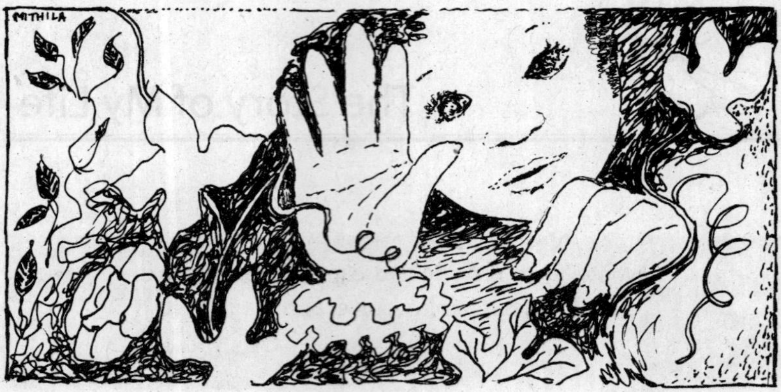

5. I am told that while I was a baby, I showed many signs of an eager, determined character. I tried to imitate everything that I saw other people doing. At six months, I could say, 'How do,' and one day, I drew everyone's attention by saying, 'Tea, tea, tea,' quite plainly. Even after my illness, I remembered one of the words I had learned in these early months. It was the word 'water', and I continued to make some sound for that word after all other speech was lost. I ceased making the sound 'wah-wah' only when I learned to spell the word.

6. They tell me I walked on the day I was a year old. My mother had just taken me out of the bath and was holding me on her knees, when I suddenly saw the shadows of leaves dancing in the sunlight on the smooth floor. I slipped from my mother's knees and began to run towards them, but I fell down and cried for her to take me up in her arms.

7. These happy days did not last long. One short spring, musical with the song of birds, one summer rich in fruit and roses, one autumn of red and gold passed by and left their gifts at the feet of an eager and delighted child. Then in the gloomy month of February 1882, came the illness which closed my eyes and ears, and I sank into a state of unconsciousness. The

doctor thought that I could not live, but early one morning I became conscious again. My family celebrated that morning, but no one, not even the doctor, knew that I would never see or hear again.

8. I can still remember something of that illness, especially the tenderness with which my mother tried to comfort me in my waking hours of restlessness and pain. I also remember how I awoke after a half sleep and turned my eyes, so hot and dry, to the wall, away from the once loved light, which came to me dim and yet more dim each day. But except for these memories, it all seems unreal, like a bad dream.

9. Little by little I got used to the silence and darkness round me and forgot that it had ever been different.

10. But during these first nineteen months of my life, I had seen something of the broad, green fields, the shining sky, trees and flowers, and the darkness that followed could not quite hide them from my memory.

11. As I got older—I was now nearly six—the desire to express myself grew. The few signs I used became less and less satisfactory to me, and my failure to make myself understood was always followed by outbursts of temper. I felt as if unseen hands were holding me, and I tried wildly to escape.

12. Then she came—my teacher, Ann Sullivan—and she set my spirit free. I am filled with wonder when I consider the difference—that of darkness and light—in my life before and after her coming. It was the 3rd of March 1887, three months before my seventh birthday.

13. I felt approaching footsteps, I stretched out my hand, as I supposed, to my mother. Someone took it, and I was caught up and held close in her arms. She had come to explain many things to me, and more than other things, to love me.

14. The morning after my teacher came, she led me into her room and gave me a doll that some little children from a special school had sent. When I had played with it for a little time, Miss Sullivan slowly spelled into my hand the word 'd-o-l-l'.

I was at once interested in this finger play and tried to imitate it. When at last I succeeded in making the letters correctly, I reddened with childish pleasure and pride.

15. I ran down the stairs to my mother, held up my hand, and made the letters for 'doll'. I did not know that I was spelling a word or even that there was such a word. I was simply making my fingers go in a monkey-like imitation. In the days that followed, I learned to spell in this un-understanding way a great many words—among them, 'pin', 'hat', 'cup'—and a few names of actions like sit, stand and walk. But my teacher had been with me several weeks before I understood that everything has a name.

16. My teacher had a fresh idea. She brought me my hat, and I knew I was going out into the warm sunshine. This thought made me jump up and down with pleasure. We walked down the path to a well where someone was drawing water. My teacher placed my hand under the cool stream and then spelled into the other hand 'water', first slowly and then rapidly. Suddenly I had a misty feeling of something forgotten—the excitement of returning thought; and somehow the mystery of language was made clear to me. I knew then 'w-a-t-e-r' was the wonderful cool something that was flowing over my hand. That living word awakened my spirit, gave it light, hope, joy, set it free! There were bars still, it is true, but bars that could in time be broken.

17. I remember many events of the summer of 1887 that followed the awakening of my spirit. I was constantly examining things with my hands and learning their names. The more I handled things and the more I got to know of their uses, the more joyous and certain grew my sense of unity with the rest of the world.

18. When springtime came, Miss Sullivan took me by the hand across the fields where men were preparing the earth for seeds. She led me to the banks of the river. Sitting on the warm grass there, I had my first lessons in the kindliness and generosity of nature.

19. I learned how the rain causes the trees to grow, many of them good for food as well as pleasant to look at; how birds build their nests and live and grow strong; how the lion, the deer and other creatures find food and shelter. As my knowledge grew, I felt more and more the delight of the world I was in.

20. I cannot explain the peculiar understanding Miss Sullivan had of my pleasures and desires. Perhaps it was the result of long companionship with the blind. Added to this, she possessed a wonderful power of description. She went quickly over uninteresting points and never troubled me with questions to see if I remembered the day-before-yesterday's lessons. The less interesting facts of science she dealt with little by little, making every subject so real that I could not help remembering what she taught.

21. Our most enjoyable walk was to Keller's Landing on the banks of the river. There we spent many happy hours. I dug riverbeds, built walls with the soil and made islands and lakes, all for fun, and never dreamed I was learning a lesson. I listened with growing wonder to Miss Sullivan's descriptions of the great round world with its burning mountains, underground cities, moving rivers of ice and many other things as strange.

22. She made raised maps of soil so that I could feel the mountain ranges and valleys, and follow with my fingers the course of rivers. So through play I learnt valuable lessons in geography.

(*The Story of My Life* by Helen Keller, London: Longman, 1948, and simplified by M. E. Carter)

Glossary

awaken	-	here, to rouse something that has been inactive or passive
cease	-	to stop
eager	-	full of interest
excitement	-	thrill
generosity	-	giving freely

gloomy	-	depressing; not bright
handle	-	here, to pick something up and touch, hold or move it with your hands
imitate	-	to copy or follow something
kindliness	-	kindness
misty	-	not clear
mystery	-	something strange or unknown
outburst of temper	-	a violent expression of anger
possess	-	to have
shelter	-	here, a place that gives protection from bad weather, danger or attack
wander	-	to walk around without a purpose

Understanding the text

EXERCISE A

Write short answers to the following questions.

1. How does Helen Keller describe her childhood home?
2. What is the meaning of 'I came, I saw, I conquered as the first baby in the family always does'?
3. How does Helen describe seasons?
4. Did Helen lose her sight and hearing at the same time? Pick out the words from the text which indicate this.
5. What was Helen's main problem when she grew older? How did she react to it?
6. How did Miss Sullivan teach Helen her first word?
7. Why does Helen refer to 'water' as a living word?
8. 'There were bars still; it is true, but bars that could be broken in time.' What does this statement tell you about Helen?
9. What did Miss Sullivan do to make Helen's geography lessons interesting?
10. What were Miss Sullivan's remarkable personal qualities?

EXERCISE B

Mark the following statements true (T) or false (F). You should be able to justify your answers.

1. Helen was blind, deaf and dumb from birth.
2. Helen had no elder sister.
3. As a baby, Helen was very active.
4. Helen lost her eyesight in an accident.
5. Helen fell ill when she was one year and seven months old.
6. Helen was six years old when her teacher came.
7. When the teacher wrote 'doll' on her palm, Helen understood what she meant.
8. Helen loved to spend time outdoors.
9. Miss Sullivan was Helen's English teacher.
10. Helen was able to speak after the teacher came.

Pronunciation

LETTERS AND SOUNDS

Effective oral communication is a combination of good interpersonal skills (which involve interest in, respect for and empathy with others), a conducive environment, suitable non-verbal cues, appropriate verbal expressions and good pronunciation. Mastery of listening and speaking skills will help us establish a good rapport with others. While communicating orally, we have to identify the spoken signals and segment the stream of speech into words made up of individual sounds. It is, therefore, a definite advantage to be aware of some of the distinctive features of English pronunciation. Such an understanding can be found in phonetics, which is the study of speech sounds.

The details given in the pronunciation section in each unit are meant to highlight the distinctive features of English pronunciation, which include the sounds of the language and the use of stress, rhythm and intonation in its spoken form. This awareness is important because English is different in many ways from our mother tongues.

One of the special features of English pronunciation is that there is no one-to-one correspondence between sounds and letters. Many letters can represent the same sound. For example:

burn
circulation
heard   } /ɜː/
insert
world

Interestingly the opposite also happens—that is, one letter can be represented by more than two sounds. For example:

- ✦ The letter 'g' has+ two sounds, /g/ and /dʒ/.

/g/	/dʒ/
graze	gentle
target	longevity
girl	ginger
get	germ

  There are words where the letter 'g' occurs twice and represents the sounds /g/ as well as /dʒ/.

  gauge
  language
  geography

- ✦ The letter 'a' can have any one of the following sounds.

/eɪ/	age
/ə/	ago
/ɔː/	all
/aː/	farm
/æ/	mat
/ɪ/	cabbage

  While using a new word with the letter 'a', take care to pronounce it correctly.

- ✦ The letters 'ch' can be pronounced in three different ways—/k, tʃ, ʃ/.

  chemistry, church, chandelier

✦ The suffix *-ed* added to verbs to form their past tense is pronounced in three different ways.

/d/	damn<u>ed</u>
/t/	match<u>ed</u>
/ɪd/	dat<u>ed</u>

Thus, while there are only 26 letters in English, the language has 44 sounds, each of which is represented by a symbol. A phonetic dictionary gives us the words in phonetic script using these symbols. All the 44 symbols are given in the Appendix for reference. (The given phonetic script is based on the British Received Pronunciation, or RP, but other phonetic realisations that guarantee intelligibility at the national and international level are equally acceptable. However, for convenience, RP is taken as the point of reference in this book.) With the help of your teacher, learn to link the symbols with specific sounds.

EXERCISE A

Identify the sounds of the letters 'o' and 'a' in columns A and B respectively.

A	B
1. look	1. architect
2. pool	2. achieve
3. hole	3. admiration
4. hot	4. angel
5. come	5. bandage
6. anatomy	6. watch
7. tomato	7. apparatus

EXERCISE B

Group the following words into three sections depending on the sound of the letters 'ch' in these words. Your teacher will then read out each word. Check if your pronunciation is right.

1. ache	11. chose
2. bronchitis	12. chronic

3. chafe
4. chaff
5. chalk
6. chaos
7. char
8. chic
9. chiffon
10. chord
13. hitch
14. machine
15. merchant
16. mechanic
17. psychiatric
18. sketch
19. technique
20. trachea

EXERCISE C

Your teacher will read out ten words to you. Listen carefully and write them down under three sections depending on which of the sounds /k/, /tʃ/ and /ʃ/ occur in them.

EXERCISE D

Work in pairs. Choose ten words each in the past tense from the unit. Make sure there are at least two examples for each type—those ending in /t/, /d/ and /ɪd/. Take turns to read out the verbs to each other. Your teacher will ask you to write down the verbs in the appropriate columns on the blackboard.

MINIMAL PAIRS

The tendency to replace English sounds with those of the language one is accustomed to is a common occurrence. For example, the sounds of English /ɒ/ and /ɔ:/ are most often pronounced /ɑ:/ or /ʊ/ by second language speakers in different parts of India. (You can try pronouncing 'college' with /ɒ/, /a:/ and /ʊ/.)

Apart from affecting the quality of speech, the substitution of one sound for another can blur the meaning, especially in words that are differentiated by just one sound. For example:

> (*overheard in a physics class*) What happens when electricity is passed through the road?

Here, /rɒd/ has been pronounced as /rəʊd/, which affects the meaning of the sentence.

These words, which are differentiated from each other just by a single sound, are called minimal pairs. For example:

calf	cough
she	see
bought	boat

Most of the minimal pairs do not occur in the same context, but it is helpful to have the support of standard diction while trying to derive meaning from a context.

EXERCISE E

Write the missing word in the minimal pairs below.

/ɪ/	/iː/	/əʊ/	/ɔː/
1. did	....	10. bone	....
2. fist	....	11. coat	....
3. tick	....	12. cloak	....
/ʊ/	/uː/	/s/	/ʃ/
4. full	....	13. ass	....
5. should	....	14. sign	....
6. would	....	15. sin	....
/ɑː/	/ɒ/	/v/	/w/
7. cart	....	16. vile	....
8. cast	....	17. veil	....
9. last	....	18. vie	....

Vocabulary

USING A DICTIONARY

Words help us convey meanings and articulate our ideas. The English language has a rich store of words which enables us to select and frame our messages in specific ways to meet the demands of a topic or situation. Words can create interest, add force and enhance the impact of communication. A dictionary gives us the range of words in a language. You would certainly have used one on many occasions.

EXERCISE A

Given below are some entries from a page of the WordMaster dictionary. Read them carefully. What information do the entries provide besides part of speech? List these.

What do you think the following abbreviations stand for:

adj.
adv.
i.
t.
u.
c.
pron.
det.

firm[1] /fɜ:m/ adj. **1** *This house has been built on a firm foundation of rock.* = strong and solid **2** *He kept a firm grip on his father's arm.* = strong and sure **3** *My decision is firm.* = strong and not changing

firm[2] noun, c. *Our firm makes medicines.* = a business company

fir•ma•ment /ˈfɜ:məmənt/ noun, u. = sky (literary)

first[1] /fɜ:st/ noun. *He got a first in the examination.* = a first class (informal)

first[2] pron. *She was the first to sing.* = before all the others

first[3] adv. *Sit down first, and then we can talk.* = before other things happen

first[4] det. **1** *She was the first speaker.* = before anyone else **2** *This is my first visit to Delhi.* = something that never happend earlier **3** *The first years in a new job are the most difficult.* = at the beginning **4** *This is the first thing to remember when you are starting your work.* = most important **first aid** = treatment given to a person injured in an accident or suddenly taken ill, before professional medical help is available. **first-class** *a first-class meal* = of the highest quality **first class** = the most expensive method of travel **first floor 1** = the rooms in a building just above the ground level (in British English and more commonly used in India) **2** = the rooms at the ground level (American English, now becoming popular in India) **first-hand** *a first-hand report* = information given by someone directly involved in an incident **first name** *Mr Sinha's first name is Ramesh.* = the part of the name which comes first, before the surname **first-rate** *This is a first-rate book.* = of the highest quality (informal)

to be on first name terms with someone = to be very friendly with someone, so that you can address him/her by the first name **to put someone or something first** *In all matters, he puts his family first.* = to consider most important

fis•cal /ˈfɪskəl/ adj. *the government's fiscal policy* = having to do with public money, especially the taxes collected by the government

fish[1] /fɪʃ/ noun, u. or c. (**fish** or **fishes**) **1** *He caught several fish./We saw three little fishes.* (c.) = an animal that lives in water **2** *Would you like some more fish?* (u.) = the flesh of a fish, used as food

fish[2] verb, i. **1** *They were fishing in the river.* = to catch or try to catch fish **2** *He was fishing around inside the cupboard.* = to search for something (informal) **fisherman** noun = a person who catches fish for a living or as a hobby **fishy** adj. **1** *a fishy smell* = like that of a fish **2** *There is something fishy about this story.* = something that causes doubt or suspicion; dishonest (informal) **a cold fish** = a person who is not friendly and does not show her/his feelings (derogatory) **to feel like a fish out of water** = to feel uncomfortable because one is in unfamiliar or unfriendly surroundings **to fish for compliments** = to try to make someone say something good about you **to fish in troubled waters** = to try to gain something from the troubles of other people **to fish out something** = to bring something out of its place after a search

fis•sion /ˈfɪʃən/ noun, u. *The first atom bomb made use of the fission of uranium atoms.* = the process of dividing or breaking up the central part (nucleus) of an atom into smaller parts (opposite **fusion**) [PHYSICS]

fis•sure /ˈfɪʃər/ noun, c. = a long deep crack in the earth

fist[1] /fɪst/ noun, c. *He clenched his fist.* = the shape of the hand with the fingers tightly clenched (closed)

fist[2] verb, t. *The goalkeeper fisted the ball away.* = to hit with one's fist **tight-fisted** adj. = a person who does not like to spend money, a miser

Source: *WordMaster: Learner's Dictionary of Modern English* Orient Blackswan, 2012, p.201.

EXERCISE B

Look up a recent edition of any dictionary of your choice and mark the following statements true (T) or false (F). Compare your answers with those of your classmates to see where your observations match those of the others and where they do not.

1. Dictionary entries are arranged in an alphabetical order.
2. Different definitions of the headword are listed in the order of frequency.
3. ▷ and □ indicate the start of the compound word section and derivative section respectively.
4. Pronunciation of the headword is given next to it.
5. The American spelling of a word is not given.
6. Sometimes there are separate entries for the same word, when it belongs to more than one class or has different meanings.
7. The past tense forms of all verbs are indicated.
8. The comparative and superlative degrees of adjectives are not mentioned.
9. Compound words are not listed with the headword.
10. The phrasal verb section gives the particle/preposition following the verb with examples of usage.

MEDICAL TERMINOLOGY

Within standard English, there are varieties that are closely linked to different specialised fields of work. Thus, for example, there is medical English, legal English, and so on. These varieties are differentiated mainly by a set of vocabulary items specific to the discipline. Preference for specific syntactical patterns can also be seen in certain varieties.

Many medical terms are coined by joining a word root to a suffix and/or a prefix. Look at the examples below.

✦ hepatoma – tumour in the liver
hepat (word root meaning 'liver') + *oma* (suffix meaning 'tumour')

- ✦ encephaloma – tumour in the brain
  encephal (word root meaning 'brain') + *oma* (suffix meaning 'tumour')

It is a definite advantage to have knowledge of the word roots, prefixes and suffixes as well as their meanings. If we are familiar with these meanings we can guess the general area referred to. If the suffix combining with a word root starts with a consonant letter, the letter 'o' is added in many instances between the word root and the suffix. For example:

- ✦ gastroplasty – surgical repair of stomach
  gastr (word root meaning 'stomach') + *o* + *plasty* (suffix meaning 'surgical repair')
- ✦ gastroscopy – visual examination of the internal part of the stomach
  gastr + *o* + *scopy* (suffix meaning visual examination of the internal parts of the body)

But if the suffix begins with a vowel, the letter 'o' is not added between the word root and the suffix. For example:

- ✦ gastritis – inflammation of the stomach
  gastr + *itis* (inflammation)
- ✦ gastralgia – pain in the stomach
  gastr + *algia* (pain)

When two word roots are combined, the letter 'o' is always inserted between them, even if the second word root begins with a vowel. For example:

- gastroenteritis – inflammation of the stomach and intestinal tract
  gastr (word root 1) + *o* + *enter* (word root 2) + *itis*
- gastroileitis – inflammation of the stomach and ileum
  gastr (word root 1) + o + *ile* (word root 2) + *itis*

Some meanings are indicated by more than one term. For example:

- *-ic/al/ar*, three suffixes meaning 'pertaining to' combining with different word roots

  gastr<u>ic</u> - pertaining to stomach
  cost<u>al</u> - pertaining to rib
  capsul<u>ar</u> - pertaining to a capsule
  derm<u>al</u> - pertaining to skin
  dermat<u>ology</u> - study of skin

A list of word roots, prefixes and suffixes are given below with their meanings. You could try coining words applying the above principles, though all combinations may not be possible or acceptable in common usage.

word root	**meaning**
aden	gland
angi	blood vessel
arthr	joint
brachi	arm
bronch	bronchus
cardi	heart
cephal	head
cerebr	cerebrum
cholangi	related to bile duct
cheil	lip
chir	hand
chondr	cartilage

col	colon
cost	rib
crani	skull
cyst	bladder
cyt	cell
derm/dermat	skin
encephal	brain
enter	intestine
gastr	stomach
gloss/lingu	tongue
haem/haemat	blood
hepat	liver
hist	tissue
hyster/uter/metr	uterus
ile	ileum
irid/iri	iris
laryng	larynx
mast	breast
mening	meninges
my	muscle
myel	spinal cord/bone marrow
nephr/ren	kidney
neur	nerve
onych	nail
ophthalm/ocul	eye
oste	bone
ot/aur	ear
phleb/ven	vein
pleur	pleura
pneumon/pneum	lung/air
pod	foot
rhin/nas	nose
splen	spleen
stern	sternum
stomat	mouth

trache	trachea
trich	hair
ureter	ureter

prefix	**meaning**
a-/an-	without
a-/ab-/abs-	away from
ad-	towards
allo-	different from
ante-	before
anti-	against
brady-	slow
brachy-	short
contra-	against
de-	down/from/opposite/removal/reversal
dia-	through/between
dys-	bad/painful
endo-	inside
exo-/extra-	outside
epi-/ep-	in addition to, over, at
hyper-	above normal
hypo-	below normal
inter-	in between
infra-	below/under
intra-	within
juxta-	near
macro-	large
meso-	middle
para-	beside/adjacent to/distinct from but similar to
peri-	around
retro-	located behind
sub-	below
supra-/super-	above

tachy-	fast
trans-	across, on the other side

suffix	**meaning**
-algia/-dynia	pain
-cele	swelling/herniation
-ectasis	dilation
-emesis	vomiting
-ectomy	surgical removal
-graphy	process of recording
-ic/-al/-ac	pertaining to
-itis	inflammation
-logist	specialist
-logy	study of
-lysis	decomposition/dissolution
-megaly	enlargement
-oid	resembling
-oma	tumour
-osis	diseased condition
-ostomy	creation of an artificial opening into a part of the body
-otomy	surgical incision
-pathy	disease
-pexy	fixing or putting together
-plasty	surgical repair
-plegia	paralysis
-rrhagia	haemorrhage
-rrhea	discharge
-rrhaphy	suturing
-rrhexis	rupture
-sclerosis	hardening/thickening
-scope	instrument for visual examination of internal organs
-scopy	visual examination of internal organs
-spasm	sudden contraction of muscles
-stenosis	tightening/narrowing

EXERCISE C

Combine the word roots with the appropriate prefixes and/or suffixes and find the words for these definitions. Write them down in the space provided.

1. inflammation of
   a. liver ....
   b. nerve ....
   c. iris ....
   d. kidney ....
   e. pleura ....
2. surgical removal of
   a. colon ....
   b. spleen ....
   c. breast ....
   d. kidney ....
   e. uterus ....
3. visual examination of the internal parts of
   a. bronchus ....
   b. larynx ....
   c. ear ....
   d. eye ....
   e. bladder ....
4. creation of an artificial opening into
   a. trachea ....
   b. stomach ....
   c. colon ....
   d. ileum ....
   e. bladder ....
5. discharge from nose ....
6. enlargement of heart ....
7. enlargement of liver ....
8. repair of lip ....
9. pertaining to kidney ....
10. pertaining to heart ....
11. rupture of a blood vessel ....

12. pain in the muscle ....
13. pain in the joint ....
14. resembling a cell ....

EXERCISE D

Based on what you have learnt, fill in the crossword below with the help of the given clues.

Down	Across
1. inflammation of the iris	3. muscle
2. eye	7. heart
3. removal of breast	8. uterus
4. pertaining to	10. hair
5. ureter	11. herniation/swelling
6. enlargement	12. pertaining to
9. against	16. spinal cord
13. ileum	17. artificial opening into colon
14. rib	19. inflammation in joints
15. ear	
18. tumour	

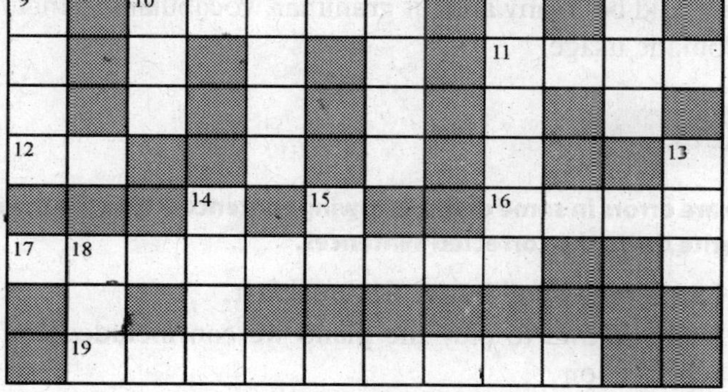

EXERCISE E

Look up the following prefixes in a medical dictionary and find out which body parts they refer to.

1. *blephar-*
2. *cor-/core-*
3. *gingiv-*
4. *rachi-*
5. *thorac-*

Grammar

LANGUAGE AWARENESS

Grammar is a set of rules that governs a language. Grammatical competence is related to the mastery of the linguistic code and contributes to accuracy in communication. Together with sociolinguistic competence, which relates language to social norms in a society, grammatical competence forms an important part of a speaker's communicative competence.

At school, you would have learnt many rules related to the various aspects of language such as active and passive voice, direct and indirect speech, complex and compound sentences, spelling, punctuation and the agreement among the different parts of speech in a sentence. Apply your knowledge and find out whether the sentences given below are correct or not. The errors could be in any area of grammar, vocabulary, punctuation or idiomatic usage.

EXERCISE A

There are errors in some of the following sentences. Identify the errors and write down the corrected sentences.

1. I took bread and butter for breakfast.
2. If she knows to play the piano we can include her in the school choir.

3. They got punishment because they never stopped stealing.
4. If you cut jokes in the class you will be punished.
5. I and my friends wanted to go for a movie last week.
6. When the chief guest came in, there was pin drop silence.
7. I told him, 'Sorry Mr, I cannot come for the meeting as I am engaged in another deal.'
8. He had come to me one or two times in the past for help but last year I never saw him.
9. Smita has bought a new car and keeps talking of it all the time.
10. The meeting will be held at 3 p.m. in the afternoon.
11. He asked me to go and fetch him a jug of milk from the canteen.
12. The painting is one of its kind and unique.
13. We left our luggages at the station. Please send someone to collect it.
14. He was not selected as he had no experiences in that field.
15. Unless you walk around you cannot appreciate the sceneries of this hill station.
16. When we went out, there were six aircraft on the runway.
17. When Ron was without a job, everyone were anxious to help.
18. One must be ready to work hard if he wants to come up in life.
19. Very few landowners will grow timber to be used for this purpose, because about forty years must elapse before he can profit by it.
20. Unless you know the English alphabets, we cannot teach you to read.
21. She plays the piano well, isn't it?
22. He was finishing his job.
23. She is waiting for a better job since last May.
24. She won the contest because she is having a nice voice.
25. The ship sails at 10 a.m. next Monday.
26. He said that he will visit me after he completing his thesis.

27. She asked Leela when was she going on leave.
28. Wherever he sees me, he inquired about you.
29. 'May I have the book'? asked Jeevan.
30. 'They come to see the principal', said Ramesh.
31. She had hurt herself accidently and so could not come for the picnic.
32. He was appointed captain of the football team from South Zone.
33. This course comprises of five areas of study.
34. He decided to take a holiday after discussing about his health with the doctor.
35. He is already picking up quarrels with the other students in the school.

EXERCISE B

Identify the grammar errors in the passage. Spot the dominant category of error and discuss it with your partner.

I am hailing from a small village and my parents are small time farmers. They believed that good education would give their children a better future. They were sending their boys to a good school and encouraged us to do well at school. They got us cycles to ride to the school 5 km away. We both were good students and in the 12th final examination I was coming first in the school and received lots off appreciation.

My parents were thrilled when I gets admission in a prestigious engineering college. It was 100 km away from our village and so they were putting me in the hostel. I like the new place but was feeling lonely. After a month I had made many friends and was happy. I was going out with them in the evenings for games or shows. I study hard and my parents were happy with my performance.

One of the favourite places for the students were the café two streets away from the hostel. It had an internet corner where people played video games. My friend and I started playing these games as a past time. I was enjoying the games very much and started spending more time there. I was staying even after my friends leave and go back to the hostel very late. Soon I was wanting to go there in the mornings also. This habit was affecting my performance and I was getting low marks in the assignments. My friends was trying hard to help me getting over this habit but I did not listen to them.

I was borrowing money to play the games. My attendance is less than 80% and they are telling me that I cannot sit for the second semester examination. They are calling my parents to meet the Principal and I am feeling ashamed. How will I face my loving parents. What can I say and do to ease their sorrow Please help me.

EXERCISE C

Without mentioning names, describe one of your friends in the class. Write about aspects like facial features, personality traits and what she is wearing on that particular day. Read out your description to your classmates and ask them to identify the person.

EXERCISE D

Discuss the contexts where the simple present and present continuous tenses occur.

Oral communication

Listening and speaking are closely interlinked language skills that help in the transfer of information. They help us interact with others and build social relationships. We communicate orally either face-to-face or through other media like telephones, radios, televisions or computers. Conversations, greetings, lectures, debates, discussions, interviews, public speeches, etc., are different forms of oral communication. We usually adapt the way we speak to suit the social, academic, formal and informal settings in which communication takes place.

An awareness of cross-cultural differences is another important factor that helps us communicate better. It enables us to connect with people from diverse cultural backgrounds in academic and work settings, both in the country and abroad. We must learn to respect the cultural differences that are reflected in verbal and non-verbal communication. It is, therefore, important that we do not dismiss or make fun of the beliefs and customs of classmates or colleagues.

Interpersonal skills, a wide vocabulary in English and a good command of the structures of the language enhance the quality of both listening and speaking. Further, matching thoughts to appropriate expressions and the logical sequencing of words and sentences contribute to clarity of speech. Finally, communicating in different styles to suit the audience, topic, place and purpose is the hallmark of a good speaker.

LISTENING

To be proficient in oral communication, we need to be good not only at speaking but also at listening. Being a good listener involves being attentive, which helps us segment a stream of speech into meaningful words and phrases that we can relate to our knowledge of the subject in order to understand what is being said. Good listeners can also identify the attitude of the speakers by paying attention to the tone and rhythm of their speech.

In social settings, listening can be tough mainly because we cannot anticipate what the speaker will speak about. Also, if we want to interact meaningfully, we have to process what we hear immediately, without a time lag of perhaps more than a few seconds. It is important that we do not switch off even when we feel we do not understand what is being said. Instead, we must pay attention to the key words and try to work it out. If we lose interest or concentration halfway through, we will completely lose the thread of what the speaker says. In academic settings, however, we usually have an idea of the topic beforehand. Such contextualised listening helps us anticipate the development of the speaker's thoughts even if we do not get all the words.

We can acquire listening skills with practice over a period of time. Listening to good soundtracks every day for ten to fifteen minutes for several months or years will help. Listening to good English regularly will activate our potential to learn the language.

SPEAKING

Good speakers of a language have a high degree of fluency and the ability to articulate words well, following the principles of pronunciation in that language. The pronunciation section in each unit in this book outlines the different aspects of pronunciation (vowels, diphthongs, consonants, stress, rhythm, intonation, etc.) on which the quality of our speech depends. But knowledge alone cannot improve our speaking skills. We must identify our shortcomings in specific areas and overcome them with the help of suitable practice activities.

Here are some tips to improve your spoken English.

- Listen to good English—spoken by teachers, friends and family and used on TV programmes and videos of a high standard. Get a feel for the English language, which is very different from our mother tongues. Clarify your doubts on pronunciation/intonation with your teacher.
- Take the time to read aloud for at least fifteen minutes every day. Practise breaking the sentences at the right places. Start with short passages focusing on stress and intonation. If possible, get it assessed by parents/friends/teachers. Recording your reading and listening to it will help you identify where you need to improve.
- Practise with tongue twisters, chants, drills, short answers, etc., to get used to the sounds specific to English.
- Learn to use contracted forms in conversations.
- Have a variety of interactive formulas at hand for routine interactions, such as greeting, requesting and interrupting.
- Remember that English is a stress-timed language with a rhythmic quality. With that in mind, practise till you get the flow of speech right. (See unit 3 for stress and rhythm.)

- Speak in English whenever and wherever possible. Do not be selfconscious. Remember that practice improves fluency.
- Build your vocabulary and grammatical structures, and use them consciously in appropriate contexts. Familiar words and constructions contribute to the smooth flow of communication.
- Good language labs, if accessible, can be of great help in self-learning of speaking skills.
- Do not be discouraged if you are unable to speak as fluently as some of your classmates. It is just a matter of time before you acquire these skills. Just start speaking in English.

For routine interactions, there are pairs of sentences/phrases that go together to effectively convey the meanings conforming to social norms. These expressions cover everyday functions like greeting, thanking, responding to introductions, apologising, and responding to an apology. Many of the responses in informal settings are not in sentences but in phrases. We are all familiar with formal greetings and their responses, for example 'Good morning. /How are you?/ Fine.' But informal greetings are more varied and dependent on our closeness to the people with whom we are communicating. A few samples are given below.

Hello! Hi!

Hi! How's it going? As usual./Oh, you can't even imagine . . .

What's up? Oh, nothing special./Something fantastic . . .

Besides the formality or informality of the context in which we speak, the choices we make in initiating and responding to such interactions will depend on (a) our *relationship* with the person we are speaking to (friend/stranger/boss/teacher), (b) the *purpose of the interaction* (social/academic/professional) and (c) the *place where the interaction takes place* (office, outdoors, meeting, interview).

Look at some examples, formal and informal, of spoken English used for the purpose of inviting, apologising, making requests and taking leave, together with their responses.

Inviting (formal and informal)

We'd be happy if you could have dinner with us on . . ./We'd love to have you over for dinner on . . .

Thank you for inviting us. We'd be happy to come.

We would love to, but unfortunately we are not free on that day.

How about joining us for dinner on Saturday?/Are you free this weekend to have dinner at our place?

Sure. When? What time?/Oh yes. Can I bring the dessert?

Wish I could, but I am not free that day./Oh, sorry. I am working this weekend.

Apologising

I am sorry, Ravi.
That's okay./No problem.

Please forgive me.
I understand. Forget it, Gopi.

Sorry about that.
Never mind./Don't let it bother you.

I really feel bad about it.
Don't. These things happen.

Making requests

Can I have a word with you?
Sure.

Can you give me a lift to the station?
No problem at all.

Excuse me.
Yes?
Could I borrow your book, please?
Of course./Sorry, Madhavan. Tina has already asked for it.

Preparing to leave and saying goodbye

Shall we make a move?/I think it's time to leave./It's time we left.

Goodbye!/Bye, bye./ See you.

Apart from the above aspects, the verbal responses in all our oral interactions must be supported by appropriate nonverbal communication. For example, greeting a person with a sour look is rude. When there is a contradiction between verbal and nonverbal communication, people tend to believe the latter. Keep that in mind when you are speaking to people. (See unit 2 for an outline of the different forms of nonverbal cues and how they affect communication.)

EXERCISE A

Match the items in column A with those in column B. Choose the best combinations. Each item may have more than one answer. Discuss with your classmates the situations in which these expressions are generally used.

A	B
1. Thank you very much.	a. Not at all.
2. Pleased to meet you.	b. No problem at all.
3. Would you like some coffee?	c. Not quite.
4. Would you mind helping me?	d. Sorry, not today.
5. I'll catch up with you later.	e. I don't mind.
6. How's it going?	f. My pleasure.
7. How far is it?	g. Don't mention it, please.
8. Do you agree with me?	h. Me too.
9. Will you join us?	i. Really well.
10. Have a great day.	j. Sure.
	k. You too.
	l. Sorry about it.
	m. Okay. Bye!
	n. Quite a distance.
	o. Not too well.
	p. See you.

GROUP DISCUSSION / EXTEMPORE TALK

EXERCISE B

1. **As a nurse, you are expected to possess certain qualities in order to perform efficiently. Have a discussion on this in groups of five and list ten qualities which you think are important for a nurse to have.**
2. **Put down these qualities on the blackboard. Other groups will do so too. With the help of your teacher select five qualities that are generally acceptable to your class.**
3. **Now take turns with your classmates to speak briefly on how you would order the selected qualities according to their importance as it seems to you.**

Communication Skills

SOFT SKILLS IN COMMUNICATION

Communication is a process of imparting and exchanging information through language or other non-verbal mediums, such as gestures, and visuals, such as drawings, maps, charts and graphs. Good communication skills play a crucial role in our personal and professional development. They enable us to acquire and share knowledge, transmit ideas, discuss issues, motivate others and increase our work output. To be able to communicate well, we need a good command of the language, knowledge in our area of work or study, and a host of qualities and attitudes that strengthen our interpersonal skills. These characteristics, often called 'soft skills' or 'smart skills', complement our linguistic and professional skills. The mastery of the language skills of listening, speaking, reading and writing enriches communication when combined with soft skills.

Many of the attributes that come under soft skills are not new to us. They are already a part of us, instilled in us by our parents, teachers or society. But we must also be aware of the importance of these qualities because they enhance our personality and communication in academic, professional and social settings. Soft skills play a positive role in interviews and when making career choices or establishing ourselves in our professions. Let us look at a few important soft skills.

Good work ethics

Honesty, reliability, dedication, loyalty and compassion are among the major attributes that constitute good work ethics. If we are conscientious, we will not make compromises in time or work output. For nurses in particular, compassion and empathy play a vital role in preparing them to fulfil their job demands, one of the foremost of which is being good caregivers. The self-discipline required to retain these qualities under all circumstances is usually the deciding factor with regard to winning or losing and greatness or mediocrity.

Team spirit

Working together well as a team involves possessing strong communication and interpersonal skills, taking criticism positively, resolving conflict, giving priority to team goals, learning from others' input, delegating responsibilities, and accepting and tolerating differences in beliefs and attitudes. The ability to work well with people from different sociocultural backgrounds, respecting their opinions and collaborating with them is a valuable asset.

Positive attitude

A positive attitude stems from believing in ourselves and our capacity to learn and get things done. Self-confidence forms the core of this attribute, which is an integral part of leadership. The quality generates positive energy and enhances communication and work output.

Ability to handle pressures

Pressures are a part of life, and it is important not to buckle under them for otherwise they will affect the quality of our performance. Exams, interviews, tight project deadlines, and public presentations are a few situations in which pressure can adversely affect our output. We must, therefore, evolve strategies to relax and keep a cool head when under pressure.

Flexibility

It is important to have an open mind when changes are introduced in our field of study or work. In today's fast-moving world, it is important that we adapt quickly to changing situations, though it must be done *without* compromising our work ethics.

Critical and creative thinking

Critical thinking and creative thinking skills are integral to life and help us generate ideas, analyse issues, interpret data, find solutions and provide coherence. Originality is the hallmark of creative thinking, and when put to good use, it can yield impressive results.

Lifelong learning

Knowledge is never static, and it is crucial that we keep ourselves updated in our field of study or work. To achieve this end, we have to become independent learners. Self-regulated learning and the ability to manage information well will be of great use to us in our academic and professional lives. This has now become easier with Massive Open Online Courses (MOOC). These courses give us the flexibility to learn at our own pace and in our own time.

Time management

All the above attributes will fail if we do not manage our time effectively. We must prioritise our tasks and learn to delegate the less important ones. We must not procrastinate*. Procrastination

---

* to keep delaying something that must be done, often because it is unpleasant or boring

has a negative impact on productivity. It is very often respect for time that determines the success or failure of a project.

EXERCISE

Can you think of an occasion when any of the soft skills discussed above helped you perform well in an academic or social context? Share your experience with the class.

Writing

DESCRIPTIVE PARAGRAPHS

EXERCISE

Helen Keller was blind and deaf. But she did not let her disabilities deter her from achieving her goals. Through her spirited battle to overcome all barriers, she reinforced the truth of her definition of life, 'Life is a daring adventure or nothing.'

Do you know anyone who, like Helen Keller, fought against odds, armed with a positive attitude and a constancy of purpose? Write a description of the person (150 words).

Appreciating Poetry

When I set out for Lyonnesse

When I set out for Lyonnesse,
A hundred miles away,
The rime was on the spray,
And starlight lit my lonesomeness
When I set out for Lyonnesse
A hundred miles away.

What would bechance at Lyonnesse
While I should sojourn there
No prophet durst declare,
Nor did the wisest wizard guess
What would bechance at Lyonnesse
While I should sojourn there.

When I came back from Lyonnesse
With magic in my eyes,
All marked with mute surmise
My radiance rare and fathomless,
When I came back from Lyonnesse
With magic in my eyes!

Thomas Hardy

EXERCISE

Write short answers to the following questions.

1. What is the poet's state of mind when he sets out for Lyonnesse, and when he returns from there?
2. Before setting out on a journey have you ever wondered what is likely to happen? Do you worry about it or do you look forward to your experiences?

UNIT 2

Deliverance

> Wherever the art of Medicine is loved, there is also a love of Humanity.
>
> —*Hippocrates*

Transplantation has the power to offer millions of dying people the precious gift of life. Read the following amazing report of a liver transplant performed successfully on a young child.

1. On an afternoon in August 1998, a family function was underway in Kancheepuram, the temple town in Tamil Nadu. The town was home to Dr M. R. Rajasekar, a consultant liver transplant surgeon, who had recently returned from the University of Chicago. The doctor was sharing his stories of complex liver transplants when a visitor asked whether a

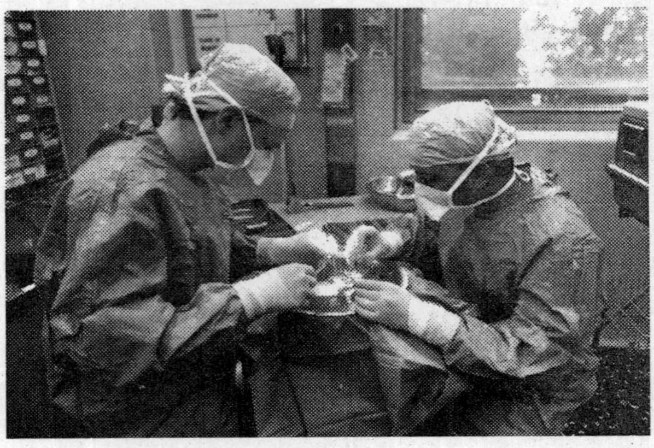

transplant would help her 18-month-old nephew, Shakthi Kandaswamy, who had severe jaundice and had not been eating properly for months. Dr Rajasekar asked her to bring the baby to him the following day.

2. When Shakthi was brought in, he was a yellow baby, suffering from biliary atresia, a congenital deformity in which there is a blockage in the ducts that carry bile from the liver to the gall bladder and the small intestine. Because of this defect, the bile secreted accumulates in the liver and damages it.

3. In such situations, if the connection between the intestine and the liver is made surgically within two months of birth, the child could live a normal life. But in this case, the surgery had not been performed on time, and the toddler had end-stage liver failure and was not able to eat properly. Dr Rajasekar asked the family to take him to Indraprastha Apollo Hospitals, Delhi, where he was working then.

4. Within two days, Shakthi was brought to the hospital where a team of liver specialists examined him. After a lot of discussion, the doctors decided to perform liver transplant surgery. It was risky, and for the team of three—liver transplant surgeons Dr Rajasekar and Dr Arvinder Singh Soin and hepatologist Dr Anupam Sibal—it was a test of all the skills and knowledge they had accumulated over the years. The department for liver transplant was set up at the hospital recently, and they tried a cadaver liver transplant on a 9-month-year-old baby in January 1996, but without success.

5. They decided to use a living donor's liver as it improves the chances of success marginally at least. It was a complicated surgery involving a lot of preparation. The child had to be prepared for the surgery nutritionally and medically. All the possible infections that could lead to complications post-surgery were to be taken into account. The operation theatre had to be sanitised and sterilised several times; a team of nurses and lab technicians had to be trained.

6. The doctors named the toddler Sanjay, meaning victory. He was immediately put on intravenous fluids, and a team of

nurses and paramedics was formed under Dr Sibal to prepare Sanjay for surgery. His nutrition and body weight had to be increased. Sanjay's father, Kandaswamy, a shopkeeper, and mother, a homemaker, were counselled about the pros and cons of the surgery. Kandaswamy agreed to donate a part of his liver.

7. The surgeons and their team of fourteen care givers performed dummy surgeries to avoid any confusion at the time of the actual surgery. This way, the team consisting of surgeons, medicine experts, anaesthetists, intensive care unit personnel and nurses could learn how to play their roles on the day of the actual surgery. By the time of the surgery, each member of the team, consisting of surgeons, medicine consultants, anaesthetists, intensive care physicians and nurses, had Sanjay's medical record information at their fingertips. 'It was like preparing for war. Everything was well planned,' says Rajasekar. He had also roped in his colleague from the US, Dr Ravi Kumar, a paediatric anaesthesiologist, who was flown in for the operation from Chicago.

8. Finally, on 15 November 1998, the team undertook the surgery that lasted for fourteen hours. Sanjay's father was first wheeled into an operation theatre where twenty-five per cent of his liver was removed; immediately, in another theatre, it was implanted in Sanjay's tiny body. Within hours of surgery, Sanjay showed improvement, his bilirubin levels started coming down, and within five days, he started eating food normally. Sanjay was kept in the ICU for three months.

9. Fifteen years on, Sanjay is hale and hearty. The class XI student is studying hard to crack the medical entrance examination next year. 'I want to become a cardiac surgeon,' he says. Sanjay, like any other boy of his age, loves to hang out with friends, is active on social media, has a Facebook account and enjoys watching action films. He loves to play basketball and badminton, has a flair for painting and has an extraordinary interest in human anatomy. 'I sometimes imagine the scene inside the operation theatre where the

surgery was performed on me. I visualise how the doctors would have performed the surgery. It is both exciting and fascinating for me,' he says.

10. The doctors, though they do not work in the same hospital now, are nostalgic when his case is mentioned. 'It was a life changing experience for all of us. We were apprehensive, but there was no other way to save the baby,' says Soin. Agrees Sibal, 'Sanjay's success was the beginning of a new surgical venture in India.' The same year the team performed another successful living donor liver transplant surgery on an adult.
11. In India, about 2,500 children suffering from chronic liver diseases need liver transplant surgery every year. Biliary atresia is the main cause of liver failure in children. If not diagnosed in time, the bile damages the liver and causes its failure. Other medical conditions where liver transplant is the only option are inherited disorders like Wilson's disease, in which copper gets accumulated and damages the liver. Other conditions that affect the liver are progressive familial intrahepatic cholestasis, liver cancer and jaundice.
12. Interestingly, liver transplant, unlike other organ transplants, if done successfully, lasts a lifetime as the liver has the ability to regenerate. 'In fact, a patient can be weaned off immunosuppressants eventually,' says Sibal. In case of paediatric transplants, a part of the liver is crafted in what is called a back-table procedure to make it fit in the child's body. In some cases, doctors may cut it into appropriate shape, according to the child's body. Arteries, veins and the bile duct are grafted according to the child's body. Then, through a microvascular surgery (done under a microscope), the doctors first connect the hepatic veins to allow blood go through the liver. That is followed by connecting the arteries and, finally, the bile duct is connected to the intestine. Within five days of the surgery, a child resumes normal food intake. The donor too can start eating normally within three days, and his or her liver will soon grow back to its normal size.

13. In the past fifteen years, liver transplant surgery has come a long way. Generally, doctors prefer to perform liver transplants on children weighing more than 7 kg. However, advancement in the medical field has also improved the chances for children who weigh less. Since Sanjay's successful liver transplant in 1998, there have been 4,000 successful liver transplants in adults and more than 400 in children in the country. 'Now we have specialised liver operation theatres which have special surgical instruments, monitoring devices and even operation tables to suit liver transplant surgery. We even use robotic and laparoscopic surgeries to remove a part of the liver from the donor's body. It hastens the recovery time for the donor,' says Soin, now the chairman of the liver institute at Medanta, Gurgaon.

14. Also, there are now better medicines to support a liver transplant. For Sanjay, the doctors procured selenium, copper and zinc supplements, which are vital to prepare the child's body for the transplant, from Christian Medical College, Vellore, as not many centres in India were treating liver diseases at that time. Now these supplements are readily available across the country. According to Sibal, the choice and quality of the immunosuppressants, which help the body in accepting the foreign liver, have also drastically improved over the years. Post-operative care is crucial in transplant surgeries. A revolution in intensive care has played an important role in making such complex surgeries a success. In fact, the hospital stay has come down from ninety days in Sanjay's case to seventeen days. Specialised liver operation theatres are available in some centres in the country.

15. What can further help transplant surgeries is awareness about organ donation. Finding a donor is difficult as it involves factoring different parameters such as age, health and size into the selection. Even today not many cadaver transplants are done in India as people are still apprehensive about donating organs. 'A liver if removed in time from a brain-dead person can be stored in a special preservative for 8–10 hours before it is transplanted in a needy patient,' says Dr Subhash

Gupta, chief liver transplant surgeon at Indraprastha Apollo Hospitals. Many more people can be saved if and when more people believe in organ donation.

Gunjan Sharma

Author's note: Shakthi has since joined medical college as a student. (*The Hindu*, 6 August 2015)

Glossary

accumulate	-	here, to gradually increase in quantity
apprehensive	-	feeling anxious
biliary atresia	-	blockage in the ducts that carry bile from the liver to the gall bladder and the small intestine
brain-dead	-	having suffered serious and permanent loss of brain function
cadaver	-	a dead human body
congenital	-	describes a disease or condition that exists at or from birth
crack an exam	-	to be successful in an exam
crucial	-	very important; necessary
deformity	-	the situation in which a part of the body has not developed in the normal way or with the normal shape
drastically	-	here, noticeably
dummy	-	something not real that is used for practice
eventually	-	in the end, especially after a lot of time and effort
hale and hearty	-	in good health
immunosuppressant	-	medicine used after a transplant operation to prevent the immune response of the body
implant	-	to put an organ, device, etc., into the body in a medical operation
jaundice	-	a disease in which excess of bilirubin, a yellow pigment found in bile, in the

		blood makes the skin and white part of the eyes yellow
laparoscopic	-	involving the use of a long thin tube put into a cut made in the body
monitor	-	to watch and check something carefully for a period of time
nostalgic	-	feeling happiness and a sense of longing for a period in the past
sanitise	-	to make something completely clean and free from bacteria
toddler	-	a child who is learning or has recently learnt to walk
wean	-	here, to make someone gradually stop using something that is bad for them

Understanding the text

EXERCISE A

Complete the following sentences by ticking the most suitable of the options given.

1. When Dr Rajasekar was first consulted about Shakthi, he was working in
   a. The University of Chicago.
   b. Kancheepuram.
   c. Gurgaon.
   d. Delhi.
2. The baby was yellow because
   a. he was premature.
   b. his bile duct was blocked.
   c. he was born without a bile duct.
   d. his liver was producing too much bile.
3. The doctors decided to perform liver transplant on the baby because
   a. the baby was at the right age for the surgery.
   b. it was the only way they could save him.

c. a liver transplant done on a baby a couple of years earlier had been successful.
d. the baby was brought to their hospital.

4. According to the doctors, using a living donor's liver
   a. greatly increased the chances of success of the transplant.
   b. only slightly increased the chances of success of the transplant.
   c. decreased the chances of success of the transplant.
   d. was both risky and expensive.
5. The donor of Sanjay's liver was
   a. a stranger.
   b. a friend.
   c. his mother.
   d. his father.
6. After the transplant surgery, Sanjay started eating normally
   a. after five hours.
   b. after five days.
   c. within five days.
   d. after five weeks.
7. Sanjay wants to be a
   a. social activist.
   b. painter.
   c. doctor.
   d. basketball player.
8. Spreading awareness about organ donation will lead to
   a. more funding.
   b. more cadaver transplants.
   c. more living donors.
   d. lower rates of transplant rejection.
9. The reason why liver transplants can last for life is because
   a. of the excellent immunosuppressants now available.
   b. of high-quality post-operative care.
   c. hospitals have specialised liver operation theatres.
   d. the liver can grow again.
10. There are not many cadaver transplants in India because
    a. most of our hospitals do not have the required facilities.
    b. people are afraid to allow the removal of organs after death.

c. people are unaware of how organ donation can save many lives.
d. people do not care about helping strangers.

EXERCISE B

Write short answers to the following questions based on paragraphs 5 to 15.

1. What were the preparations that had to be made for Sanjay's liver transplant?
2. What steps did the doctors take to get the young child ready for the transplant?
3. Why did they do dummy surgeries?
4. What was Sanjay's post-operative condition?
5. What are Sanjay's present interests?
6. What, according to you, is likely to have influenced Sanjay in his decision regarding his future career?
7. Besides biliary atresia, what are some other conditions that could cause liver failure?
8. What are some of the improvements that have helped doctors get good results in liver transplant operations?

Pronunciation

WORD STRESS

Stress within a word and in a sentence is an important aspect of English speech. A word can be divided into sounds which are called syllables. Each syllable usually has a vowel although /l/ and /n/ are also syllabic. A word can be monosyllabic or polysyllabic. The syllable which is said with greater breath force gains more prominence, or is stressed, which is indicated by a vertical mark above the syllable. In monosyllabic words no stress mark is indicated.

time
burst } monosyllabic words

be.ˈgun (2)
ill.ˈness (2)
ˈtea.cher (2)
ˈfam.i.ly (3)
be.ˈgin.ning (3)
ˈcon.sci.ous (3)
ˈab.so.lute.ly (4)

} polysyllabic words

The English stress pattern is fixed and can fall on any syllable of a word. For example:

ˈmelancholy	(stress on the 1st syllable)
reˈmarkable	(stress on the 2nd syllable)
diploˈmatic	(stress on the 3rd syllable)
impossiˈbility	(stress on the 4th syllable)
personifiˈcation	(stress on the 5th syllable)

It is difficult to learn the stress pattern through theoretical rules, but repeated listening to the language can give us a general idea. A few clues can be of help.

- A weak prefix like /ə/ is not stressed. For example:
  aˈlone
  obˈtain

- Suffixes like *-age, -ness, -tion* are not stressed. For example:
  ˈrudeness
  ˈwastage

- Polysyllabic words ending in *-tion* are stressed on the last but one syllable. For example:
  consulˈtation
  qualifiˈcation

- When some words are used both as nouns and verbs, stress and vowel changes can occur according to the function of the word. For example:

noun	**verb**
ˈdecrease	deˈcrease

ˈdigest	diˈgest
ˈpermit	perˈmit

But there are words which are stressed on the same syllable whether they are used as nouns or verbs. For example:

conˈsent
exˈperience
ˈnotice

✦ Stress shifts also happen in the derivatives of some words. For example:

ˈphotograph
phoˈtographer
photoˈgraphic

✦ Some consonants are said with different degrees of force even when they are a part of a stressed syllable. For example, 'put', 'pull', 'push' and 'pound' are said with greater force than 'pure', 'pale', 'power' and 'puff'.

EXERCISE A

Listen to your teacher read the following sentence and mark the stress in the italicised words.

Suddenly I had a misty feeling of something *forgotten*—the *excitement* of *returning* thought; and somehow the *mystery* of language was made clear to me.

EXERCISE B

In the following pairs of sentences, the underlined words show stress shift. Mark stress in each pair of words by placing [ˈ] before the appropriate syllable.

1. a. I <u>object</u> to your statement.
   b. Identify this <u>object</u>.
2. a. We <u>produce</u> textiles of export quality.
   b. The agricultural <u>produce</u> this year has been satisfying.
3. a. They will <u>decrease</u> the bonus this year.

b. There should be a decrease in our population if we want to progress.

EXERCISE C

Mark the stressed syllable in the following words.

1. concern (noun)
2. delight (verb)
3. education
4. tiny
5. determined
6. singers
7. splendid
8. suspect (verb)
9. character
10. wonderful

EXERCISE D

Practise reading the following minimal pairs aloud. Ask your teacher or look up a dictionary whenever necessary to get the meaning and pronunciation of the word right.

	A	B	C
1.	look - luck	light - late	leap - loop
2.	fair - fear	far - fir	fill - fall
3.	corn - cone	came - come	curd - cord
4.	father - further	fool - full	fog - fig
5.	dam - dim	dig - dug	dirt - dot
6.	grim - grime	game - gum	guest - gust
7.	hot - heart	hurt - heat	hole - hall
8.	leap - lop	lick - leak	lock - luck
9.	make - mock	mile - male	mole - mall
10.	pack - peak	pull - pool	plate - pleat

Vocabulary

HOW TO INCREASE YOUR WORD POWER

Words help us express our thoughts, feelings, ideas and reactions when we interact with others. If we have a rich vocabulary, we can communicate fluently and accurately. The right choice of words not only adds depth and force to our communication but also contributes to precision and clarity, which are basic to a good style of speaking and writing. If we have an extensive vocabulary, we can easily understand what we listen to or read.

At the college entry level, many students have a fairly large vocabulary. Extensive reading will help in acquiring new words that will further expand it. A wide vocabulary will enhance your learning capacity and communication skills. However, learning a word means more than knowing its meaning, spelling and pronunciation. What is crucial is your ability to use it in appropriate contexts.

Remember the following points while building your vocabulary for the purposes of study and work.

- Academic communication requires a good command of standard English. Avoid using colloquialisms and slang in formal contexts.
- When you choose vocabulary items, be sure of the exact meanings of the words/phrases. A word can have multiple senses or different shades of meaning. For example, look at some of the meanings of the word 'flat' in different contexts.

  She lives in a *flat*. (a set of rooms for living in)

  Keep the glass jar on a *flat* surface. (level)

  Life in the new town we moved to was rather *flat*. (uninteresting/ without excitement)

  The car battery is *flat*. (without electrical power)

  He spoke in a *flat* voice. (monotonous)

  Our request was met with a *flat* refusal. (complete)

Father drove me to the airport in ten minutes *flat*. (exactly)

- ✦ Sometimes different words are very close in their meanings, varying only in the degree of intensity. For example:

  accident: a bad incident that happens unexpectedly and unintentionally, resulting in damage or injury

  mishap: an unlucky accident

  disaster: a serious accident resulting in great harm, damage or death

- ✦ The relationship between English pronunciation and spelling is complex, and so you must make sure that you get both right for every word. Thus, some words, called 'homophones', which have different spellings and meanings, are pronounced the same way, for example 'site' (place), 'sight' (vision) and 'cite' (quote), all pronounced /saɪt/.

  Some words, called 'homonyms' are pronounced and spelt the same way but have different meanings, for example: 'lie' /laɪ/ means (a) to be in a horizontal position and (b) to speak falsely.

- ✦ It is best to learn words in context. The words that come immediately before and after a word or phrase will help you discover its meaning for use in similar situations. Collocations and idiomatic usage should be learnt as chunks. Collocations are words that normally go together in spoken and written English. They involve all parts of speech, but there are no rules to specify why some combinations are acceptable and others are not. Look at some examples below.

  Losing the match to his student was *a bitter pill to swallow*. (something that is very unpleasant but must be accepted)

  I did not want to *break the news* of the accident to my sister. (to tell someone about something unpleasant)

  He has *chronic arthritis*. (continuing for a long time)

  The woman is *acutely ill*. (extremely ill)

- The best source of all such details about a word or phrase is a standard dictionary or a grammar book. You can pick up useful phrases by listening to formal and informal lectures by good speakers in English. Well-written books are also rich sources of commonly used expressions in context.
- Prepare flash cards with words/phrases on one side and the necessary details on the other and keep them to aid your memory.
- Practise new words/idioms/patterns by using them in the right context in everyday spoken and written communication. Repeated and regular use is the most effective way to learn a new item. Once acquired, the expressions are at your disposal to use in appropriate situations.

BRITISH ENGLISH AND AMERICAN ENGLISH

Apart from formal and informal English, regional varieties of English also exist. The main ones are the British English and American English. The difference between these two varieties is manifested mainly in pronunciation and spelling. There are also a few variations in grammar.

Many words are spelt differently in British English (BrE) and American English (AmE). Most dictionaries include both spellings.

BrE	*AmE*
centre	center
colour	color

In some cases BrE and AmE have different words for the same meaning.

BrE	*AmE*
biscuit	cookie
chemist	drugstore

EXERCISE A

List ten to fifteen words that are spelt differently in British and American English. Use a dictionary if necessary.

EXERCISE B

Write the American equivalents of the following words in British English.

1. queue
2. lift
3. flyover
4. dressing gown
5. nappy
6. torch
7. full stop
8. dustbin
9. holiday
10. flat
11. postbox
12. mobile phone
13. curriculum vitae
14. autumn
15. pavement
16. lorry

THESAURUSES

Apart from the general dictionaries, there are specialised ones covering specific study disciplines. A medical dictionary would give you all the technical terms and many other relevant words associated with health care.

The *thesaurus* is another useful book that we can use to enrich our vocabulary. For easy reference, it groups together all the synonyms of a word, with different shades of meaning ranging from the positive to the negative. For example, look at some of the words grouped in a thesaurus under the words 'thin' and 'strong-willed' respectively.

slim/lean/slender/slight/willowy/svelte (all convey a positive sense)

skinny/gaunt/emaciated/stick-like/scrawny (all convey a negative sense)

firm/strong/resolute/tenacious/persistent (all convey a positive sense) obstinate/inflexible/stubborn/pigheaded/dogmatic/fanatical (all convey a negative sense)

Some thesauruses list the words expressing a range of meanings, from similar to opposite. This makes it easy for us to choose the right word, which is essential in order to be accurate. For example:

Susan *never/hardly/occasionally/sometimes/often/always* goes jogging in the park.

By grouping together the synonyms and antonyms of words, a thesaurus makes it easy for us to write and speak using a variety of expressions. It is very useful when we are drafting formal speeches or essays. It will help us introduce variety and vitality into our speech and writing, and in the course of time, the new words will become a part of our vocabulary.

EXERCISE C

Look up the following words in a thesaurus and list a minimum of six synonyms for each of them.

1. compassionate
2. difficult
3. pain
4. competent
5. change

EXERCISE D

Complete the following sentences by filling in the blanks with one word that has a similar meaning to the word/phrase underlined. For example, 'He is an <u>outstanding</u> surgeon and also a *brilliant* artist.' Sometimes there may be a change in word class (noun ←→ adjective). For example, 'He is a <u>famous</u> writer, but his *popularity* never made him proud.'

1. She was crippled in an accident but has courageously learnt to live with her ....
2. The cut is extremely painful. The doctors are worried about the .... pain.
3. You must be attentive in class. Unless you are ...., you will miss the important points.
4. After her fifth delivery, she barely has strength to walk. We must build up her ....
5. The nurses warned him about being out in direct sunlight. They .... him against taking the instructions lightly.
6. The hospital has a group of sincere staff. The .... are known for their dedicated work.
7. Mild airway obstruction can worsen if edema increases. We must prevent such ....
8. Approximately 360 ml IV fluid is needed. The .... amount can be bought at the chemists.
9. He has advised me on many occasions when I needed .... on career prospects.
10. She has no liking for food. I am worried about her loss of ....
11. He is sleepy. The drug has made him ....
12. His intake of salt is too much. Anything in .... will affect our health.
13. His condition is slowly deteriorating. It is frightening to watch the .... decline in health.
14. The play received unfavourable reviews. These .... comments have affected the director terribly.
15. The sudden beginning of the epidemic caught them unawares. The .... of the disease has affected the whole village.

Grammar

AGREEMENT

You would have learnt at school about nouns, verbs, pronouns, adjectives, adverbs, conjunctions, etc., and how words belonging to these groups come together in various combinations to form sentences. It is important that in a sentence there is agreement (concord) among the units. To take subject–verb concord, for example, it means that when the sentence is in the simple present tense, third person singular nouns take a different verb form from the rest of the noun forms. But there are quite a number of exceptions to this rule depending on the type of linking words and nouns in use.

Given below are some rules that govern subject–verb concord.

- Two singular subjects linked by 'and' usually takes a plural verb. For example:

  Cynthia and Sneha *are* good at singing.

- However, when the two items are always thought of together, the verb is singular. For example:

  The bread and butter in the fridge *is* fresh.

- When the two nouns in a sentence refer to the same person, the verb is singular. For example:

  The renowned painter and sculptor *was* honoured by the Arts Academy.

  (If the painter and sculptor are two individuals, the article 'the' should precede the second noun as well.)

- When two singular nouns are linked by 'either . . . or/neither . . . nor', the verb is singular. For example:

  Either Kala or her sister *is* meeting me.

- However, if one of the nouns is plural, the verb is plural, and the plural noun should be placed next to it. For example:

  Either Kavita or her sisters *are* meeting me.

- When there is no clue to the number of the nouns mentioned, a singular verb is used. For example:

  Neither Asif nor his friends *are* coming.
  but Neither of them *is* coming.

- In sentences with linking words 'together with/along with/ as well as/not only . . . but also', the form of the verb depends on the number of the first noun. For example:

  The *captain* as well as the players *is* ready to go.

  The *players* as well as the captain *are* ready to go.

- The words 'each' and 'every' take a singular verb even when followed by plural nouns. For example:

  Each of them *is* ready to play.

- Words referring to money take a singular verb. For example:

  Five hundred rupees *is* a lot of money.

- Collective nouns take singular or plural verbs depending on whether they are thought of as a whole or as a collection of individuals. For example:

  The committee *has* decided to pass the bill.
  The committee *are* arriving at different times this morning.

  For the sake of clarity it is preferable to rewrite the second sentence as:

  The committee members *are* arriving at different times this morning.

- Titles of books take a singular verb. But if it is a collection of tales, the singular or plural form can be used. For example:

  'Pride and Prejudice' *is* my favourite novel
  'Aesop's Tales' *is/are* very popular.

- Uncountable nouns, such as 'furniture' and 'crockery', take singular verbs. For example:

  The furniture *is* made of teakwood.

- Words such as 'police', 'clergy' and 'cattle' take plural verbs. For example:

  The police *were* very helpful.

- When a plural noun within inverted commas is the subject, the verb is singular. For example:

  'Senior citizens' *means* people over sixty.

- When a clause forms the subject, the verb is singular. For example:

  What you think *is* important to me.

- When a phrase forms the subject, the choice of verb will depend on the number of the headword. For example:

  A *study* of his poems *reveals* his concern for the poor.
  My *plans* for my sister *have* finally come through.

- Phrases with the words 'some', 'more than', 'any', 'majority', 'percentage', etc., follow the rule of proximity—that is, the number of the noun preceding the verb decides the choice of the verb. For example:

  Some of them *are* willing.
  but Some of it *is* spoilt.

  The majority of the students always *win*.
  but The majority of the class always *wins*.

  More than a thousand people *have* been affected by the strike.
  but More than one person *has* offered to help.

  In fact, in informal communication, the rule of proximity seems to decide the choice of verbs even in the case of 'each', 'every', 'either . . . or', 'neither . . . nor', 'none', etc.

English, like other languages, is dynamic and rules of grammar change to match popular usage. But the process is very slow, with both forms existing side by side until over the years a particular usage gains preference. In formal and academic writing, it is advisable to follow standard rules of English unless they are considered outdated.

EXERCISE A

Fill in the blanks in the following sentences with one of the verb forms given below. Discuss your answers with the teacher.

is **are** **has** **have**

1. The difficulty of obtaining pure milk and other household articles .... too much.
2. Several books and magazines .... on sale today.
3. The problems related to his lifestyle .... affected his health.
4. Measles .... spreading fast in the southern regions.
5. The treasurer and the manager .... come to the party.
6. The treasurer and manager .... organising the function.
7. The police .... done an excellent job.
8. The team .... playing very well.
9. A large percentage .... come with their children.
10. Ten percent of my income .... for charity.
11. Bread and butter .... my favourite breakfast.
12. Either of them .... capable of setting a new record in athletics.
13. Either Sheeba or her friends .... completed the job.
14. Neither Ravi nor his brother .... capable of organising this.
15. Every one of the boys .... willing to help.
16. The leader along with his followers .... come.
17. Ramesh together with his colleagues .... organised the show.
18. Tamil as well as foreign languages .... taught in our college.
19. Not only the captain but also the players .... ready to take up the challenge.
20. Not only my friends but also my sister .... come for the party.
21. Some men .... agreeable to our suggestion.
22. Some help .... to be given to the poor.
23. The majority of them .... gone home.
24. More than fifty persons .... signed the petition.
25. More then one class .... decided to help out.

INTERROGATIVES

In the medical field, questions play a vital role in history taking, gathering current information, clarifying doubts and establishing a rapport with patients. Questions are formed by placing the verb in front of the subject or by the initial positioning of an interrogative or a *Wh*-word. For example:

> Are you there?
> Can I help you?
> Do you want the book?
> When can I meet you?

According to the types of answers expected, questions are divided into three categories.

Yes–No questions

In Yes–No questions, the answers will be either yes or no. For example:

> Do you want to come to the zoo?
> Are you ready?

Wh- questions

In *Wh*- questions, the answers will supply information. For example:

> Why are you staring at that man?
> What made you jump down?

Alternative questions

In alternative questions, the answers will be one of the options presented. For example:

> Will you be at home or in the library?
> Would you like to go to the museum or the cinema?

While communicating, we use a combination of all types of questions depending on the purpose.

EXERCISE B

Frame five questions using 'who', 'where', 'how', 'why' and 'when' to bring out the information in the sentence given below.

Indira is going by train to Kanpur today to meet her sister.

EXERCISE C

Do as directed.

1. He spoke well. (Frame a question using 'how'.)
2. She likes travelling. (Frame a question using 'what'.)

EXERCISE D

Frame Yes–No questions using 'do', 'does' or 'did'.

1. They danced for our college day.
2. Balu organises concerts to raise funds.
3. They run very fast.
4. They worked hard for the final examination.
5. He planned to go abroad.
6. She meets Sowmya near the school.
7. He participates in all the tournaments.
8. Priya practises every day.

EXERCISE E

Frame Yes–No questions by the inversion method.

1. He can join us.
2. She was late for the class.
3. They are going on a picnic.
4. She has agreed to represent our school.
5. They have searched all the rooms.

EXERCISE F

Is there a way of forming a question without placing the verb in front of the subject? Discuss.

EXERCISE G

Read the passage given below and write 8–10 questions of different types (using Wh- words, modals, etc.) that would elicit the information in the passage.

I am Divya. Ever since I can remember, I have been curious about the way people think and behave. When I was in Class XI, I was introduced to the subject of psychology: I was captivated. I continued studying it through Classes XI and XII, after which I decided that I wanted to study Psychology in college. With every semester I became more and more interested in the discipline, as I learnt about various aspects of the theory and practice of psychology.

My professional aim is to develop centres that cater to the requirements of children with special needs – their education, the therapy they need and counselling for their caregivers, among many other things. I feel that there is very little awareness in India about children with special needs, and the amount of support they receive is negligible.

I am passionately committed to bringing about a change in special education in the Indian context. I believe that my avid interest in psychology along with my keenness to understand people will help me develop into someone who can further this dream and turn it into reality.

I believe that psychology has had and will have a huge role in shaping me into someone who can not only understand but also help differently abled children attain their full potential. It would be a privilege to get a chance to do my Masters in Psychology, and I will work steadily towards this.

TAG QUESTIONS

Tag questions are short questions added on to statements for the purpose of asking for agreement or confirmation. A tag question has a verb and a pronoun that corresponds to the subject of the statement. Where the finite verb in the statement includes an auxiliary verb (e.g., 'was sleeping', where 'sleeping' is the main verb and 'was' is an auxiliary verb), it is the auxiliary that appears as the verb in the tag question (in this case, ' . . . wasn't she/he?'). If, on the other hand, the finite verb in the sentence consists of only a main verb (e.g., 'dances'), the auxiliary verb 'do' functions as the verb particle in the tag question (which here would be 'doesn't she/he?'). For example:

Benjamin <u>is not teaching</u> journalism, *is he?*
Spring always <u>follows</u> winter, *doesn't it?*

Note that in an affirmative sentence, the tag is negative, and vice versa. It must also be remembered that the question tag appears in the same tense as the preceding statement. For example:

They <u>were singing</u> well, *weren't they?* (*not* 'aren't they?')

Rajan usually <u>comes</u> home for Deepavali, *doesn't he?* (*not* 'didn't he?')

Sheela <u>will not have left</u> for Sri Lanka, *will she*? (*not* 'has she?')

EXERCISE H

Add tag questions to the following sentences.

1. Francis did a good job.
2. Farida has come from Delhi.
3. The children are joining us.
4. Sheila cannot accept her failure.
5. Your friends will come with us.
6. You travel a lot.

7. The watch is not expensive.
8. Mukesh is getting discharged from the hospital today.
9. The umpires came early to meet the board members.
10. Vijay is eager to learn music.

Speaking

THE ROLE OF NONVERBAL COMMUNICATION

Nonverbal communication is the transmission of a message without the use of words. It occurs mostly in conjunction with verbal messages and includes aspects such as general appearance, eye contact, use of voice, facial expressions, posture and gestures, which convey a variety of messages. Silence, distance and touch too are forms of language conveying acceptance and caring or indifference. We should be sensitive to nonverbal cues and learn to interpret them correctly and integrate them with verbal messages.

While communicating in our mother tongues, we effectively integrate the nonverbal cues, and it is important that we do the same while communicating in English. But the manner in which nonverbal modes of expression are used and interpreted is often dictated by cultural, ethnic and individual differences, and these differences need to be understood. Otherwise we may make invalid assumptions unintentionally.

For example, when faced with death, some people express their sorrow through loud wails and spoken words. In such cases, empathising verbally would help them. But for others in similar situations, silence and a gentle touch would be perhaps more meaningful than words. Nonverbal cues take on different meanings depending on the context. Think of other situations where people may react differently to nonverbal communication.

EXERCISE A

What do the following nonverbal cues convey? You could give more than one answer. For example, clean clothing and good grooming

convey a sense of respect and caring for oneself and for others. The first three are done for you.

1. glancing frequently at the watch during a conversation *usually indicates that the person is either not interested or is in a hurry.*
2. frowning *could mean impatience, doubt or concern*
3. good posture *shows confidence*
4. arms crossed over the chest ....
5. hands on hips ....
6. shifting uncomfortably while talking ....
7. tapping feet and drumming fingers ....
8. eye contact with the interlocutor ....
9. holding the interlocutor's hands ....
10. standing very close to a person while talking ....

GROUP WORK/DISCUSSION

Being in college offers students many opportunities to interact in academic and social settings with friends, classmates, seniors and teachers. You need good interpersonal skills to work in teams. Soft skills, such as team spirit, flexibility, critical thinking and the ability to handle pressure, contribute positively to building a good rapport with the others in your team. Conversational skills are crucial to win over your teammates and make them understand and accept your point of view. Here are a few tips and language expressions that you can use to hold conversations with more confidence.

✦ A conversation or a discussion involves taking turns so that all the speakers have equal opportunities to express their thoughts. The skill of knowing when to start and finish a turn in a conversation without being dominated or dominating helps a conversation flow smoothly. You must stop at appropriate intervals to allow others to take their turns. Pauses and a drop in the pitch at the end of an utterance indicate the end of a speaker's turn and signal others to participate in the conversation.

- Facilitate interaction by drawing out silent or shy participants with questions like *What do you think?*, *Would you like to say/add something?*, *Have you anything else to say?* and *Let us hear what Naveen has to say.*
- You can politely interrupt the dominating ones so that you save time and encourage participation across the board. A few expressions that can be used to interrupt politely are *Excuse me*, *Do you mind if I say something?*, *I just want to say . . .*, *Can I have a word, please?* and *Just a moment.*
- Express your point of view/opinion politely without being rude or aggressive. The following expressions will help you do it.

  The way I see it, . . .
  In my opinion, . . .
  As far as I'm concerned, . . .
  I think (that) . . .
  I honestly feel (that) . . .
  I strongly believe (that) . . .
- You can disagree but do not argue. Put it across politely with statements like *I don't think that is the way to go about . . .*, *Don't you think that it would be better if . . .?*, *I'm afraid I don't agree . . .*, and *Shouldn't we consider . . .?*
- Some expressions you can use to convey the degree of your agreement with a particular point of view are *I really agree with you*, *I think you are right*, *I am with you on that*, *What you say is partly true* and *I agree with the first part of what you said.*
- Use open-ended questions starting with *why*, *what*, etc., for seeking clarifications. Paraphrasing is another tool that can be used for the purpose (e.g. *Are you saying that . . .?*).

EXERCISE B

Your college is planning to raise funds to offer scholarships for school students in an orphanage. Some of your classmates want to have a variety entertainment programme to raise funds, whereas others

feel a food fair will be a better idea. It is decided to present the matter at the college students' union meeting. Take a stand and have a discussion on the issue.

INTERVIEW

EXERCISE C

Imagine you are going to interview Ms Ann Sullivan for television. Prepare a set of ten questions for the interview and enact the scene.

EXERCISE D

Work in two groups. The first group thinks of a famous person. The second group tries to guess the name of the person by asking a maximum of twenty Yes–No questions. Repeat the exercise so that the first group gets to ask the questions.

EXERCISE E

1. **Look at the picture below from a nursing journal. Guess the title of the article that goes with it. Discuss the title with your teacher.**
2. **Suggest five ways to achieve the goal related to the title.**

Writing

EXPRESSING VIEWS

EXERCISE

What do you think is the most important quality a nurse should have? Write a paragraph on the topic in about 100 words.

Appreciating poetry

Warblers

When we wrestle soft old people
into their beds, clawing and shriveled,
I can't help thinking freedom is instinct
and falling is no worse
than flying without wings.

In wheelchairs, they become reels
of silent movies, gray and terribly sad,
dressed in flapping arms
and pale blue gowns.

Hasn't the sky already tumbled?
Their ribs are paper kites
lonely for sunset
and lunging in short bursts
from their chests.

What can I do but catch this string,
fasten to our steel, keep them
from blowing into thickets
or over the edge of boulders.

I find it impossible not to imagine
them before—pink and round and barefoot—
racing each other in cool spring air,
where, suddenly, their cries become warblers
who can't stop calling for help
before the cat creeps back
grinning, waving his midnight tail.

Hortense Wood

EXERCISE

Write short answers to the following questions.

1. What is the mood of the poem?
2. Do you agree with what the poet is saying? Discuss.

UNIT 3

Jimmy Valentine

> The true measure of a man is how he treats someone who can do him absolutely no good.
>
> —*Samuel Johnson*

Read the story of Jimmy Valentine and complete it using your own ideas.

1. Jimmy Valentine was busy making shoes in the prison shoe shop. He had almost served ten months of his four-year sentence. With many influential friends, he usually managed to get out of prison faster. This time, after the Spring Field robbery, Ben Price had arrested him and Jimmy's friends had a tough time getting the Governor's pardon for him. He was released only after ten months. Jimmy went back to the cafe which belonged to his friend Mike Dolan.
2. He got his key and went upstairs, unlocking the door of a room at the rear. Everything was just as he had left it. There on the floor was Ben Price's collar-button, which was still lying as it had been torn from that eminent detective's shirt band when they had overpowered Jimmy to arrest him.
3. Pulling out a folding-bed from the wall, Jimmy slid back a panel in the wall and dragged out a dust-covered suitcase. He opened this and gazed fondly at the finest set of burglar's tools in the East. It was a complete set, made of specially tempered steel, the latest designs in drills, punches, braces and

bits, jimmies, clamps and augers, with two or three novelties invented by Jimmy himself, in which he took pride. Over nine hundred dollars they had cost him to have them made at a place where they make such things for the profession.

4. In half an hour Jimmy went downstairs through the cafe. He was now dressed in tasteful and well-fitting clothes, and carried his dusted and cleaned suitcase in his hand.

5. A week after the release of Valentine there was a neat job of safe burglary done in Richmond, Indiana, with no clue to the burglar. A scant eight hundred dollars was all that was stolen. Two weeks after that, a patented, improved burglar-proof safe in Longansport was opened like a cheese to the tune of fifteen hundred dollars currency; securities and silver were untouched. That began to interest the rogue catchers. Then there was another burglary in the old-fashioned bank of Jefferson City, and there was a loss amounting to five thousand dollars. The losses were now high enough to bring the matter up to Ben Price's class of work.

6. By comparing notes, a remarkable similarity in the methods of the burglaries was noticed. Ben Price investigated the scene of the robberies, and was heard to remark, 'That's Dandy Jim Valentine's autograph. He's resumed business. Look at that combination knob—jerked out as easy as pulling up a radish in wet weather. He's got the only clamps that can do it. Jimmy never had to drill more than one hole. Yes, I guess I want Mr Valentine. He'll do his bit next time without any short time or clemency foolishness.'

7. Ben Price knew Jimmy's habits. He had studied them while working on the Spring Field case. Long jumps, quick getaways, no confederates and a taste for good society; these ways had helped Mr Valentine to become noted as a successful dodger of retribution. It was made known that Ben Price had taken up the trail of the elusive cracksman, and other people with burglar-proof safes felt more at ease.

8. One afternoon Jimmy Valentine, carrying his suitcase, climbed out of the mail-hack in Elmore, a little town five miles off the

railroad down in the black-jack country of Arkansas. Jimmy, looking like an athletic young senior just home from college, went down the sidewalk towards the hotel.

9. A young lady crossed the street, passed him at the corner and entered a door over which was the sign 'The Elmore Bank'. Jimmy Valentine looked into her eyes, forgot what he was, and became another man. She lowered her eyes and coloured slightly. Young men of Jimmy's style and looks were scarce in Elmore.

10. Jimmy cornered a boy who was loafing on the steps of the bank as if he were one of the stockholders, and began to ask him questions about the town, feeding him dimes at intervals. Eventually, the young lady came out, looking royally unconscious of the young man with the suitcase, and went her way.

    'Isn't that young lady Miss Polly Simpson?' asked Jimmy, with not-so-true charm. 'Naw', said the boy. 'She's Annabel Adams. Her pa owns this bank.'

11. Jimmy went to a hotel and registered as Ralph D. Spencer. He studied the business situation at Elmore and found there would be good business. Mr Ralph Spencer, the phoenix that arose from Jimmy Valentine's ashes—ashes left by the flame of a sudden attack of love—remained in Elmore and prospered. He opened a shoe store and did good business. Socially too he was a success and made many friends. And he accomplished his heart's wish. He met Miss Annabel Adams and became more and more captivated by her charms.

12. At the end of a year, the situation of Mr Ralph Spencer was this: he had won the respect of the community, his shoe store was flourishing, and he and Annabel were engaged to be married in two weeks. Mr Adams, the typical plodding country banker, approved of Spencer. Annabel's pride in him almost equalled her affection. He was as much at home in the family of Mr Adams and that of Annabel's married sister as if he were already a member.

13. One day Jimmy sat down in his room and wrote this letter, which he mailed to the safe address of one of his old friends in St Louis:

Dear Pal,

I want you to be at Sullivan's place, in Little Rock, next Wednesday night at nine o' clock. I want you to wind up some little matters for me. And, also, I want to make you a present of my kit of tools. I know you'll be glad to get them—you couldn't duplicate the lot for a thousand dollars. Say, Billy, I've quit the old business—a year ago. I've got a nice store. I'm making an honest living and I'm going to marry the finest girl on earth two weeks from now. It's the only life, Billy, the straight one. I wouldn't touch a dollar of another man's money now for a million. After I get married I am going to sell out and go West, where there won't be so much danger of having old scores brought up against me. I tell you, Billy, she's an angel. She believes in me; and I wouldn't do another crooked thing for the whole world. Be sure to be at Sully's, for I must see you. I'll bring along the tools with me.

Your old friend,

Jimmy

14. On the Monday night after Jimmy wrote this letter, Ben Price jogged unobtrusively into Elmore in a livery buggy. He lounged about town in his quiet way until he found out what he wanted to know. From the drug store across the street from Spencer's shoe store, he got a good look at Ralph D. Spencer.

'Going to marry the banker's daughter, are you, Jimmy?' said Ben to himself, softly, 'Well, I don't know!'

15. The next morning Jimmy had breakfast at the Adams'. He was going to Little Rock that day to order his wedding suit and buy something nice for Annabel. This would be the first time he would be leaving town since he came to Elmore. It had been more than a year now since those last professional 'jobs', and he thought he could safely venture out.

16. After breakfast quite a family party went down town together. Mr Adams, Annabel, Jimmy and Annabel's married sister with her two little girls aged five and nine. They came by the hotel where Jimmy still boarded, and he ran up to his room and brought along his suitcase. Then they went on to the bank. There stood Jimmy's horse and buggy and Dolph Gibson, who was going to drive him over to the railroad station.

17. All of them went inside the high, carved oak railings into the banking room, Jimmy included, for Mr Adam's future son-in-law was welcome anywhere. The clerks were pleased to be greeted by the good-looking agreeable young man who was going to marry Miss Annabel.

18. The Elmore Bank had just put in a new safe and vault. Mr Adams was very proud of it and insisted on an inspection by everyone. The vault was a small one, but it had a new patented door. It fastened with three solid steel belts thrown simultaneously with a single handle, and had a time lock. Mr Adams beamingly explained its workings to Mr Spencer, who showed a courteous, but not too intelligent interest. The two children, May and Agatha, were delighted by the shining metal and funny clock and knobs.

19. While they were thus engaged, Ben Price sauntered in and leaned on his elbow, looking casually inside between the

railings. He told the teller that he didn't want anything; he was just waiting for a man he knew.

20. Suddenly there was a scream or two from the women, and a commotion. Unperceived by the elders, May, the nine-year-old girl, in a spirit of play, had shut Agatha in the vault. She had then shot the bolts and turned the knob of the combination as she had seen Mr Adams do.

21. The old banker sprang to the handle and tugged at it for a moment, but it wouldn't open because the clock hadn't been wound, nor the combination set. Agatha's mother screamed again, hysterically.

    'Hush!' said Mr Adams, raising his trembling hand, 'Everyone be quiet for a moment.' 'Agatha!' he called as loudly as he could, 'Listen to me.'

    During the following silence they could just hear the faint sound of the child wildly shrieking in the dark vault in a panic of terror.

22. 'My precious darling!' wailed the mother, 'She will die of fright. Open the door! Oh, break it open! Can't you men do something?'

    'There isn't a man nearer than Little Rock who can open that door,' said Mr Adams in a shaky voice, 'My God! Spencer, what shall we do? That child, she can't stand it long in there. There isn't enough air, and besides, she will go into convulsions from fright!'

23. Agatha's mother, frantic now, beat the door of the vault with her hands. Somebody wildly suggested dynamite. Annabel turned to Jimmy, her large eyes full of anguish but not yet despairing. To a woman nothing seems quite impossible to the powers of the man she worships.

    'Can't you do something, Ralph?'

(adapted from the story 'Retrieved Reform' by O. Henry)

Glossary

accomplish	-	to fulfil
buggy	-	here, a light carriage pulled by one horse
burglar	-	thief
captivate	-	to attract and hold the attention and interest of someone
clemency	-	mercy, especially when giving a punishment
confederate	-	someone you work together with in a secret, sometimes illegal, activity
dime	-	a coin
dodger of retribution	-	one who escapes deserved punishment
elusive cracksman	-	a thief difficult to catch
eminent	-	famous and respected
investigate	-	to examine all facts about a crime, accident, etc.
loaf	-	to spend one's time in an aimless, idle way
lounge	-	here, to stand in a relaxed way
mail-hack	-	a hired horse-drawn carriage carrying mail and passengers in the past
novelty	-	a new unusual thing
old score	-	an old mistake
overpower	-	to defeat or overcome with superior strength
phoenix	-	a mythical bird that sets fire to itself every five hundred years and is born again from its ashes
prosper or flourish	-	to become successful financially
shriek	-	to shout in a high pitched voice
tug	-	to pull
unobtrusively	-	unnoticeably
vault	-	a room protected by locks, thick walls, etc., used to keep money or valuable things safe

Understanding the text

EXERCISE A

Write short answers to the following questions.

1. What lay hidden in the suitcase in Jimmy's room?
2. Why was detective Ben Price sure that Jimmy was responsible for the robberies?
3. How did Jimmy's way of working help him escape punishment?
4. How did Jimmy find out the name of the young woman he saw outside the Elmore Bank?
5. What was Jimmy's life in Elmore like?
6. Why did Jimmy want to give away his tools?
7. Why did Jimmy go to the Elmore Bank with Annabel's family?
8. What made Agatha's mother scream?

EXERCISE B

Complete the story using your own ideas and the following questions to guide you.

- Was Agatha saved?
- Did Jimmy open the safe?
- Was Jimmy arrested by Ben Price?
- Did Annabel marry Jimmy?

Pronunciation

SENTENCE STRESS AND RHYTHM

English words belong to two categories—content words and function words. In connected speech, only content words are usually stressed.

Nouns, verbs, adjectives and adverbs are content words which give us important information and express ideas and feelings. Apart from these, there are a few other words that are also key to understanding what is written or spoken. These include the negative 'no', demonstrative pronouns 'this', 'that', 'these' and 'those', and question words 'what', 'where', 'which', 'when', 'how' and 'why'. These words are also stressed in oral communication.

The function words in a sentence help us connect the meaning conveyed by the content words and thus help us understand what is expressed. Function words include auxiliary verbs, articles, conjunctions and pronouns. Auxiliary verbs are used to mark the tense of the main verb, prepositions show relationships in time and space, articles tell us that something referred to is specific or one of many, and pronouns refer to nouns mentioned earlier. These words are sometimes stressed to make the meaning clear or to add emphasis or to bring out a contrast.

I don't want to talk to ˈher.

I wanted to see ˈhim, not ˈyou.

EXERCISE A

Underline the content words in the following sentences

1. Geeta has started a new business.
2. He's flying to London next week.
3. I don't understand this theorem.
4. The children are at the swimming pool.
5. We decided to go to a concert.
6. The best time to study is early in the morning or late in the evening.
7. The trees along the lake are beginning to bloom.
8. Our friends called us yesterday and asked if we'd like to visit them next month.
9. You'll be happy to know that Maria's got distinction in English.
10. I have decided to join the tennis club.

EXERCISE B

Read the given sentence six times, stressing each time a different word. Does it make any difference to the meaning conveyed? Discuss.

1	2	3	4	5	6
I	thought	you	were going	home	today.

WEAK FORMS

Each language has its own rules with regard to its pronunciation. English is a stress-timed language, which means that when speaking in English, the time taken to pronounce the words between the stressed syllables is the same. For example, read the two sentences given below stressing only the content words.

> It was fˈascinating to ˈphotograph the ˈbeautiful ˈmountain near the ˈlake.
>
> She can ˈcome on ˈSaturdays as long as she ˈdoesn't have to do ˈhomework in the ˈevening.

Though the second sentence is longer than the first, the time taken to read the two will almost be the same because most of the words in the second sentence are unstressed function words. We usually use the weak forms of these words when we speak. Some of these are listed below.

auxiliary verbs

am	/əm, m/
can	/kən, kn, kŋ/
is	/ɪz, s/
shall	/ʃəl, ʃl, ʃə, ʃ/
will	/l/
would	/wəd, əd, d/

conjunctions

and	/ənd, ən, nd, n/

prepositions

for	/fə/

of /əv, v, f/

pronouns

her /ɜː, hə, ə/

his /ɪz/

them /ðəm, ðm, əm/

articles

an /ən, n/

However, knowledge of the sounds and stress pattern alone will not make us good speakers of English unless one learns to pronounce them and get the rhythm right while communicating orally. The rhythm produced by the combination of stressed and unstressed syllables is one of the main features of spoken English.

English spoken with only strong forms has the wrong rhythm, sounds unnatural and does not help the listener to distinguish emphasis or meaning. The learner who can maintain the rhythm of the language will sound both natural and fluent.

Many factors contribute towards getting the rhythm of spoken English right. Some ways of ensuring smooth flow of speech are dropping sounds, gliding over function words and leaving even some content words unstressed.

Speed is also a characteristic feature of fluency. When we speak quickly, especially in conversations and informal speeches, we tend to utter groups of words together so that they are heard as a continuous stream, without pauses between them. However, it is certainly not worth achieving fluency at the cost of clarity, so we must moderate the speed of our speech to ensure that we are understood.

EXERCISE C

Read the given lines from the poem 'Daffodils' by William Wordsworth twice, first using the weak forms of the unstressed

words, and then with their strong forms. Comment on the difference in the flow of speech in the two versions.

I wandered lonely as a cloud
That floats on high o'er vales and hills,
When all at once, I saw a crowd
A host of golden daffodils;
Beside the lake, beneath the trees,
Fluttering and dancing in the breeze.
Continuous as the stars that shine
And twinkle on the Milky Way,
They stretched in never-ending line
Along the margin of a bay:
Ten thousand saw I at a glance,
Tossing their heads in sprightly dance.

INTONATION

Intonation is related to the variations in pitch that occur while speaking. We have a falling or rising intonation or a combination of both within a word or spread over a sentence. They are indicated by slash marks as shown below.

1. She doesn't like it. (falling intonation)
2. Give it to me, please. (rising intonation)
3. You say she is clever. (falling and rising intonation)

Complete and definite statements, strong commands and exclamations take a falling intonation. Incomplete statements, requests and greetings take a rising intonation. Falling and rising intonation is used in sarcastic comments or statements implying doubts.

One-word questions, *Wh*- questions asked in a neutral way and alternative questions use falling intonation. Rising intonation is used with Yes–No questions demanding an answer, questions conveying surprise (e.g. 'Really?') and *Wh*- questions asked in a friendly way.

In short, intonation reveals the attitude and emotion of the speaker and draws attention to the important word by emphasising it.

EXERCISE D

Read the following sentences and identify the attitude of the speaker (sarcastic, neutral, authoritative, friendly, polite, doubtful, etc).

1. Give it to me.
2. Did you see her?
3. This is great.
4. What do you want?
5. Take this to my room.

Vocabulary

HOMONYMS, HOMOGRAPHS AND HOMOPHONES

Words that have the same form (spelling) and pronunciation but different meanings are called *homonyms*. For example:

word	pronunciation	meaning
bank	/bæŋk/	a. ground near river
		b. establishment for custody of money
grave	/greɪv/	a. serious
		b. place of burial; tomb

Words that are spelled the same but pronounced differently are called *homographs*.

word	pronunciation	meaning
lead	/led/	a. metal
	/li:d/	b. show the way by going in front
row	/rəʊ/	a. propel (a boat); arrangement in straight lines
	/raʊ/	b. quarrel

Words that have different spellings and meanings but are pronounced the same way are called *homophones*. For example, 'sole' (the underside of a person's foot) and 'soul' (the spiritual part of a person) are both pronounced /səʊl/.

EXERCISE A

Categorise the following words under homonyms and homographs. What are the two meanings and pronunciations of the words?

1. bow
2. excise
3. ground
4. critical
5. minute
6. swallow
7. wind
8. tear
9. sow
10. buffet
11. fair
12. host
13. left
14. ring
15. bark
16. change
17. fast
18. content
19. genial
20. invalid
21. lie
22. stool
23. trip
24. bolt
25. trunk

EXERCISE B

Your teacher will read out words which can be spelt in two different ways, as for example, 'queue' and 'cue'. Listen carefully and write down both the words. Discuss the difference in their meanings.

EXERCISE C

The following words are taken from paragraphs 1, 2 and 5 of the story of Jimmy Valentine. Each word has different meanings. Frame sentences to bring out the difference in meanings. Change in word class (noun verb, noun adjective, etc.) is allowed.

1. sentence para 1
2. back
3. room para 2
4. just
5. still
6. safe para 5

7. tune
8. interest
9. class
10. notes

WORD GAME

EXERCISE D

Find the hidden roots and suffixes of medical words in the grid below. The words may be hidden left to right, top to bottom, vertically, horizontally or diagonally.

a	B	S	S	I	T	I	L	E	Y	M	S
b	H	I	S	T	E	C	T	O	M	Y	E
c	D	T	N	E	U	R	O	C	E	L	E
d	E	I	O	T	O	R	R	H	E	A	M
e	P	T	V	R	F	E	L	C	Y	N	Y
f	H	A	P	M	P	S	O	G	I	C	O
g	U	M	R	H	A	T	J	D	L	E	L
h	S	O	I	Y	A	C	I	G	K	P	O
i	I	T	B	P	O	O	A	P	O	H	G
j	S	S	E	R	T	S	H	D	M	A	Y
k	A	H	I	S	T	M	O	T	Y	L	A
l	T	H	O	R	I	L	H	M	A	O	I
m	C	C	I	H	O	D	O	G	E	S	G
n	E	C	O	G	A	T	E	R	E	C	L
o	B	A	Y	L	O	M	E	N	I	O	A
p	E	N	T	E	O	T	O	T	O	P	D
q	L	V	L	I	R	T	I	N	H	Y	I
r	H	I	G	A	S	T	O	C	I	H	R
s	P	N	A	S	A	L	P	M	Y	H	I
t	A	Y	M	O	T	C	E	T	Y	C	R
	1	2	3	4	5	6	7	8	9	10	11

GRAMMAR

PARTS OF SPEECH

Words are grouped into the different categories of nouns, pronouns, verbs, adjectives, adverbs, articles, prepositions, conjunctions and interjections mainly according to the functions they have in sentences. These units are called 'parts of speech'. You must have learnt the definitions and functions of these parts of speech at school.

EXERCISE A

Based on your knowledge about parts of speech, mark the following sentences true or false.

1. Verbs express action or indicate states of existence.
2. Pronouns take the place of nouns.
3. Adjectives modify nouns and pronouns.
4. Adverbs modify a verb, an adjective or another adverb.
5. Prepositions link words.

EXERCISE B

Some words have multiple meanings and may belong to different parts of speech. For example, 'by' functions as an adverb in the first sentence and as a preposition in the second.

He hurried *by* without talking to me.
He lives *by* the river.

Write sentences using the words below as indicated in brackets.

1. sentence (as a noun and a verb)
2. very (as an adjective and an adverb)
3. left (as a noun, an adverb and an adjective)
4. back (as a noun, a verb, an adjective and an adverb)
5. round (as a noun, a verb, a preposition, an adjective and an adverb)

EXERCISE C

Fill in the blanks in the sentences below with suitable verbs. You can choose from among the given nouns, which can function as verbs as well. Use the verbs in their present tense forms except in sentences 1, 5 and 9.

axe	inch	buttonhole
man	cash	map
coat	mirror	dwarf
pot	elbow	referee
foot	ship	head
shoulder	house	table
tax		

1. The prime minister .... the government scheme for drought relief.
2. He .... spices abroad.
3. He is brilliant and .... everyone into insignificance.
4. He .... very well.
5. She .... her way through the crowd.
6. They .... people and make them listen to their stories.
7. The minister .... unnecessary expenditure.
8. The boys .... my patience.
9. The detective .... his way along in the dark.
10. He always .... responsibility.
11. She .... the delegation.
12. I .... out our holidays in advance.
13. He .... in on his popularity.
14. This article .... the public opinion.
15. Father usually .... the bill.

COHESION

Cohesion relates to unity of thought and contributes to clarity in communication. A wide variety of words/phrases belonging to different parts of speech are used to link ideas together. Some link ideas within a sentence, and others connect sentences. All the words in a group may not suit the same contexts. For example, some of them can be used only at the beginning of sentences. Look at the following list of a few connecting words/phrases and their functions.

and, moreover, in addition, as well as, along with, just as, similarly, besides	to list additional items or indicate the continuation of an idea
therefore, as a result, consequently, because, since, due to, so	to give a cause
however, nevertheless, but, in contrast	to present contradicting ideas
regarding, with regard to, as for	to indicate the subject being referred to
if, only if, unless	to indicate a condition
just as, similarly, in comparison, on the other hand, whereas	to compare

EXERCISE D

Use suitable words from the list above to fill in the blanks in the following sentences. There may be more than one appropriate word in each case.

1. It has been proved that smoking is dangerous for our health .... many continue to smoke.
2. Prem speaks five languages .... he is now learning Japanese.
3. .... we agree to their conditions, they will lend us the money we need to open a bookshop.
4. This shopping complex is well known for jewellery .... electronic goods.
5. .... your request, I need some time to get all the details.
6. Varun got the highest score in class in mathematics .... did badly in the English test.
7. She was in hospital for six months .... she could not attend classes.

8. I love to play cricket .... my friends prefer football.
9. I am too tired to go shopping now ...., I have to leave for the airport at five tomorrow morning to catch a flight.
10. He came late for the interview .... was not selected.

COHERENCE

Coherence refers to the unity of theme achieved in a passage through logical development of thought. Even in the absence of linking words, logical development of thought can lend unity to a text. Grouping relevant ideas in a paragraph and developing its meaning without contradiction are essential for effective presentation.

EXERCISE E

The sentences given below are in jumbled order. Arrange them in the right order. (Identify the introductory and concluding sentences first.) Now organise the text into paragraphs. Give it an appropriate title.

1. It is said to be a native of the Mediterranean but is now cultivated in many parts of the world including India, Europe and Australia.
2. Lavender flowers are generally purple but the shrubs also come with white, blue and pink flowers.
3. All over the world people are familiar with lavender's gentle fragrance that provides the undertones of many perfumes.
4. Many farms cultivate lavender on a large scale because of the demand for the produce and the products.
5. The essential oils soothe nerves and relieve pain in the muscles. It is used in aromatherapy along with herbs.
6. Lavender is one of the most versatile plants in the world. It is part of the mint family and belongs to the genus Lavendula.
7. It has pretty, fragrant flowers, attractive foliage. Blooms come in various shapes and sizes and are mounted on long spikes or short stems.
8. These flowers will bring butterflies and other pollinating insects into our garden.
9. Lavender is commercially grown primarily for its essential oil, extracted from the oil glands in the stem, which is not

only fragrant but also has antiseptic and anti-inflammatory properties.

10. It is widely used in cosmetics because of its fragrance. Dried flowers are used in potpourris and as fresheners (tied in sachets).
11. Occasionally they are blended in green and herbal teas and used in kitchen as a culinary herb.
12. Lavender flourishes best in well drained, dry, hardy soil. The plants are drought resistant.

Speaking

DISCUSSION

EXERCISE A

Study the pictures below to get an idea of some of the work that children in rural areas are often made to do. Work in pairs. One of you can take the role of a social worker, the other that of a villager who works in the fields and has three sons and four daughters all below the age of twelve. Enact the roles and have a discussion on child labour.

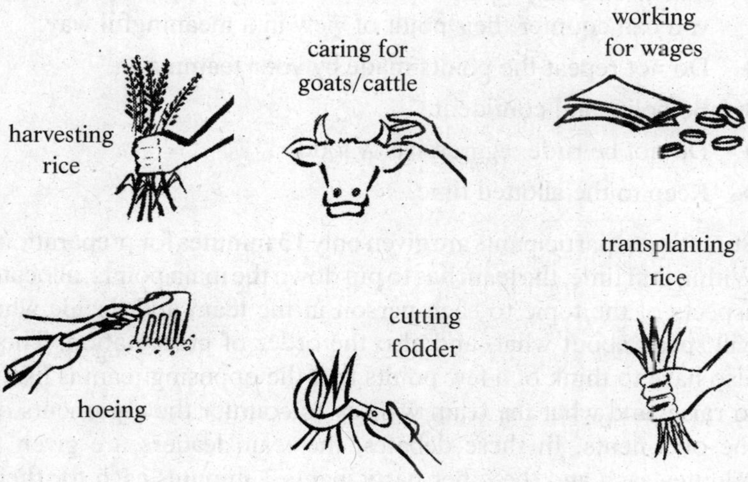

fetching water

caring for younger children

caring for chickens/ducks

DEBATE

A debate is a discussion of a proposition on a controversial topic of current interest. It involves two teams with three to four members in each who present opposing points of view. The success of your team will largely depends on how well you work together collecting, sharing and organising the data you collect, and how you present it as a team. The following pointers will be helpful:

- Research the topic, collect data from various sources and prepare logical arguments.
- Keep a list of supporting evidence and examples for the position you have taken.
- Anticipate counter-arguments and prepare rebuttals.
- Listen carefully to the speeches of your opponents so that you can counter their point of view in a meaningful way.
- Do not repeat the points made by your teammates
- Be polite and confident.
- Do not be rude, aggressive or loud.
- Keep to the allotted time.

Sometimes, participants are given only 15 minutes for preparation. Within that time, the team has to put down the main points, allocate aspects of the topic to each person in the team and decide who will speak about what, and also the order of presentation. They also have to think of a few points that the opposing team is likely to raise, and what the team will say to counter the arguments of the opponents. In these debates, the team leaders are given 5 minutes each and the other participants 3 minutes each for their presentations. The leaders have the opportunity to sum up their points at the end of the debate. A moderator is present to keep time and intervene if necessary.

Debate topics could be in the form of questions or statements. After the debate the audience or the judges vote to decide which side has won.

Debates offer an excellent opportunity to practise formal spoken English. They not only enhance one's knowledge and speaking skills but also teach us qualities like team spirit, cooperation, time management, positive attitude and leadership qualities. Participation in such activities are good preparation for interviews or lectures.

EXERCISE B

Conduct a debate on the following topic.

Preparation time: 20 minutes

Are online academic courses better than conventional classroom courses?

EXERCISE C

Look at the following topics. Your teacher will divide the class into groups and assign one of the following topics to each group. Read about it and prepare your arguments as a group. Assign tasks and plan your presentation. Present to the class on the assigned day. Your classmates will judge which team won (for each topic).

Preparation time: One week

1. Does Indian society practice gender equality?
2. Sports or academics: What are the choices?
3. Encouraging creativity in children: Beginning of a dream or a waste of time?

EXERCISE D

Here are two pairs of proverbs that have been handed down to us from the past. Can you see the contradictions of thought? What is your point of view? Take a stand and have a debate.

1. a. The pen is mightier than the sword.
   b. Action speaks louder than words.
2. a. Birds of a feather flock together.
   b. Opposites attract.

WRITING

ESSAY WRITING

An essay is a piece of writing on a particular topic. Essay writing, through which our knowledge of subjects is assessed, is part of the academic curriculum. Articles in academic journals are essentially essays on topics related to specific subject areas and readers. Some essays published in newspapers and magazines are written on controversial or topical subjects that are of interest to the general reader.

The purpose of writing an essay may vary—to narrate, give information, explain, present an opinion supported by arguments, etc. However, since all these kinds of essays need substantial content, we must read for information and collect relevant data before writing them. Writing essays involves focusing on the main idea and purpose, planning and presentation. To be good at essay writing, we have to work hard in a systematic way just as we do when preparing to give a lecture. Most of the guidelines given below are, therefore, common to essay writing as well as public speaking, which is discussed in unit 6.

- ✦ Understand your target audience (the readers for whom you are writing)—their age, interests, level of knowledge about the topic, etc.
- ✦ Be sure of the purpose of writing. Is it to introduce a topic, describe a process or explain a new concept? It can also be to convince the readers about an idea or opinion or contradict

a belief. Select your content and style of writing to suit the purpose of your essay.

- Collect data from all possible sources (books, journals, newspapers, personal experience, internet, etc.) and get a thorough in-depth understanding of the subject. Check on the authenticity of the material. Make a note of your sources.
- Anticipate the doubts the target audience is likely to have and present sufficient material to clarify them.
- When writing about a controversial topic or one with different points of view, take a stand and state it clearly. Think of arguments others may use to refute or undermine your position. In the case of such essays, you will need plenty of data to defend your stand and will also have to use a persuasive style of writing. Persuasive writing is all about making the audience agree with your point of view through logical discussion. It requires strong points to sustain your arguments and convince the reader that your opinion is correct.
- The tone of persuasive writing can be positive, negative or neutral. A positive tone is enthusiastic, optimistic, lively, assured and respectful. On the other hand, a negative tone is aggressive, bitter, sarcastic, bullying and threatening. The neutral tone is formal, matter-of-fact, controlled, forthright and official. Avoid using a negative tone. You can effectively get across to the readers by using a mix of positive and neutral tones.
- Organise your material into an introduction, the body of the essay in at least two or three paragraphs, and a conclusion.
- State the main idea or your stand in the introduction and grab the attention of the reader right at the beginning. You can also start with a relevant quotation or a short anecdote or facts that make the main idea of your essay clear to the audience.
- Present ideas logically and clearly in the paragraphs that follow the introduction. Every paragraph in the body of the essay must have a topic sentence, which expresses its main idea. Develop each paragraph carefully, using clear, relevant examples and rational, convincing arguments. Remember to acknowledge the sources of all quoted material.

- Make appropriate use of linking words/phrases that connect discourse within and between paragraphs. For example:
  - 'similarly', 'likewise', 'besides' and 'in the same way' to express similarity
  - 'in contrast', 'on the other hand', 'however', 'yet', 'nevertheless' and 'while' to express contrast
  - 'furthermore', 'moreover', 'for instance' and 'additionally' to add to a point
  - 'therefore', 'as a result', 'consequently', 'thus', 'for this reason', 'eventually' and 'in conclusion' to express a logical progression of ideas

  These signposts draw attention to similar or contrasting ideas, signal their progression and help in sequencing them. When correctly used, these linking expressions help the readers understand the essay better. Furthermore, connectors can add elegance to your writing. However, be aware of the attitudinal meanings conveyed by some of these words so that you can use them appropriately.
- Critical thinking will help you analyse facts and ideas and present them in a coherent manner. Creative thinking will help in expressing your ideas in an original manner.
- Use the concluding paragraph to sum up your ideas or arguments presented in the body of the essay clearly, arrive at a conclusion or restate your opinion. Do not repeat sentences used in previous paragraphs.
- Use grammatically correct English with a wide range of sentence structures. Enhance the flow of thought by using linking devices and appropriate vocabulary. Do not use slang in essays, which are formal pieces of writing. Avoid using jargon, which is vocabulary specific to different fields/ subjects, in essays meant for the general reader. Also, use the dictionary, the thesaurus and the spell check program on your computer to ensure accuracy and variety in the use of words.
- Make sure the length of your essay is within acceptable limits.

- Read the draft of your essay and edit it. You may need to do it more than once in order to fine-tune it until you are fully satisfied.
- Finally, remember that practice is the best way to improve your writing skills, and that is true for essay writing as well.

EXERCISE A

Read the following sentences and identify the tone of writing (neutral, positive or negative).

1. Nadal's victory speech after the Wimbledon finals was gracious and a fantastic example of sportsmanship. His compassion and respect for his opponent was stirring. That is what great sport is all about.
2. So the government is going to solve the financial crisis by showering people with money. Why has nobody thought of this spectacular plan earlier?
3. Stray dogs are a menace to society. They are accidents waiting to happen and should be destroyed. Ignore the protests of stray dog lovers and bring in legislation to kill such animals.
4. We all want what is best for our community, and the only way forward is to work together to overcome the problems in our society.

EXERCISE B

Write an essay in about 300 words expressing your view on the topic "Social Networking: Boon or Bane"

EXERCISE C (ASSIGNMENT)

Prepare an essay (in about 1000 words) on any one of the following topics and submit it in 2 weeks.

1. Geriatric care in India: Past, Present and Future
2. Euthanasia: The ongoing debate

Research the topic referring to different sources, and write an essay. Your teacher may ask you to present the salient points of your essay to the class so prepare a list of important points and arguments.

Just like libraries, computers too are a valuable resource for study and research. Now read about the advantages of using computers.

Computers

Computers are electronic devices that process data and produce accurate information.

They furnish immediate responses to the input of signals. They give us a lot of information through different lanes of access like texts, videos, graphics, voice etc. Computers can be programmed to perform a wide variety of tasks and have impacted on our lives in many ways.

Advantages

- Computers give us access to vast quantity of information with a high level of accuracy.
- They can help you access information from any part of the world and help people manage work from home.
- They offer us information from a vast variety of sources on a wide range of topics. They are electronic encyclopaedias.
- For study, they offer large amounts of resources and interactive material for practice and we can learn new skills at home at our own pace.
- Distance learning programmes now use virtual classrooms which are made interesting with power point presentations and multimedia inputs.
- Governments use computers for their planning, control and law enforcement activities. In defence, computers are used in tracking incoming missiles, in targeting enemy forces, in controlling unmanned aircrafts, etc.

- Computers have enhanced productivity in the business world. Sales and marketing are increasingly happening online.
- In the entertainment sector too their impact is tremendous. Computer generated graphics have become a part of books, advertisements and films.
- Computers are used in sports to design safety equipment, digital scoreboards and in recording the matches for replay and appraisal.
- Mobile phones, digital watches, cameras etc., are computerised and act as mini computers offering easy access to information when we travel.
- Computers have revolutionised the way people communicate: emails, SMS, social networking sites, chat rooms, helplines, videoconferencing, etc., are some of the common services that most of us with computers and connectivity use. We can share via text, photos, audios and videos.
- Computers are machines and may sometimes malfunction. Ensure that all important information is backed up regularly in a different computer or in the Cloud.

While computers have great benefits they can also become a source of distraction. Users have to be careful not to lose focus or to become addicted to its use and lose touch with the world around us.

USE OF COMPUTERS IN MEDICINE

- Many hospitals have computerised many of their processes, such as admission of patients, their records (history, symptoms, diagnosis, medication), doctors' schedules, etc. Appropriate software is installed to suit each hospital's needs.
- In-patient monitoring systems such as for vital signs, respiratory rate, etc., alert the staff if the values are abnormal.

- Scanning and diagnostic testing equipment like ultrasound, CT, MRI, ECG etc., are heavily dependent on computers for imaging and interpretation of findings.
- Hospitals must ensure that their computerised systems are patient friendly and help run the institution smoothly.

It is important to remember that while computers can perform many mechanical functions they cannot replace the human mind, or human attributes like concern and empathy, especially in fields like medicine. Institutions should not become overly dependent on computers, and ignore the human interaction required in patient care.

Email

Email is a near-instant mode of communication; it is cost-effective and potentially paperless. We can use it for both personal interaction (with friends) and professional communication (at our workplace). Given below are some guidelines for writing emails.

- In formal emails use grammatically correct language. Be precise and use simple language. Do not use informal abbreviations.
- In business communication use the formal formats expected in each setting.
- Additional information, such as images, documents, or audio/video files can be sent as attachments to the email. Send these only if absolutely necessary.
- You can use informal language in informal personal communications, say to a close friend or a relation.
- You can send a mail and copy it to many people simultaneously, using the Cc tab. Copy your letter to people only if they really need to see it.
- Email ids can be saved under Contacts. Update these frequently. Make sure you save them with the full name of the contact since there may be multiple people with the same first name in your contact list: you could send the mail to the wrong person!

- If the address you have sent the mail to is wrong you will get an immediate notification regarding this. However if the address is right but you have unintentionally sent it to the wrong person, you cannot do anything about it once it has left your Outbox.
- You can save mails that you are typing in the Drafts box and send them later.
- You can delete mails: they will go to the 'Trash' bin.
- If you get unsolicited mail (that is, promoting products or asking for your bank or other details), report them as 'Spam'.
- Do not use capitals when typing a mail: it is considered rude, and is the equivalent of shouting in a conversation.
- There is provision to automatically attach your signature at the end of the mail.
- If you will not be checking mail for some days you can turn on the 'Vacation response' to automatically inform senders of emails of the response you have preset.
- You may want to separate your business correspondence from personal emails. This can be done by either creating folders or by maintaining two separate email accounts (ids).
- Safeguard your passwords and change them at regular intervals to ensure privacy and prevent hacking.
- Check your emails regularly but don't become addicted to checking your account every few minutes.
- Many smartphones allow you to check your emails on the phone itself: this can be convenient but it could also be dangerous if you lose or misplace your phone.

Disadvantages

- We cannot predict when emails will be checked by the recipients. If you wish a mail to be seen immediately, you may have to call/message the person to let them know.

- Bogus and spam mails can easily avoid filters in the computer. Do not share confidential data with strangers.
- Attachments may contain viruses. Make sure your computer is protected with appropriate anti-virus software.
- Despite all precautions, your email account may be hacked into. If this happens, immediately inform your contacts that since your account has been hacked into, they should not respond to any communication from that id.

EXERCISE D

Which five aspects of computer technology do you value the most (in order of preference)? Work with a partner. Compare your lists and explain to each other why you chose them.

Appreciating poetry

All the World's a Stage

All the world's a stage,
And all the men and women merely players;
They have their exits and their entrances;
And one man in his time plays many parts,
His acts being seven ages. At first the infant,
Mewling and puking in the nurse's arms;
Then the whining school-boy, with his satchel
And shining morning face, creeping like snail
Unwillingly to school. And then the lover,
Sighing, like furnace, with a woeful ballad
Made to his mistress' eyebrow. Then a soldier,
Full of strange oaths, and bearded like the pard,
Jealous in honour, sudden and quick in quarrel,
Seeking the bubble reputation
Even in the cannon's mouth. And then the justice,
In fair round belly with good capon lin'd

With eyes severe and beard of formal cut,
Full of wise saws and modern instances;
And so he plays his part. The sixth age shifts
Into the lean and slipper'd pantaloon,
With spectacles on nose and pouch on side,
His youthful hose, well sav'd, a world too wide
For his shrunk shank; and his big manly voice,
Turning again toward childish treble, pipes
And whistles in his sound. Last scene of all,
That ends this strange eventful history,
Is second childishness and mere oblivion;
Sans teeth, sans eyes, sans taste, sans everything.

William Shakespeare

EXERCISE

Write short answers to the following questions.

1. In which play of Shakespeare does this poetic verse appear?
2. Who speaks these lines in the play?
3. What do 'exits and entrances' refer to? (line 3)
4. What is the meaning of 'seeking bubble reputation even in the cannon's mouth'? (lines 14 and 15)
5. Why is the last stage referred to as 'second childishness'? (line 27)

UNIT 4

Bird Song in Your Drawing Room

> Poetry is the echo in the human heart of the melody of the universe.
>
> —*S. Radhakrishnan*

Reading well involves speed among other things. A good reader is one who reads fast and with a high degree of comprehension. Let us first use the passage below to assess your reading speed and then discuss ways to improve it. Work in pairs and take turns to note down the time (in minutes and seconds) taken by you and your partner to read the passage. After you finish, pick out the correct answer to the questions given at the end of the passage.

You can start the timer now.

1. One of the memorable experiences in my years of bird watching has been listening to the song of a *shama*, listed among the world's most famous songbirds. In the Kandala bird sanctuary, near Bombay, standing transfixed behind a rock that misty morning and listening, I had wondered if anyone could record this ethereal sound of the forest.

2. Young Sivaprasad of Coimbatore has done just that. A computer engineer by profession, he had spent years watching the birds of the Western Ghats. In the recent past, he has been roaming the wilderness around Coimbatore and Wyanad with a microphone in hand and has recorded the calls of sixty-six birds, ranging from the crested hawk eagle to the mottled wood owl. His cassette 'An Audio Guide to the Birds of South India: Part One', just released in London, is drawing impressive notices. This cassette, a landmark

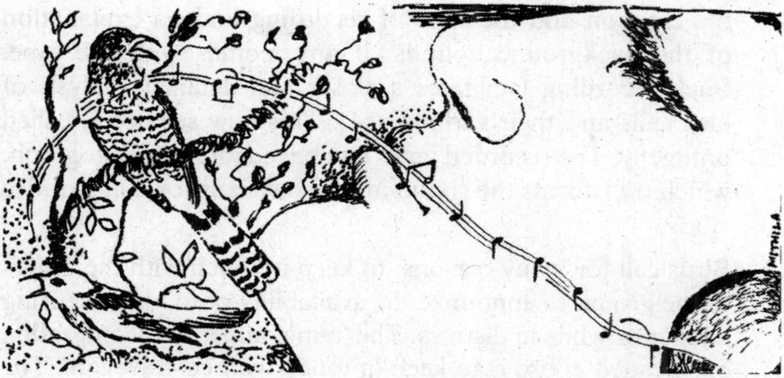

in bird studies in India, is the first work of its kind in the subcontinent and Sivaprasad has achieved this almost single-handedly. The cassette is the first of the series he plans to bring out.

3. Recording the calls of birds is new to Indian ornithology. The only information on bird calls available to us is in bird books, which give the nearest sounding English words. Calls of certain birds struck the early birdwatchers, all British, as very similar to some English words, and they described these calls with those words. For instance, the call of a yellow-wattled lapwing was described as 'did-he-do-it' or the call of the common-hawk cuckoo as 'brain-fever, brain-fever'. Such descriptions do not give an exact idea of the call. Moreover, some species which look very much alike but sound different—kingfishers, for instance—can be easily identified by their clearly distinct calls. In dealing with nocturnal birds like owls and nightjars, calls are critical. The call of a bird is a surer guide to its identification than its colour or flight. But then one has to be well acquainted with bird calls.

4. That is where Sivaprasad comes in. His audio guide introduces the calls of different birds. An announcement of the popular and scientific name of the bird, done impeccably by Krys Kazmiereczak, precedes each recording. Then comes the call. A booklet giving the names of the birds, the number assigned to each of them in Salim Ali and Ripley's *Handbook*,

the location and the time of recording and an explanation of the background sounds, if any, comes with the tape. Such recording facilitates a closer and detailed analysis of bird calls and their various uses. This new science is called ontogeny. The recorded tapes can be fed into a spectrograph, which transforms the sound into visual signs for comparative study.

5. Birds call for many reasons: to keep in touch with the others of the group, to announce the availability of food, on sensing danger or while in distress. The 'aung, aung' of the migrating bar-headed goose is to keep in touch with co-travellers. The koel's popular song is a call for mating. An ornithologist observed that a starling's heartbeat was faster when it heard the distress call of another starling. Among the nocturnal birds like owls and night herons, calls are much more consequential. They rely entirely on sound to locate mates and rivals. Understandably, their calls are distinct and carry far. Birds in dense vegetation, where visibility is limited, also have loud and distinct calls.

6. A bird's song has been described as an audible fence. Usually associated with breeding, a song is different from a call. The bird announces that the territory has been occupied and that it will be defended. A song can often be an invitation to mate and breed. The magpie robin's song, which can be heard even in our urban gardens, is part of its effort to impress the female. While birds of the open country, like peacocks and sarus cranes, indulge in elaborate dances to woo the mate, birds of the forest sing.

7. To record birds calls, you need enormous patience in addition to equipment like directional microphone and parabolic reflector. First of all, you should be knowledgeable about bird behaviour and should know where to look for a species. You should also anticipate calls. Sivaprasad says he has waited many times without success for a whole day to record a single call. The recordist should be alert and should have a steady hand or else handling noises will also be recorded. The

right season should be chosen. For example, in summer, you cannot find a single spot in the forests of south India where you do not have cicadas or bush crickets keeping up their chorus.

8. The recording in this 90-minute tape is of high quality. Sivaprasad has managed to capture on tape the calls of rare species like the Malabar trogon, a colourful bird that inhabits the interior of rain forests. It is difficult to even spot it. The calls of birds like the heart-spotted woodpecker evoke the ambience of the forests of the Western Ghats very effectively.
9. Dim the lights, play this tape in your music system and let the trilling song of the Malabar whistling thrush fill your drawing room. A truly transcendental experience.

S. Theodore Baskaran

Stop the timer now. Tell the teacher how long it took you to read the passage and find out what your reading speed is. Are you a slow or fast reader?

Glossary

ambience	-	the atmosphere of a place
consequential	-	important
dense	-	crowded closely together; thick
ethereal	-	in a way that seems not to be real or of this world
evoke	-	to bring to mind a memory or feeling
impeccably	-	perfectly
landmark	-	here, an event marking an important stage in something
nocturnal	-	of or in the night
ornithology	-	the study of birds
transcendental	-	relating to a spiritual level of existence

transfix	-	to make someone unable to move because of wonder, horror or astonishment
vegetation	-	plants in general or those found in a particular area or habitat

Understanding the text

EXERCISE

Tick the statement which you think most accurately summarises the main idea of the above passage.

1. Listening to bird songs is a fantastic experience.
2. One can identify a bird accurately by its call rather than by its other features.
3. Birds call to keep in touch, while in distress, on sensing danger or to announce the availability of food.
4. Sivaprasad's audio guide is of high quality and gives valuable information about bird calls.
5. Sivaprasad took a lot of effort to produce the audio guide.
6. The audio guide is a landmark in ontogeny.

Proficiency in reading has a great impact on academic excellence and communication.

Tips to Improve Reading Skills

- Strike a balance between speed and comprehension. Try to guess the meanings of word you do not know from the context they are in.
- Adjust the speed of reading to suit the purpose. Study (academic) reading needs more concentration and time than reading for pleasure.
- Be interested in what you read.
- Read silently without moving your lips. You will be able to read faster if you read silently.

- Your eyes should scan a range of words, and move smoothly across word groups and lines. Do not read word by word.
- Do not go back to what you have already read. If you read with concentration you will not need to do this.
- Build a range of vocabulary. Practise using them so you do not need to memorise meanings.

A person who reads widely can converse knowledgeably on diverse topics. This is an asset particularly while taking English proficiency examinations like IELTS, TOEFL, etc. or other qualifying exams like GRE, GMAT, etc. These exams assess the candidates' abilities in speaking, listening, writing and reading comprehension. People who are in the habit of reading will definitely be at an advantage in these situations. During job placement interviews too, proficient readers score over others because of general awareness and fluency. The wealth of knowledge you gain through reading can also make you a good conversationalist in social settings.

Pronunciation

SILENT LETTERS

Many English words have consonant letters that are not pronounced. For example:

honest /ɒnəst/
know /nəʊ/

The letter 'r' is almost always silent except when followed by a vowel sound. For example:

bird /bɜ:d/
form /fɔ:m/
bright /braɪt/
try /traɪ/

EXERCISE A

Working in pairs, identify words in the list below that have silent consonant letters in them and underline the letters. Take turns to read the words aloud.

1. badge
2. corpse
3. breathless
4. edgy
5. sandwich
6. benign
7. debris
8. hourly
9. gadget
10. serve
11. brink
12. debt
13. exhausting
14. grudge
15. comb
16. banquet
17. depot
18. thirsty
19. receipt
20. subtle

EXERCISE B

Take turns with your partner to repeat the following tongue twisters.

1. Very well. Very well. Very well.
2. Peter Piper picked a peck of peppers.
3. Three grey geese in the green grass grazing.

Vocabulary

WORD FORMATION

One way of forming new words in English is by adding a prefix or a suffix to a word base, with or without a change in the word class. For example:

understand (v) – misunderstand (v)
friend (n) – friendly (adj)

There are time prefixes, locative prefixes, prefixes of attitude, etc. Many English antonyms are formed by affixation. We have to be careful as to which prefix/suffix combines with the base to form its antonym. For example, in the words 'inaccurate', 'incapable' 'inequality' and 'inessential', the prefix is used to give the antonym of the base form. However, this is not always so. Thus, the meaning of the word 'invaluable' is not 'something that is not valuable' but 'something of great value'.

EXERCISE A

Write the antonyms of the following words by adding an affix.

1. alignment ....
2. clockwise ....
3. courteous ....
4. discreet ....
5. fortune ....
6. legible ....
7. limited ....
8. normal ....
9. plausible ....
10. remediable ....

EXERCISE B

Write the meanings for the following words (1–15) and abbreviations (16–30).

1. antenatal ....
2. antibacterial ....
3. brachycheilia ....
4. bradycardia ....
5. apnea ....
6. tachypnea ....
7. dyspnea ....
8. intercostal ....
9. infra-axillary ....
10. hyperthyroidism ....
11. hypocalcemia ....
12. retronasal ....
13. sublingual ....
14. hypoglossal ....
15. extracystic ....
16. inj. ....
17. tab. ....
18. cap. ....

19. stat. ....
20. prn. ....
21. BD ....
22. t.i.d ....
23. q.i.d ....
24. q.6h ....
25. q.8h ....
26. AD ....
27. IM ....
28. ID ....
29. IV ....
30. S/C ....

EXERCISE C

A part of each of the following sentences is underlined. Fill in the blanks in each sentence with words or phrases with meanings similar to that of the underlined parts. These words or phrases can be coined by combining the appropriate items from columns A and B given below. Answers can be single words, hyphenated compound words or phrases. Every word must be used only once.

e.g.: You have spent beyond the amount allotted. It is not good to .... this way. (Answer: overspend)

A	B
high	swings
up to	the mark
stream	rooted
mood	lock
spin	going
short	hill
deep	date
up	colour
dead	long
off	off
on	term
life	risk

over	standers
grief	line
by	spend
	colour
	stricken
	lined
	draw
	come

1. The new tutor has organised the programme methodically. He has .... the whole session.
2. His condition is such that there is great possibility of a harmful outcome. Such .... cases have to be handled with utmost care.
3. The fluctuations in his temperament irritate me. He is known for his extreme ....
4. I am determined to succeed in this difficult task. I can definitely .... the problems.
5. He is unwell and should have a thorough check up. He has been .... for quite some time.
6. You mustn't be affected by the difficulties faced during this limited period of time. These .... problems can be sorted out soon.
7. This has been a continuous problem. We should do something to stem this .... course of events.
8. We can't take him off the ventilator because it is absolutely essential for his existence. At the moment the ventilator is a/an .... for him.
9. The woman's untimely death plunged her family into great sorrow. Her .... family finds it difficult to cope with the daily routine.
10. In spite of all our efforts, we totally failed to reach an agreement. It is difficult to break the ....
11. This is an additional benefit of the new discovery. The new antibiotic is a/an .... from this research on a cancer drug.
12. He struggled a lot to come up in life. It was a/an .... job.

13. His prejudice cannot be easily removed. It is ...., and he is stubborn by nature.
14. There are too many onlookers around the accident victim. Ask the .... not to crowd around the injured child.
15. His paper consisted of the most recent information on AIDS. He had access to a good library, and so could get these .... details.

Grammar

IRREGULAR VERB FORMS

One of the ways in which verbs, forming an integral part of sentences, can be classified is as helping and main verbs. Main verbs can be transitive (those that can take an object and that can be changed into passive) or intransitive. Another form of grouping is based on the way they form their past tense. Those verbs which form their past tense and past participle by adding *-d, -ied* or *-ed* to the stem are called regular verbs. Irregular verbs form their past and past participle in different ways.

Some verbs have the same form for present, past and past participle. For example:

cut cut cut

In other verbs, the past tense and the past participle have the same form. For example:

keep kept kept

In others, all three are different. For example:

write wrote written

There are also verbs whose present tense and past participle forms are the same. For example:

run ran run

It is important that we use the correct forms in our writing. Past participles are used in passive constructions and in perfect tenses.

A list of irregular verbs with their past and past participles is given at the end of the book.

EXERCISE A

The verb phrases in some of the following sentences are wrong. Identify the errors and rewrite the corrected sentences.

1. He bleeded to death.
2. The news was broadcast yesterday.
3. They burst crackers last night.
4. He was stang by a scorpion.
5. She shaked in fear on seeing the snake.
6. The rice should be grinded to a paste.
7. He laid still.
8. It cost me Rs 1000 when I bought it last year.
9. He slided down the staircase.
10. My ankles were swollen when I stood up.
11. The clothes shrunk after the first wash.
12. He has strived very hard to come up in life.
13. The rowdies beated him up yesterday.
14. The child clang to her mother.
15. He speeded along the highway.

ACTIVE AND PASSIVE VOICE

Past participles are used in passive constructions along with the auxiliary verbs 'is', 'was', 'are', 'were', 'can be', 'may be', 'has been', 'is being', etc. For example:

The book *is written* by Rohan.
The book *has been written* by Rohan.

In scientific writing, where the action is of more relevance than the person performing the act, the passive voice is usually used, with the emphasis on the action. When nurses record their interventions in the charts of patients, the same principle is followed. Nursing interventions should be recorded accurately and briefly, making use of the passive voice. Specific collocations such as the following can aptly express these actions.

The patient	-	*was admitted.*
	-	*was weighed.*
	-	*was oriented to the ward.*
	-	*was fed.*
	-	*was dressed and groomed.*
	-	*was helped to sit up/walk.*
	-	*was ambulated.*

Only those verbs that take an object can be converted into passive sentences. Such verbs are called transitive verbs. Transitive verbs can have direct and indirect objects. For example:

Shyla presented	*the book*	to *Raja*.
	(dir. obj.)	(indir. obj.)

Answers to the questions 'what' or 'to whom' after the verb will give us the direct and indirect objects in the sentence. But if the answer to these questions is the subject itself, the words following the verb do not take an 'object' but a 'complement'. For example:

She is *my teacher*.
(comple.)

In such cases, the sentences cannot be changed into passive. Verbs that cannot be changed into passive voice are called intransitive verbs. For example, 'come', 'go', 'laugh', 'jump', 'sit', 'reach' and 'travel'.

Many verbs can be both transitive and intransitive. For example:

She *grows* tulips. (transitive)
Tulips *grow* well here. (intransitive)

I *read* J. K. Rowling's latest novel last week. (transitive)
J. K. Rowling's latest novel *reads* well. (intransitive)

A passive sentence is formed by putting the auxiliary verb 'to be' in the same tense as the main verb in the active sentence and adding the past participle of the main verb. The table below gives you examples of active sentences and their equivalent passive constructions (the doer or performer of the action is not mentioned).

S. no.	Tense	Active	Passive
1.	simple present	He *writes* a book. He *writes* books.	A book *is written*. Books *are written*.
2.	present continuous	He *is writing* a book.	A book *is being written*.
		He *is writing* books.	Books *are being written*.
3.	present perfect	He *has written* a book.	A book *has been written*.
		He *has written* books.	Books *have been written*.
4.	simple past	He *wrote* a book.	A book *was written*.
		He *wrote* books.	Books *were written*.
5.	past continuous	He *was writing* a book.	A book *was being written*.
		He *was writing* books.	Books *were being written*.
6.	past perfect	He *had written* a book.	A book *had been written*.
		He *had written* books.	Books *had been written*.

Active verbs with auxiliary–infinitive combinations take a passive infinitive. For example:

I *will buy* the house.
The house will be bought.

You *must accept* the presents.
The presents must be accepted.

EXERCISE B

Rewrite sentences 1–10 in passive and sentences 11–20 in active forms. Make sure you choose the right past participle and tense and that you follow the rules of concord.

1. She sang a beautiful song.
2. They are congratulating him.
3. Suresh completed the essay.
4. He draws beautiful pictures.
5. She has written many short stories.
6. The captain is encouraging the players.
7. I had posted the letters before Nina arrived.
8. My friends were helping the victims.
9. Malini will definitely invite us.
10. We inflated all the balloons.
11. These pictures were taken by Subhash yesterday.
12. The essay has been chosen by the teacher.
13. The fruit trees are being planted by me.
14. Many books on medicine are published by our medical college.
15. The shield was won by my team.
16. The animals are fed by the gardener.
17. The news should be communicated by you.
18. Many plans had been made by us.
19. At every show, new tricks are being shown by the magician.
20. The biscuits were eaten by the cats.

EXERCISE C

Answer each question first in active and then in passive voice, using the words given in brackets.

1. What did he buy? (mangoes)
2. Who gave the books to Raja? (Mukesh)
3. Who has arranged the party? (I)
4. What do we need for the house? (furniture)
5. Who is teaching the children maths? (Ms Nina Menon)

EXERCISE D

Complete the passage with the active or the passive forms of the verbs in brackets.

Baby in a Briefcase

The first years of a baby's life (1) .... (be) in many ways the most critical for the development of language, cognitive and emotional skills. Hearing difficulties (2) .... (deter) a child from realising his/her full potential, so it is vital that any impairment (3) .... (detect) as soon as possible.

Now the hearing of a baby just a few days old (4) .... (test) using a revolutionary new equipment developed after extensive research by Hillingdon Hospital and Brunel University in London. In the past, the time and expense it involved (5) .... (mean) that only babies deemed to be at obvious risk through rubella or physical abnormalities (6) .... (can screen) in the earliest days of their lives. As a result many babies (7) .... (suffer) undetected deafness until it (8) .... (detect) at a much later date when the problems were more difficult to rectify.

The new, highly portable Auditory Response Cradle (ARC) which when closed, (9) .... (resemble) a briefcase, means that the hearing of all newborns (10) .... (can test). The just-fed baby (11) .... (lie) in the cradle and a range of audio signals (12) .... (transmit) through earphones. The baby's response (13) .... (pick) up by the sensitive meter and head unit and (14) .... (measure) by computer-recorded behavioural reactions. If the test, which only (15) .... (take) a few minutes, (16) .... (show) a possible problem, the baby (17) ....

(refer) for more extensive tests. If hearing loss is not too great, all that (18) .... (may need) in the baby's first months of life (19) .... (be) for the mother and other adults to speak to the baby in a louder voice so that he/she (20) .... (learn) vital, early language skills or so that early fitting with hearing aids may help linguistic and cognitive development. Babies who (21) .... (pass) the early detection tests will still (22) .... (need) the standard screening tests at other stages of their development, as progressive and acquired hearing losses (23) .... (cannot detect) at the neonatal stage.

The main purpose of screening for hearing impairment in new born babies (24) .... (be) detection of severe loss. In a long-term evaluation study, the ARC (25) .... (find) to have a high detection rate for severe hearing loss.

('London Pictures Service' in the *Hindu*, 19 March 1995)

Speaking

PSYCHOSOCIAL ASPECTS OF COMMUNICATION

Good pronunciation, rich vocabulary and grasp of grammar definitely enhance clarity in communication. But in the healthcare setting, where communication is the basic component of good interpersonal relationship, we need to integrate competence in language skills with enabling qualities like cooperation, mutual understanding and respect, ability to adapt, etc. These enabling skills will promote a psychological climate that strengthens interpersonal relationship. They encourage attentive listening and expression of genuine feelings without hurting others and sharpen our sensitivity to other's feelings. As a result, while communicating we reassure, clarify, validate and focus on the needs of people we interact with. These skills, therefore, are good facilitators of communication.

On the other hand, selfishness and narrow-mindedness are reflected in language in the form of angry remarks, threats, orders, moral strictures, criticism, etc., which are barriers that block communication.

Thus, in learning to speak a language, interpersonal negotiation skills need to be cultivated consciously if our communication is to be effective either in the mother tongue or in the second language. For more on these skills, refer to the section on the topic in unit 8.

EXERCISE A

Four students Rekha, Saila, Mary and Mumtaz of the BSc nursing class share a room in the student nurses' hostel. Rekha and Mumtaz are friendly by nature and many friends drop in at their room to listen to music or for a chat. Saila and Mary consider it an intrusion into their privacy and decide to express their feelings. Here are two statements conveying the message. Which do you think is more effective and why?

1. We are angry with you for encouraging your friends to come to our room. It is always crowded and noisy. We never have it to ourselves. You are so thoughtless. It'll be good if you show some consideration for your roommates. If this continues we'll report the matter to the warden.
2. We would like to discuss certain things with you. It's about your friends visiting our room at odd times. Can we evolve a system so that we can have the room to ourselves, say after 8 p.m.? That will give us time to organise things and complete our work without distraction. Do you think that will be a workable arrangement?

EXERCISE B

Work in groups of five. Each group can select a problem and enact the situation highlighting communication facilitators and barriers that will solve or worsen the problem.

GROUP DISCUSSION/DEBATE

EXERCISE C

Your college has organised an AIDS awareness campaign in the town. Refer to the sample below and work in groups to prepare posters that would convey the message effectively.

Have a debate in class on the topic 'Should AIDS victims be segregated or not?'

EXERCISE D

Study the picture below and identify the four ways in which AIDS is spread. Have a class discussion on the subject.

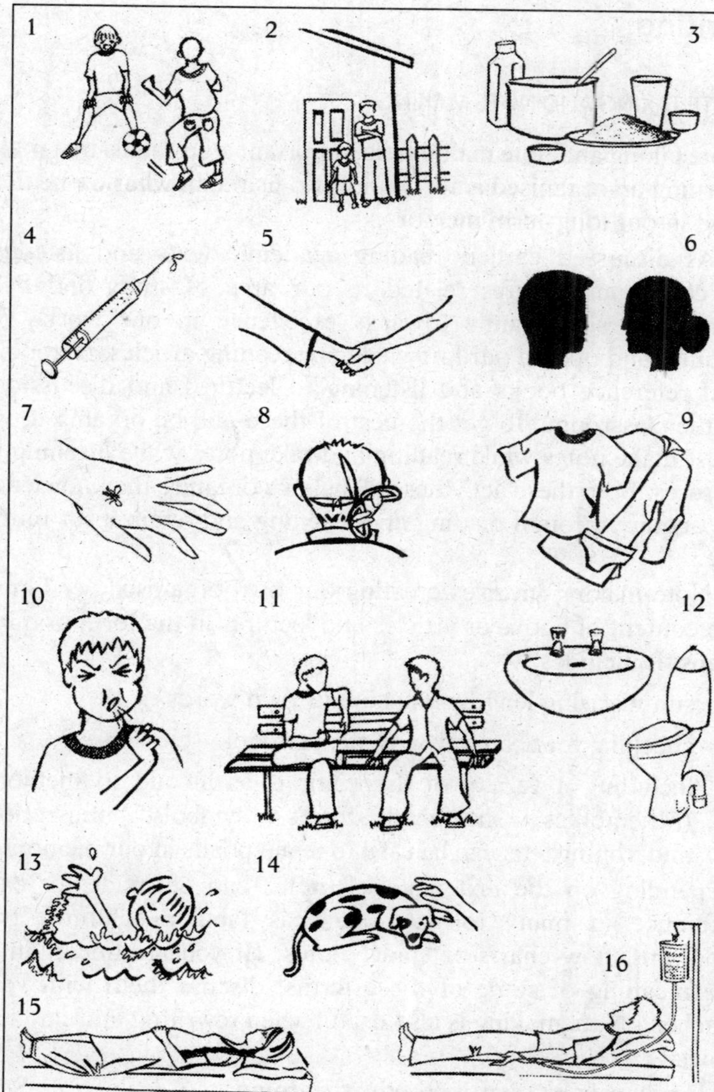

(Voluntary Health Association of India)

Writing

NOTE TAKING AND NOTE MAKING

Note taking and note making are important study skills that make learning an organised activity and help us retain what we hear or read in our long-term memory.

As discussed earlier, reading academic texts and listening to classroom lectures related to our area of study and field contribute significantly towards excellence in our work. We acquire and update our knowledge by reading articles, textbooks and reference books and listening to lectures and discussions in the classroom. To get the best of these and be organised, we must make notes while reading and take notes while listening to lectures. Both these activities will help us organise the knowledge we acquire through reading and listening and retain it for future use.

Note making involves creating our own organised version of the content of books or articles and lectures in the form of mind maps. It includes:

- summarising lengthy texts in our own words
- checking for accuracy with the textbook
- including a variety of associations as an aid to memory. (Mnemonics, shortened forms, symbols, numbering, underlining, etc. can be used to retain points in our memory.)

Depending on the text material, notes can be made for easy reference in many formats, such as tabular columns, tree diagrams, flow charts or spider notes. (If you are uncertain of the meaning of some of these terms, discuss them with your teacher.) Note making is also useful when rewriting unclear class notes.

Develop your own method of learning and stick to it. Self-discipline and a good method make the difference between winning and losing as well as between greatness and mediocrity. Therefore, make these learning tools a natural part of your life as a student and enjoy the benefits.

EXERCISE A

Read the following passage and make notes by filling in the blanks in the table below it.

Leukaemias

Leukaemias are malignancies of haematopoietic stem cells. There are many different kinds of leukaemias, and it is important to differentiate one from the other because the treatment for each is different and the prognosis also varies.

In blood, there are different types of cells—RBCs, WBCs and platelets. The WBC can be broadly divided into lymphocytes and granulocytes. Leukaemias arising from lymphocytes are called lymphatic leukaemias and those arising from granulocytes are called myeloid leukaemias. Each of these can be either acute or chronic. Let us take a quick look at the clinical and laboratory features which help us to distinguish one from the other.

Both acute lymphatic leukaemia (ALL) and acute myeloid leukaemia (AML) are leukaemias of young adults and children. AML occurs in the age group 15–40 and ALL in children of about 4 years of age. Those affected present clinically with fatigue, fever and bone pain and bleeding from sites like nose, gums, etc. On examination they are anaemic. There is enlargement of lymph nodes, liver and spleen which is more marked in ALL than AML. The lab findings common to both ALL and AML are anaemia, a low platelet count and a marked increase in the WBC count. However, in ALL the cells which predominate are lymphoblasts or immature lymphoid cells whereas in AML the predominant cells are myeloblasts or immature myeloid cells.

Chronic leukaemias on the other hand present in much older age groups. Chronic myeloid leukaemias (CML) usually occur in adults. Clinically the symptoms are weight loss, easy fatiguability and weakness. Many complain of a dragging sensation in the abdomen caused by massive enlargement of the spleen. Laboratory findings include mild anaemia, a marked increase in platelet count and a very high WBC count. Granulocytes in different stages of maturation are seen.

Patients with chronic lymphocytic leukaemias (CLL) fall into the 60–70 age group and are often asymptomatic. They may have non-specific complaints like loss of weight, weakness, etc. On examination they have lymph node enlargement and their liver and spleen are also often enlarged. Blood smear shows a very high WBC count. The WBCs are mostly mature lymphocytes. Platelet count is normal and there is no striking anaemia.

Treatment of choice for acute leukaemias and CML is bone marrow transplantation if an HLA identical donor can be found. Patients with CLL survive (without any problem) for ten years or so after diagnosis and so are treated with low dose chemotherapy.

Type	**Age of occurrence**	**Signs, symptoms**	**Lab features**	**Prognosis**	**Treatment**
CLL	60–70	1. fatigue 2. weakness 3. weight loss 4. lymph node, spleen, liver en-largement	1. increased WBC, mainly mature lymphocytes 2. normal platelet count 3. very mild anaemia	fairly good	low-dose chemo-therapy
CML					

ALL					
AML					

TRANSFERRING INFORMATION: GRAPHS, TABLES, DIAGRAMS AND CHARTS

Graphs, tables, diagrams and charts are some types of pictorial representation of data. They are used to present huge amounts of data in a concise and clear format. It is important that we learn to interpret them correctly and present the information they contain in writing. This is an essential skill needed for writing research articles or project proposals on subjects in different specialised areas.

Many national and international admission tests include questions on report writing based on interpretation of data presented in bar graphs, flowcharts, tree diagrams, etc. It is important that we use appropriate words and phrases to compare and contrast and to describe trends. Using a variety of expressions for the purpose will help us score well.

EXERCISE B

Based on the diagram below, write a short paragraph on the life cycle of the hookworm to be included in a textbook for Class 12.

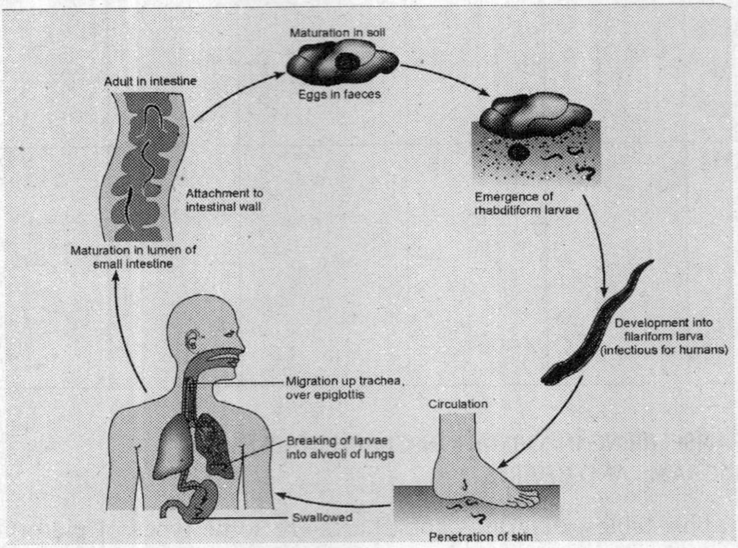

EXERCISE C

The bar diagram and graph given on the next page present the data regarding different kinds of organisations handling maternity cases in Tamil Nadu over eight years and the maternal mortality ratio there during that period. What were the major changes that happened and what effect did they have on maternal health? Transfer the information given in visual form to a short written report of about 100 to 150 words. Make brief, precise comparisons using some of the expressions given below.

the drift is towards	in favour of
lean/is inclined towards	steady increase
slight dip	sharp/gradual rise
rose dramatically	most striking feature

displays/denotes/reveals/points to/illustrates/draws attention to

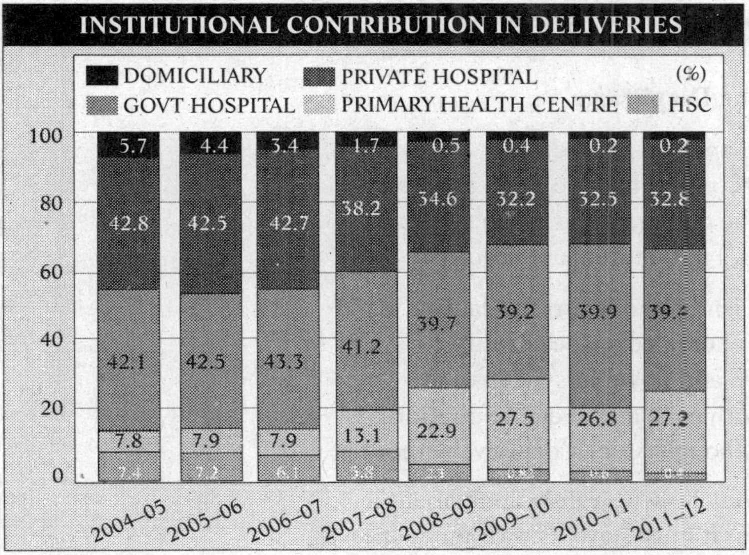

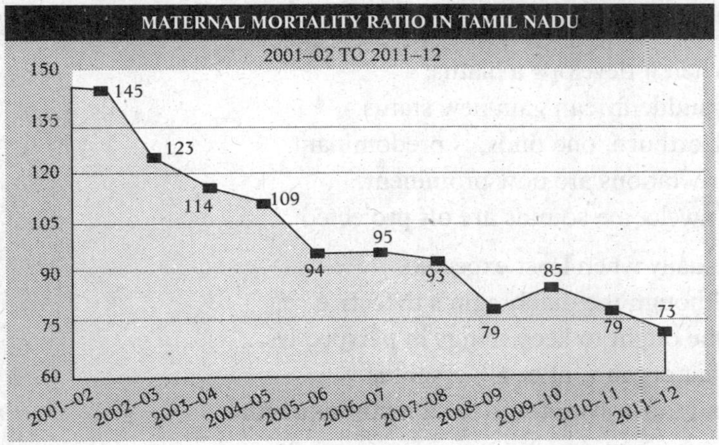

('Better Equipped PHCs Deliver' by Ramya Kannan in the *Hindu*, 22 February 2013)

Appreciating poetry

The Diaphragm

In any sort of a recital
Of organs that we think are vital
The diaphragm is much neglected.
(It's not entirely unexpected.)

It isn't famous for its beauty;
Unheralded it does its duty—
Up and down in syncopation
With each and every respiration.
Although we can't survive without it,

Somehow we rarely think about it
But it must have its own uniquenesses,
Anomalies and strengths and weaknesses.
Yet somehow it stays, underrated—
Unless, of course, it's herniated!

When it develops a hiatus,
It suddenly can gain new status.
Heartburn, one finds, is predominant
Eructations are now prominent.
Unwelcome sounds are oft projected,

Usually when least expected.
Although the diaphragm's defective,
One ought to keep things in perspective.
That organ's, after all, essential
And those symptoms seem inconsequential.

Still, patients may be inconsolable
Because those sounds are uncontrollable,
And such a minor impropriety
Could banish them from high society!

Benjamin Midler

EXERCISE

Write short answers to the following questions.

1. Pick out aspects of the poem that make it humorous.
2. Based on the features you have identified, write a humorous plea in four lines for any other organ in the body.

UNIT 5

Down and Out, Yet Standing!

> You will never find a rainbow if you are looking down.
>
> —*Charlie Chaplin*

Have you ever wondered what you would do if you were to lose everything and had to start life all over again? Read the inspiring story of a brave and determined sportswoman who proved that it is possible.

1. At 1 a.m. on 11 April 2011, national volleyball player Arunima Sinha lay between two railway tracks on the Lucknow–Delhi route. A few minutes earlier, she had been thrown off a train by robbers when she resisted their attempt to snatch her gold chain. Arunima's hands were fractured, and the bones in her right leg, which were crushed, tore through her trousers. Her spine was fractured in three places, and she could not feel her left leg, which had been run over by a train. She lay there for over seven hours, losing blood all the while and trying to shield herself from trains that were coming from both directions.

2. At dawn, a villager spotted her, and help finally arrived. Arunima held on to life as she was being moved from one hospital to another. She bore the pain when her left leg was amputated without giving her any anaesthesia. Arunima was finally taken to the All India Institute of Medical Sciences in New Delhi, where she received good care. Once her wounds healed, Arunima was fitted with an artificial limb. Many

thought this was the end of her sporting career. But a dream was taking shape in Arunima's mind as she lay in her hospital bed. She was tired of the pitying attitude that people had towards her. She wanted to prove that she was still the same spirited girl she once was.

3. However, more than her physical strength, what counted was her determination to put her life back on track. 'When I was in the hospital, I was broken as anyone could be,' says Arunima. She had lost all her certificates when she was pushed out of the train. The railway police guard on duty at the time of the accident shirked responsibility by putting the blame on Arunima, saying she was trying to commit suicide. The remark pained her, but she was not disheartened. 'The more they tried to weaken my spirit, the more determined I became. Though the future looked bleak, I knew I had to live without being pitied. I thought I would chose the toughest sport and come out a winner. I decided to climb Mount Everest.'

4. With the help of her elder brother, she started looking for people who could help her achieve her goal. She got in touch with Bachendri Pal, the first Indian woman to climb Everest. Her brother gave up his job with the CRPF to help her, and they went to Uttarakhand to train under the experienced mountaineer. Initially, Bachendri Pal also doubted whether Arunima was really serious. 'But when she saw that I had gone to Jamshedpur the second day I was discharged, she realised my determination and sincerity,' says Arunima. The young sportswoman knew that there was a big difference between having a dream and achieving it. She started training within months of being fitted with an artificial limb. Initially, each step was painful, and Arunima would be the last one to reach the top among the mountaineers she trained with. 'Many a time, I was asked to turn back even before reaching the summit, and it used to break my heart,' says Arunima.

5. Gradually, her stamina and strength improved, and she would be among the first to reach a summit, sometimes in spite

of her bleeding stump.She trained hard for two years and then climbed several mountains in Uttarakhand under the guidance of Bachendri Pal. She climbed the difficult Chamser Kangri, the third highest peak in Ladakh, in 2012. For a year and a half, she kept climbing other peaks in the Himalayan range, including Surya Top and Madhav Kunj. Arunima also managed to find a sponsor—Tata Steel.

6. Preparations over, on 1 April 2013, Arunima started her dream climb and, on 10 April, reached the treacherous Island Peak, which is 6,160 m above sea level. The journey to the top of the world was not smooth. On her way to the summit from camp 4, Arunima realised that her oxygen supply would not last. But she refused to give up. 'I believed that if I did not die in spite of lying on the train tracks for seven hours, I would not die on the way to Mount Everest because it was not time for me to go,' she says. Fortunately, fate intervened. On their way to the top, Arunima and her Sherpa saw a British mountaineer give up the climb, leaving behind his oxygen cylinder. Arunima continued her climb with that cylinder.

7. On 21 May 2013, she stood on the top of the world, literally. She had successfully climbed Mount Everest and became the first female amputee to do so. An incredible feat, especially

since even able-bodied people would find it tough to accomplish such a strenuous feat. The day she reached the top was the happiest ever for her. 'I was so happy! I wanted to tell all those who had doubted my capabilities that I achieved my goal,' says Arunima. Today the 25-year-old sportswoman is busy giving motivational speeches and raising funds for an academy she plans for specially-abled children in Uttar Pradesh.

8. Arunima's story is a testament of how willpower and determination can change a person's life. Instead of brooding over fate, she believed in her dream and worked hard to achieve it. 'I turned my pain into opportunity. If I had not changed my mindset, I would not even have managed to come out of my room,' she says. Like Arunima, many other people have risen above terrible situations to emerge as winners because they were optimistic.

9. Optimism is defined as a tendency to expect the best possible outcomes or to keep thinking about the most hopeful aspects of a situation. For optimists, setbacks are temporary, while pessimists think they will last forever. According to Martin Seligman, professor of psychology and co-founder of the discipline of positive psychology, 'Optimists believe defeat is not their fault; circumstances, bad luck or other people brought it about. Such people are unfazed by defeat and when confronted by a bad situation, they perceive it as a challenge and try harder.'

10. Optimists have positive expectations from the future and change their behaviour when the outcomes do not match their expectations. It is also found that optimists deal directly with the problems that can be solved, but when facing an irrevocable situation, they use strategies like acceptance and humour and look afresh at the situation positively. 'Optimism is the ability to find a broader range of solutions, believing that new paths can open up. It is believing in life and our abilities,' says Sadia Raval, founder and chief psychologist of Inner Space Counselling in Mumbai.

11. However, optimism comes with its own pitfalls, which must be avoided. Optimists may underestimate risks and hazards and fail to take the necessary precautions. It is not wise to throw caution to the winds in the name of optimism. True optimism means being realistic about a situation, believing that things will get better and working to make them so.

12. Here are a few tips given by psychologists for nurturing optimism: Challenge your negative beliefs and cultivate positive thoughts; have a purpose and engage in something meaningful; learn to count your blessings; relax and calm your mind; believe in yourself; develop a good network of friends and well wishers.

(adapted excerpt from 'Down and Out . . . Standing!' by Swagata Yadavar in *The Week*, 22 June 2014)

Author's note: Arunima has since hoisted the Indian flag on the Pennine Alps in Switzerland. (*The Week*, 6 June 2015)

Glossary

amputee	-	a person who has had an arm or leg amputated, or cut off
bleak	-	with little or no hope.
broken	-	here, suffering terrible emotional pain because of something bad that happened to you
brood	-	to think for a long time about things that make you sad, worried or angry
count	-	here, to be important
cultivate	-	to learn to develop
disheartened	-	without confidence and hope
feat	-	something difficult needing a lot of skill, strength, courage, etc., to achieve
hazard	-	something that is dangerous
incredible	-	difficult to believe
intervene	-	to become involved in a difficult situation in order to improve it or prevent it from becoming worse

irrevocable	-	impossible to change
mindset	-	a person's way of thinking
nurture	-	to help develop
optimist	-	a person who always believes that good things will happen
pessimist	-	someone who feels that bad things are more likely to happen than good things
pitfall	-	a likely problem in a situation
shirk	-	to avoid something difficult or unpleasant
spirited	-	enthusiastic and determined
strategy	-	a plan of action meant to achieve something
stump	-	here, the part of a limb that is left after most of it has been removed
testament	-	proof
treacherous	-	here, dangerous
unfazed	-	not worried or affected

Understanding the text

EXERCISE A

Basing yourself on paragraphs 1 to 5, mark the following statements true (T) or false (F).

1. Arunima Sinha, who was thrown off a moving train by robbers, was a college student.
2. Besides other injuries, her left leg felt numb because it had been run over by a train.
3. Arunima was rushed to AIIMS in Delhi immediately after the accident.
4. While recovering in the hospital, Arunima pitied herself and gave up hope of being able to achieve anything in the future.
5. The railway police guard on duty in the train from which she was thrown off lied that Arunima had tried to kill herself.
6. Her elder brother, a CRPF employee, agreed to train her to be a mountaineer.

7. Arunima started training after a year of being fitted with an artificial leg.
8. The first few months of learning to climb mountains were very difficult, but Arunima did not give up.
9. After completing her training, the young woman climbed several mountains in the Vindhya Range under the guidance of Bachendri Pal.
10. Arunima was fortunate to be sponsored by an NGO.

EXERCISE B

Write short answers to the following questions based on paragraphs 6 to 12.

1. What was a major problem Arunima faced while climbing Mount Everest and how was she able to solve it?
2. What made Arunima's achievement of climbing the world's highest mountain really extraordinary?
3. How did the young sportswoman's way of thinking help her fulfil her dream?
4. What is a main difference between optimistic and pessimistic people?
5. According to psychologists, how do most optimists deal with their failures?
6. Why is the quality of flexibility an important part of being optimistic?
7. How can people's optimism sometimes cause them problems?
8. Which three tips among those given by psychologists for developing optimism do you think are most useful?

Pronunciation

VOWEL SOUNDS

Some people have difficulty in differentiating between the following vowel sounds.

/ɜː/ as in bird
/ɑː/ as in bard

/əu/ as in bone
/ɔ:/ as in bought
/ɒ/ as in got

EXERCISE A

Listen to your teacher read out a list of words and group them in the five columns below according to their vowel sounds.

/ɜ:/	/ɑ:/	/əu/	/ɔ:/	/ɒ/

EXERCISE B

Look through the unit and pick out at least three examples each of words with the vowel sounds given in the above exercise.

Vocabulary

PRECISION AND ACCURACY

Precision is integral to scientific writing. When you record facts, you should avoid redundancy. Also, substitute phrases with single words. Finally, be brief and direct. For example, in the first sentence given below, the word 'halves' is not necessary, just as in the second sentence, the italicised phrase could be replaced with the word 'now'.

Divide the cake equally into two *halves*.
He is sleeping *at the present moment*.

EXERCISE A

Rewrite the following sentences avoiding unnecessary words.

1. This necklace is unique; it is the only one of its kind.
2. Her car is black in colour.
3. When the bad news reached his ears, he was filled with apprehension.
4. Although there isn't enough food, yet people won't starve.
5. He reached the hotel first, ahead of others.
6. She is suffering from a chronic disease that has continued for a long time.
7. In the event of his visit, I will take leave.
8. I want the cash without delay in order to buy the house.
9. I have an appointment with the doctor in the afternoon at 3 p.m.
10. There are sixty boys in the class, and Anand is the best of the boys in the class.
11. In many cases, the answers lacked clarity.
12. Because of unfavourable climatic conditions, we cancelled our picnic.
13. We used to meet near the school on a regular basis.
14. The lawyer said that there was not going to be any possibility of winning the case.
15. The committee decided to give consideration to our request, provided we made a few more changes.
16. He submitted all the true facts.
17. This is a free gift from the government to all the farmers.
18. He spoke to me only for a brief moment.
19. His comments on our performance were totally unecessary.
20. Will you repeat that again, please?

Another important feature of recording and reporting facts and processes is accuracy, which includes using words correctly in the right contexts.

EXERCISE B

The errors in the following sentences are because of the wrong choice of words. Write down the corrected sentences in your notebook.

1. My parents wanted me to choose nursing as my carrier.
2. I will like to meet you latter at the auditorium.
3. She is very interested in the currant topic of debate.
4. In spite of working hardly, she was not selected.
5. She did not wish to loose her place in the team.
6. The film was quiet interesting.
7. The doctor wanted her to report if there was mucous in the sputum.
8. He won an award presently for the best eye surgeon in India.
9. She advised the students to adopt to the new environment.
10. Beside singing, she participates in debates and dance competitions.
11. He was anonymously selected as the president of our club.
12. He charged me a very high prize for these books.
13. He wore a business suite to the meeting.
14. The patient is suffering from the affects of overmedication.
15. It is very hard to destroy bad habits.
16. He has a flare for singing.
17. The vocabulary section in our book proceeds the grammar exercises.
18. We listened to the music concert with wrapped attention.
19. I stopped to buy some stationary on my way back from the college.
20. He is known for flaunting the rules.

The above exercise illustrates the point that in English there are many words that are similar in their spellings but are different in their meanings. Be careful in your choice of such words.

Further, there are other words, called homonyms, which are used in different contexts with different meanings. For example, look at the meanings of the word 'tongue' in the sentences below.

Don't stick your *tongue* out. (a part of the human body)

The *tongues* of fire rose high and engulfed the house. (a jet of flame)

Push in the *tongue* of the shoe. (the flap under the laces in a shoe)

We camped at the *tongue* of the island. (a narrow strip of land jutting out into the sea)

When the *tongue* of the bell strikes it, a ringing sound is produced. (the swinging metal piece inside a bell)

What is your native *tongue*? (the first language you learn as a baby)

EXERCISE C

Find out five different meanings of 'scan' and write a sentence each to illustrate them. The word can be used in different parts of speech.

COLLOCATIONS

Collocations are words that normally go together in written and spoken English. There are no rules to explain why some combinations are acceptable and others are not. Look at the examples below.

a high mountain peak or a tall man, *but not* a tall mountain peak or a high man

fully recovered, *but not* absolutely/totally recovered

strong tea or weak tea, *but not* vigorous tea or lean tea

heavy drinker/rain/traffic, *but* strong criticism/opinion/sense of duty

Collocations can involve different parts of speech in a phrase. For example:

language/trade barrier (*noun with noun*)

have/take a bath (*verb with noun*)

a fatal/deadly/infectious/contagious/curable disease (*adjective with noun*)

deeply/greatly/bitterly regret; vary slightly/considerably/greatly/widely; nearly/almost always (*adverb with verb, adjective or another adverb*)

Sometimes, when both the words in a collocation have the same meaning , they are referred to as Siamese twins, for example 'bits and pieces', 'spick and span', 'nuts and bolts', 'kith and kin', 'rant and rave'.

Basically, English collocations have to be learned and used regularly in speech and writing. By reading standard books and listening to good English, we get a feel for these collocations. The exposure will imprint a lot of natural speech patterns on our minds.

EXERCISE D

Match the words in columns A and B, choosing the best combinations.

A	B
1. ample	a. plan
2. colossal	b. opportunity
3. extensive	c. difference
4. gigantic	d. scope
5. vast	e. increase
6. immense	f. waste
7. sound	g. improvement
8. meagre	h. satisfaction
9. marginal	i. stride
10. splendid	j. damage

EXERCISE E

Fill in the blanks in the sentences with words that are usually used with those that follow them. One is done for you.

1. He is ..*under*.. the influence of his brother.
2. I broke the vase .... mistake. I am sorry.
3. I have not met them .... years.
4. The factory workers are .... strike.
5. We have to .... an exam at the end of every semester.
6. They made a .... offer on our plot of land, so we accepted it.
7. Do you think the office will .... my contract for another year?
8. The doctors .... supported the nurses' demands.
9. Sarita .... a shock when she saw the mess the children had made.
10. Have you .... the problem of getting an electricity connection yet?
11. We were asked to organise a meeting .... short notice.
12. Work hard to .... your goal in life.
13. The scientist started by giving us a .... outline of his talk.
14. Mother .... a happy smile on her face when she came home.
15. There are many new paintings .... display at the museum.

Grammar

TENSE

Tense is related to the time aspect of an action, activity or state. Broadly speaking, we have the present and past tenses. Future time is indicated in English in different ways, which include the use of the simple present and present continuous tense forms as well as the auxiliary verb 'will'. Within each of the above, distinctions are conveyed through the simple, continuous, perfect and perfect continuous tenses. Specific situations and points of time demand the use of particular tenses. However, it is often found that English allows both flexibility and overlapping in the case of some tense forms. The forms and usage of two tenses — the present and past — are listed below.

The simple present tense is used:

- to indicate universal truths (e.g., 'The earth *revolves* round the sun.');
- to convey habits (e.g., 'Asha and Kiran *go* for a walk every evening.');
- in commentaries covering live events (e.g., 'Sachin *sends* the ball across the boundary for an amazing six runs!');
- in news paper headlines (e.g., 'Finance Minister *presents* budget in Parliament.');
- for historic past (e.g., 'Shakespeare *is* a great dramatist.');
- to indicate a future action which is very definite (e.g., 'I *fly* to Mumbai tomorrow.' The sentence indicates a very definite future action when compared to 'I *will fly* to Bombay tomorrow.');
- with stative verbs (e.g., 'adore', 'value', 'desire', 'hear', 'know', 'own' and 'possess') which cannot be used in the present continuous. Thus, 'I *know* him well.' But some of these stative verbs acquire a different meaning when used in the present continuous tense as in 'I *value* it' for 'It is precious to me', and 'I *am valuing* it' for 'I am assessing its worth.')

The present continuous is used:

- to convey an action happening at the time of speaking (e.g., 'Look! The boat *is sinking*.');
- to indicate a definite arrangement in the near future (e.g. 'I *am leaving* at 3 p.m.');
- to indicate a action, activity or event that is done or that happens regularly over a period of time starting prior to the present moment of speech and continuing to do so in the present (e.g., 'Prakash *is studying* hard' indicates that Prakash

is studying hard not only at the moment of speech but also as a rule in recent times.)

The present perfect tense is used:

- to indicate that an action that began sometime in the past has been completed in the present (e.g., 'Tony *has finished* his dinner.');
- to convey a past action or event whose effect is felt at the present moment of speech (e.g., in 'Amrit *has won* many prizes in swimming when at school', the use of the present perfect 'has won' implies that the subject of the sentence is, therefore, a good swimmer in the present.);
- with stative verbs to indicate a state of being of long duration, beginning in the past and continuing up to the present moment of speech (e.g., 'I *have been* asthmatic since 1975.');
- with other verbs also in place of the present perfect continuous (e.g., 'Salim *has waited* since morning for his friend' implies that Salim is still waiting.).

The present perfect continuous is used:

- to indicate an uninterrupted action or activity of long duration, starting in the past and continuing into the present moment of speech (e.g., 'I *have been waiting* at the bus stop since 7 a.m.');
- to convey intermittent actions that have become habits (e.g., 'He *has been going* to Kashmir twice a year.').

The simple past indicates actions and events that have been completed in the past (e.g., 'Last year Lata *won* the first prize in the English essay writing competition', and 'Sharad *was* always punctual in coming to school.').

The simple past and past continuous combination indicates a time span within another event. (e.g., 'When I *went in* Victor *was reading*', indicates that the activity of reading was ongoing at the time the speaker went in.).

When two events or actions or activities that have occurred in the past are referred to, the verb indicating the one that occurred earlier in the past appears in the past perfect form while the one that happened later in the past appears in the simple past form (e.g., in the sentence 'By the time Roy *arrived* at the station, the train *had left,*' the train leaves at an earlier point of time in the past while Roy arrives at a later point of time in the past.) The past continuous and past perfect are thus linked to a simple past verb either in the same sentence or in consecutive sentences.

The prediction that an action or activity will occur in the future is indicated by the use of the auxiliary verb 'will' along with the base form of the main verb (e.g., 'Sama *will take* us shopping'), and, as said above, also by the simple present and present continuous tenses.

EXERCISE A

Discuss the different shades of meaning in the following pairs of sentences.

1. a. Nishu always writes long compositions.
   b. Nishu is always writing long compositions.
2. a. I am meeting Anand tomorrow.
   b. I will meet Anand tomorrow.
3. a. I saw the book in the library.
   b. I have seen the book in the library.
4. a. He had breakfast at 8 a.m.
   b. He was having breakfast at 8 a.m.
5. a. For many years, they were manufacturing radios.
   b. For many years, they have manufactured radios.
6. a. They talked about Tina when I went in.
   b. They were talking about Tina when I went in.
7. a. Is he stupid?
   b. Is he being stupid?
8. a. Tell me when he comes.
   b. Tell me when he will come.
9. a. I listen to classical music.
   b. I am listening to classical music.
10. a. He practises every day.
    b. He is practising every day.

EXERCISE B

Fill in the blanks with the appropriate tense forms of the verbs in brackets.

1. My friend is annoyed with me for being late. He .... (wait) for me since morning.
2. The baby .... (scream). I am sure something has bitten her.
3. Udit is always successful because he .... (work) hard.
4. You can trust him. I .... (know) him for ten years now.
5. Every year the floods .... (ruin) our crops, and every year we request the government to help us.
6. They constantly .... (fight) over small things. So, finally, they were dismissed yesterday.
7. Gopi .... (rush) home to convey the good news he has just received.
8. Tigers .... (run) very fast.
9. I went to the shop to buy a pen because I .... (lose) mine.
10. When I reached the platform, the train .... (approach) the station.

We (11) .... (buy) the farm in 1984. Since then, we (12) .... (try) to develop it. Finally we (13) .... (succeed) and now we (14) .... (enjoy) the benefits. Hard work always (15) .... (help) one succeed.

Speaking

TELEPHONE CONVERSATIONS

Telephones and mobiles have become indispensable to communication in the current era. Given below are some guidelines for telephone etiquette:

PHONE ETIQUETTE

Clarity, brevity and courtesy are the hallmarks of good telephonic communication.

- Answer calls promptly and identify yourself by name or by professional identity.
- Adopt the appropriate level of formality, depending on who you are talking to and whether the call is personal or professional.
- Be clear and audible. Do not mumble.
- When you initiate a call, start with a greeting, such as 'Good morning' or 'Hello'.
- Address the caller by name or title (Mr Sharma, Dr Rao, Sir, Madam).
- Be clear why you are calling: explain the purpose to them.
- In professional settings, plan your message so it is be direct and specific. If you have a lot of points to discuss, jot these down before making the call. Keep a notepad and pencil handy to take down the answers.
- If you need time to collect/access the information the other person wants, explain this to the caller and give them the option either to hold or to call back. Do not place them on hold indefinitely.
- Never bang the phone down or disconnect without concluding the conversation politely.
- Speak clearly, confidently and respectfully.
- While on the phone, focus on the conversation. Do not be distracted by conversations or music around you. If it is inconvenient to talk at the time, either change your location or say you will call back at a more appropriate time.
- Do not shout on the phone or be aggressive or rude.
- Do not eat or drink while talking.

COMMON EXPRESSIONS RELATED TO TELEPHONE CALLS

1. I **made the call** to invite him; I **rang him up**. (contacted)
2. I **rang off** after conveying the news; I just **got off the line** after congratulating him. (finished calling)
3. Please **put me through** to Ravi. (connect me)
4. I finally **got through** to Ravi. (managed to contact)
5. I'll **get back** to you by evening. (call you back)

HOW TO RESPOND TO REQUESTS, QUESTIONS AND APOLOGIES

1. May I speak to Suresh please?
   a) Just a minute...
   b) Hold on...
   c) Hang on, please... (I'll call him)
   d) Please be on the line; I'll put you through to him. (on the extension line)
   e) He is not yet in. Can I take a message?
   f) Sorry, he is on leave. (unable to contact)
2. May I come to your office at 9 am tomorrow?
   a) By all means...
   b) Sure, no problem...
   c) Please make it 11 am. I have a meeting at 9.
3. Would a meeting next week be OK for you?
   a) Definitely...
   b) I am not sure. Let me check with the manager and get back to you.
4. May I leave a message for Dr. Sudha?
   a) Please wait. I'll take it down...
   b) Just a minute. I will write it down and pass it on to her when she comes.
5. Can I take a message?
   a) Sure. Please tell Ram that Varun called; he's leaving for the UK tonight.

b) It doesn't matter. I'll call later. Thank you.

6. Will you hold on a minute please?
    a) Sure...
    b) OK.
    c) No problem.
    d) Sorry, I'm in a rush. Please tell her I'll call at lunch time.
7. Could you please repeat it?
    a) Sure...
    b) No problem.
8. I didn't catch what you said. Could you please speak a little louder?
    a) Sure.
    b) ... Is it OK now?
9. Sorry, I couldn't be of much help.
    a) No problem. Thanks anyway
10. I have another call coming. I'll speak to you again soon.
    a) Thanks for calling.
    b) Sure.

TELEPHONE CONVERSATIONS IN HEALTH CARE SETTINGS

While on duty, avoid taking private calls unless absolutely necessary. It interrupts the flow of work and is unprofessional. Mobiles should be on silent mode during work hours. We can always call back the callers later. Some hospitals ban the use of private mobile phones in the wards as they can be a source of infection.

We have to be careful while answering work related calls inside or outside the hospital setting. Privacy is an important aspect in health care. Patient information is confidential and should not be shared with others. Often, it is passed on unconsciously when we discuss cases with colleagues face to face or over the phone. Every effort should be taken to ensure patient privacy. Remember that patient information cannot be shared even with their friends and relatives without patient consent.

While documenting telephonic orders/instructions from superiors, write down the instruction first and read it back to the caller to ensure that it is correctly recorded. Then record the doctor's name and telephone number. Print your name and sign with time and date.

SAMPLE PHONE CALL

Situation

Three-year-old Master Kesavan, a known asthmatic on treatment, is admitted in the hospital after a bad wheeze. Suddenly he becomes breathless and Monisha, the nurse in charge of the Paediatric Emergency Unit, wants to contact the unit doctor on rounds in another ward. She keeps Master Kesavan's chart and a notepad nearby and makes the phone call.

Monisha : Dr Kiran, I'm Monisha, staff nurse in B ward. I'm calling about Master Kesavan, 3-year-old boy, admitted with a severe wheeze under you on Wednesday, 21 Feb. When I was assisting him in breathing exercises he suddenly became breathless. His respiratory rate is 58 per minute and work of breathing is more with use of sternocleidomastoid muscles.

Dr Kiran : Is there an audible wheeze? How are his vital signs? What medication is he on?

Monisha : Yes, there is an audible wheeze. His respiratory rate is 58 per minute, temperature is 100.8 degree Fahrenheit, heart rate is 104 mt, BP is 100/70 mmHg. He is on inj. Aminophylline 8 mg (IV) Q6H. Is there anything specific you would like me to do?

Dr Kiran : Stop the exercises. Start him immediately on Oxygen. Continue inj. Aminophylline as recommended. Continue to monitor vital signs. I'll be there soon.

Monisha : Okay, doctor. Please come as soon as you can.

Dr.Kiran : I'll be there in five minutes.

Nurse : Thanks you, doctor.

EXERCISE A

Read the situation given below. Enact it as a telephonic conversation between Mr Kannan and the ward sister.

SITUATION

Mr. Kannan, 70 years old, was admitted in the medical ward with diabetes mellitus. He was treated with inj. Insulin 40 units OD. He was advised on health related issues like diet control, exercise, and medication. He was discharged after a week when his blood sugar was under control.

After a month Mr. Kannan rings the ward sister Mrs Aruna Ramesh to clarify some of the doubts related to his condition. His morning sugar was high on that particular day and he wanted to know whether his insulin dose needs to be increased and also whether anything can be done to reduce pain at the injection site.

Writing

PRÉCIS

Précis writing involves summarising a passage, usually to one-third of its length. The first step is to read the passage carefully and understand its gist. This is to be followed by condensing it without missing out any of the main points. Direct speech (if present) should be changed into indirect speech. If the passage is in first person, change it into third person. A précis is usually written in one paragraph even if the given passage has many paragraphs. You must also give the précis a suitable title. Make a rough draft first, read through it closely and make the necessary corrections and changes before writing the fair copy. Mention the number of words in your final draft.

Two passages, A and B, and their précis are given below as samples.

A. After every Holi I can't help wondering—we celebrate the festival of colours by throwing bright and vibrant colours all over each other and then what happens? We end up looking like complete horrors! Many species of birds too celebrate the coming of spring by adorning themselves in equally bright and vibrant colours—and end up looking stunning!

What's the reason behind all these dazzling colours and displays—not that anyone is complaining! Well, the first reason is that the birds' colours serve as a badge of identification for the species (and for us) and ensure that no dreadful inter-breeding mistakes are made. Secondly, male birds are snappy, flashy dressers in order to impress the female birds and to better their chances of breeding. (Of course, there is also the song and dance that follows to clinch the deal!). Female birds, on the other hand, are more soberly clad because it won't do to be gaudily multicoloured while sitting on a clutch of eggs or chicks—that would be like a restaurant's neon invitation to a passing predator.

Colours even help in chick feeding. Most young birds have yawning gapes, usually in bright papaya colours, to help their mothers put the food in the right place. In some cases, you can say the compliment is returned: The chicks of the herring gull for example, know where their meals are by the red spot on the bills of their parents. Many birds, especially seabirds and those that fly great distances, have dark or black tipped wings because the pigments that cause the black colour make them more resistant to wear and tear. (271 words)

(adapted from an article by Ranjit Lal in the *Hindu*, 15 April 2005)

Colours in birds

In spring, many birds look stunning in vibrant colours. Colours help them and us identify the species. They help avoid inter-breeding mistakes. Colourful males are impressive and gain mating partners easily. Females have sober colours which camouflage them from predators during breeding seasons. The bright oral cavities in the young help the mothers while feeding. The red spots on the beaks of herring gulls help the chick to know where the food is. The pigment in the dark wings of seabirds helps them fly long distances with minimum wear and tear.

(91 words)

B. Three aspects, simple but overwhelmingly strong, have governed my life: the longing for love, the search for knowledge, and the unbearable pity for the suffering of mankind. These passions, like great winds, have blown me hither and thither, in a wayward course, over a deep ocean of anguish, reaching to the very verge of despair.

I have sought love, first, because it brings ecstasy—ecstasy so great that I would often have sacrificed all the rest of life for a few hours of this joy. I have sought it, next, because it relieves loneliness—that terrible loneliness in which one shivering consciousness looks over the rim of the world into the cold unfathomable lifeless abyss.

With equal passion I have sought knowledge. I have wished to withstand the hearts of men. I have wished to know why the stars shine. And I have tried to apprehend the Pythagorean power by which number holds sway over the flux. A little of this, but not much, I have achieved.

Love and knowledge, so far as they were possible, led upward toward the heavens. But always pity brought me back to earth. Echoes of cries of pain reverberate in my heart. Children in famine, victims tortured by oppressors, helpless old people—a hated burden to their sons, and the whole world of loneliness, poverty, and pain make a mockery of what human life should be. I long to alleviate the evil, but I cannot, and I too suffer.

This has been my life. I have found it worth living, and would gladly live it again if the chance were offered me. (269 words)

(extract from Bertrand Russell's autobiography)

Great passions in life

Longing for love, thirst for knowledge and compassion for the suffering were the dominant passions in Bertrand Russell's life. He wanted love because it brought ecstasy and relieved loneliness. He loved to seek knowledge in different disciplines and achieved this in some measure. Both love and knowledge uplifted him. Pity for the poor, famished children, victims of torture, helpless old people and the lonely affected him. Because he could not alleviate their problems, he too suffered. Despite all this, he found life worth living.

(84 words)

EXERCISE

Write précis of the following passages.

1. Butterflies can be seen fluttering over flowers in the Himalayas, in the Gangetic plains or deep down in the villages in Tamil Nadu. These beautiful creatures are useful pollinators. Their wings are formed of pigments of red, yellow, black and white, while the blues, the greens and the metallic iridescent hues are the result of refraction. The patterns on butterfly wings are created by a mass of tiny coloured scales which overlap almost like the tiles on a roof. Their antennae are used primarily to find food and mates. They are covered with microscopic sense organs and moved by basal muscles. Through these, they perceive odours, changes in temperature, humidity in the air and certain other stimuli.

A fascinating aspect of these insects is their protective colouring. Most of them have colouring that blends with their background (for example, green caterpillars on grass or foliage). In some, the familiar outlines of the body are concealed by irregular patterns and patches. Some resemble the bark on which they rest and in others the colour, shape and pattern of leaf veins are imitated. Some butterflies, while chased, suddenly fold their wings revealing the drab outside. The quickness of the action and the sudden hiding of their brilliant colours seem to make them invisible.

In some cases, the wings appear ripped and tattered like dry leaves. There are also species with transparent wings which enable them to melt into the background. In some species with dull colours, the protection device is flash colouration. The butterfly suddenly opens its wings to display a flash of bright colours, which startles the predator and gives the prey enough time to escape. Some caterpillars have prominent black and yellow marking to advertise their nasty taste. Some resemble the seed pods of the plants on which they feed and grow. (300 words)

(extract from an article by J. Banerjee in the *Hindu*, 27 October 1996)

2. Wetlands are the womb from which our ancestors emerged. In the Devonian Age, 360 million years ago, the first amphibians crawled out of the sea and begun to breathe the damp air of the ancient wetlands.

Sadly mankind often forgets the great protecting, recycling, purifying and generating power of the wetlands and allows them to be drained for so-called development. If our mangroves and wetlands had been protected, the tsunami might not have created such havoc. Mangroves absorb the destructive power of waves, whereas wetlands deter human settlement within reach of the sea's fury.

A stunning example of ecological rejuvenation is the London Wetland Centre. The famous naturalist Sir Peter Scott transformed the stagnant reservoirs of the Thames river water into an innovative eco-park. Set in 125 acres, it has a great lake with some of the centre's 170 species of birds living free against the backdrop of London. The centre's great expanses of water bodies, landscaped grounds and winding paths are divided into World Wetlands with 14 different habitats with their own wild fowl. So here we see the paddy fields of East Asia along with the mountain streams of New Zealand. They are windows into the watered wilderness of the earth.

This eco-park offers much more than spectator entertainment. It shows us how to create our own sustainable gardens and how to preserve the environment by strengthening its ecology.

There are fascinating shows conducted for children. They listen with rapt attention when the guide speaks about some of the 350 species of moths and 20 species of dragonflies found in the wetlands. Children are allowed to feed ducks and birds at specific times. Side by side, they are made aware of the dos and don'ts related to the preservation of the environment. The wetland centre makes them environmentally conscious from a very young age. This should be one of the major objectives of eco-parks in every country. (320 words)

(adapted from the original article by Hugh and Colleen Gantzer in the *Hindu*, 17 April 2005)

Appreciating poetry

If

If you can keep your head when all about you
Are losing theirs and blaming it on you,
If you can trust yourself when all men doubt you,
But make allowance for their doubting too;
If you can wait and not be tired by waiting,
Or being lied about, don't deal in lies,
Or being hated, don't give way to hating,
And yet don't look too good, nor talk too wise:

If you can dream—and not make dreams your master;
If you can think—and not make thoughts your aim,
If you can meet with Triumph and Disaster

And treat these two impostors just the same;
If you can bear to hear the truth you've spoken
Twisted by knaves to make a trap for fools,
Or watch the things you gave your life to, broken,
And stoop and build 'em up with worn-out tools:

If you can make one heap of all your winnings;
And risk it on one turn of pitch-and-toss,
And lose, and start again at your beginnings
And never breathe a word about your loss;
If you can force your heart and nerve and sinew
To serve your turn long after they are gone
And so hold on when there is nothing in you
Except the Will which says to them: 'Hold on!'
If you can talk with crowds and keep your virtue,
Or walk with Kings—nor lose the common touch,
If neither foes nor loving friends can hurt you,
If all men count with you, but none too much;
If you can fill the unforgiving minute
With sixty seconds' worth of distance run,
Yours is the Earth and everything that's in it,
And—which is more—you'll be a Man, my son!

Rudyard Kipling

EXERCISE

Write short answers to the following questions.

1. What is the essence of the poet's advice to his son?
2. Do you think the title of the poem is an appropriate one? Why?

UNIT 6

Helping Hands

> The measure of a man is the way he bears up under misfortune.
>
> —*Plutarch*

It is said that pain and suffering are inevitable parts of life but being miserable is optional. Do you think compassion for others can help us cope better in times of adversity? Read the account below to find out.

1. In 1962, when 10-year-old Ramachander started getting blue patches and bruises on his body, his parents thought that it was due to nutritional deficiency.
2. But Ramachander was diagnosed as suffering from haemophilia due to factor VIII deficiency in his blood and was treated with plasma transfusion. When Ramachander's father was posted in Washington, the boy received treatment by plasma and powdered form of cryoprecipitate of factor VIII.
3. Recalling how she met her husband Ramachander, Ranjana Ramachander, General Secretary, Bangalore Chapter of the Haemophilia Society (affiliated to the Haemophilia Federation of India, or HFI) said, 'I met Ramachander at a wedding when I was nineteen and he was twenty-six'. Ranjana married Ramachander in 1979. 'I underwent relevant blood tests to make sure that I was not a carrier of the haemophilic gene,' she said. Ranjana also underwent relevant pre-natal

screening tests during her pregnancies—both her daughter and son are normal and non-haemophilic.

4. Settled in Bangalore, Ramachander received timely transfusion of factor VIII. By the early 1990s, Ramachander suffered severe episodes of bleeding and painful knee joints.

   'That phase in our life was most challenging for both of us and my in-laws, especially because till then we had had quite an active life attending get-togethers, going for long drives, hosting my painting exhibitions! When the haemorrhagic episodes in my husband's knee joints became quite frequent and troublesome, we left for Canada to seek the advice of haematologist Dr Martin Wood to explore the possibility of whether my husband could have a knee replacement surgery. But the doctor advised us against the surgery. When we returned to India, we continued my husband's treatment with imported factor replacement therapy,' says Ranjana.

5. In 1962, Ranjana and Ramachander started the Haemophilia Society at Cunningham Road in Bangalore. 'We interacted with haematologist Dr Cecil Ross at St John's Medical College Hospital, and that in a way mitigated our sorrow because he enlightened us about there being many others in Karnataka who had been diagnosed and registered as haemophilic at the hospital's haematology department. Our discussion with Dr Ross was an eye opener since most of the haemophilics could not afford expensive timely transfusions.'

6. The couple also met several other persons with haemophilia (PWH) who had started self-help groups not only in Bangalore but also in Kerala and other states. The Society for Haemophilia added more meaning to Ramachander's life since he had started interacting and counselling other PWH.

   'My husband started putting behind his own suffering, once he became busy with networking with other PWH from all over Karnataka. My in-laws provided enough funds for the Haemophilia Society to take off and progress.'

7. In 1999, one night after his dinner, Ramachander died of cardiac arrest. Says Ranjana, 'The stress of having had to deal with haemophilia right from his childhood probably took a massive toll on my husband. When the reality of his departure started sinking in my mind, I was numb and felt for several months that I would not be able to carry on the work of the Haemophilia Society without his guiding force. But he had taught me to forget our pain by counselling other people and extending a helping hand to PWH who could have a problem getting the right treatment and medicines. I continued with the activities of the society and a couple of years later got further motivated by Sarojini (the late Jeeva Raj Alva's sister, whose son Prem is a PWH) when she gave a lecture on mind and body healing in haemophilia-afflicted persons.' In November 2002, Ranjana shifted her office to the infrastructure provided free at Bangalore Mahaveer Jain Hospital in Vasanth Nagar.

8. A woman of grit, Ranjana believes that all the events in one's life work to provide a certain design to it. She says her life has been moulded to deal with the manner in which she has had to live.

9. Her commitment to the Haemophilia Society is evidently deep, and her message to PWH and their families is reflected in the quotation written by a volunteer in her office, which reads 'Disability does not mean inability—well or ill, you live only once.'

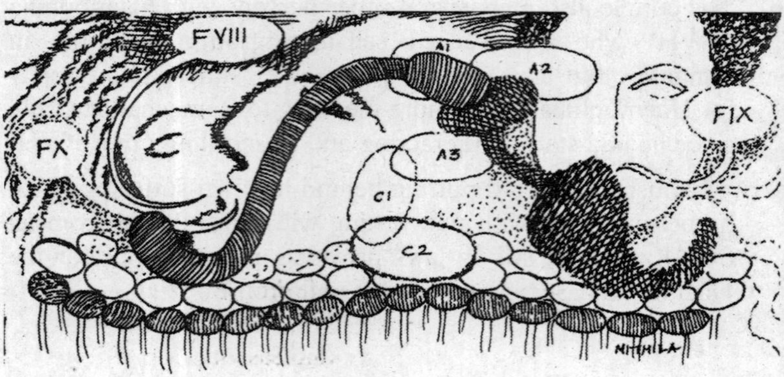

10. Ranjana, a torch bearer to several PWH, is no doubt a woman of substance and is capable of making a haemophilia sufferer's journey meaningful and tolerable through the services of the society which she has been heading.

('Holding a torch' by Veena Bharathi in *The New Indian Express*, Bangalore edition, 22 February 2005)

Glossary

afflicted	-	affected
bruise	-	an injury in which the skin is discoloured but not broken
commitment	-	a willingness to give a lot of time, energy, etc., to something you believe in
cryoprecipitate	-	precipitate formed when plasma of patients with autoimmune diseases is stored at 4°C
deficiency	-	a state of not having something that is needed
design	-	plan
episode	-	here, a period in which someone is affected by a particular illness
evidently	-	obviously
grit	-	courage and determination in spite of difficulties
haemophilia	-	a blood disease characterised by greatly prolonged coagulation time, which leads to abnormal bleeding
infrastructure	-	basic facilities like building, water, etc.
mitigate	-	to make less bad
mould	-	to shape
network	-	to interact with others to exchange information and develop professional or social contacts
numb	-	incapable of feeling or acting
sink in	-	to slowly start to believe or understand something unpleasant or surprising

take off - to start to be successful
take a massive toll - to cause a lot of suffering or harm

Understanding the text

EXERCISE A

Based on paragraphs 1 to 6, mark the following statements true (T) or false (F).

1. Nutritional deficiency causes blue patches on the body.
2. Haemophilia is caused by plasma transfusion.
3. Haemophilia Federation of India is affiliated to the Bangalore Chapter of Haemophilia.
4. Through blood tests, one can find out if one is a carrier of the haemophilia gene.
5. Factor VIII deficiency leads to bleeding.
6. The 'challenging' time mentioned in paragraph 4 refers to the couple's anxiety about their children.
7. Dr Martin Wood came from Canada to treat the patient.
8. Haemophilia affects the knee joints of patients.
9. Starting the Haemophilia Society helped to reduce the stress that Ramachander and his family were going through.
10. In India blood transfusions are not expensive.

EXERCISE B

Write short answers to the following questions.

1. What is haemophilia?
2. Mention two contributions of the Haemophilia Society.
3. What is the meaning of 'mind and body healing' mentioned in para 7?
4. What is the message of the Haemophilia Society to PWH?
5. Do you know any other person who has contributed to the welfare of others despite his/her physical limitations and suffering? Write a short note of about 50 to 100 words on the person.

Pronunciation

LETTERS AND SOUNDS

EXERCISE A

The letter 'n' is pronounced in two different ways: /n/ and /ŋ/, as in the words 'win' and 'anxiety' respectively. Write down ten more such words each in the two columns below.

/n/	/ŋ/

EXERCISE B

The letter 'x' is pronounced as /ɪks/, /eks/ or /ɪgz/ when it follows the initial 'e' in a word. Your teacher will read out a list of words. Listen carefully and write them down in the right columns below, depending on the sound that 'x' has in the words.

/ɪks/	/eks/	/ɪgz/

EXERCISE C

Read aloud the short rhyme given below. What is the sound of the letter 's' in it?

Leisure without measure
Is a doubtful pleasure.

Vocabulary

PLURAL FORMS OF NOUNS

English plurals are formed in a variety of ways. These are shown in the table below. Also note how the plural forms of compound nouns are formed.

Singular	Plural	Change in form
sheep	sheep	no change
calf	calves	'f' changes to 'ves'
proof	proofs	addition of 's' after 'f'
hoof	hooves/hoofs	both patterns above
solo	solos	addition of 's'
echo	echoes	addition of 'es'
lady	ladies	'y' changes to 'ies'
valley	valleys	addition of 's' after 'y'
crisis	crises	internal change
goose	geese	internal change
cherub	cherubs or	addition of letters
	cherubim	
chateau	chateaux	
ox	oxen	
larva	larvae	
memorandum	memoranda (also, memorandums)	
radius	radii	

taxi driver	taxi drivers	change in the second noun
mother-in-law	mothers-in-law	change in the first noun
woman teacher	women teachers	change in the both the nouns.

EXERCISE A

Write down two more examples of each type given above.

WORD GAME

EXERCISE B

In each group of words below, four items share a common aspect—related to meaning or pronunciation or grammar or medical terminology. Find the odd word that does not belong to the group and explain the reason for your choice.

1. little, sparse, ample, meagre, scanty
2. tense, disturbed, on edge, jittery, weary
3. warm, damp, tepid, lukewarm, hot
4. indisposition, ailment, infirmity, deceased, diseased
5. witty, astute, childish, sharp, judicious
6. receipt, depot, subtle, coup, drain
7. cleverer, better, brighter, shrewder, wiser
8. advice, information, luggage, shopping, experience
9. malleus, incus, cochlea, cornea, stapes
10. spatula, pustule, shears, retractor, forceps

EXERCISE C

Fill in the blanks with the right words or phrases chosen from those given below. Discuss the meanings of the expressions with your teacher.

by and large	lightheaded	point-blank	titbit
blanket rule	foolhardy	dropouts	pell-mell
round the clock	hangover	taskmaster	offhand
watertight			

1. He is suffering from a .... after the party.
2. We are .... happy with the service at the hotel.
3. The angry crowd rushed .... towards the dais.
4. The doctors worked .... to save his life.
5. He felt .... after the accident.
6. Father works for an organisation that helps school ....
7. The manager's .... refusal to consider their request angered the workers.
8. The university has a .... prohibiting smoking on campus.
9. His .... behaviour with the customer has landed him in trouble.
10. Aunt Rita always had some .... for us when we returned from the school.

Grammar

SIMPLE, COMPOUND AND COMPLEX SENTENCES

A sentence is a group of words that has a subject and a finite verb and that conveys complete meaning. Verbs (v), nouns (n), adjectives (adj.), adverbs (adv.), articles (art.), prepositions (prep.) and conjunctions (conj.) are the elements of a sentence. These occur in different combinations and with specific functions (subject, object, predicate, complement, etc.) to convey meaning accurately. For examples, look at the sentences below.

He	gives	me	presents	every year.
subj.	verb	indir. obj.	dir. obj.	adverbial

She is a scientist.
subj. verb art. complement

Sentences with more than one clause could have main clauses that can appear as independent sentences outside the larger sentence and subordinate clauses that cannot be meaningful sentences on their own.

Based on the clauses they contain, sentences are labelled as simple (with just one main clause) or compound (two or more main clauses linked by coordinating conjunctions) or complex (subordinate clauses linked to a main clause). For example:

I met John. (simple)
main clause

I went to school *and* met John. (compound)
main clause 1 main clause 2

When I went to school, I met John. (complex)
subordinate clause main clause

Some sentences may have more than two main as well as subordinate clauses. Here they are classified as complex sentences.

The words 'and', 'but', 'still', 'so', 'yet', 'or' and 'not only . . . but also' are samples of coordinating conjunctions. The words 'although', 'because', 'if', 'that', 'since', 'until', 'where', 'while', 'when', 'as', etc., are subordinating conjunctions.

In some compound sentences, nouns, pronouns and verbs can be dropped if they occur in both or all the main clauses that are linked. For example:

She is pretty and witty. (pronoun and verb dropped in the second clause)
Suresh composes and sings songs. (noun dropped in the second clause)

In some complex sentences, the subordinating markers may be absent. For example:

I suppose he is right. (*for* I suppose that he is right.)

Simple sentences can be converted into compound or complex ones by changing a noun/phrase/infinitive/participle into main or subordinate clauses and linking them with suitable conjunctions. For example:

My friend Sheila has come to see you. (simple)
noun phrase
Sheela is my friend and she has come to see you. (compound)
Sheela, who is my friend, has come to see you. (complex)

We stayed at home *because of the rain*. (simple)
phrase
It rained and so we stayed at home. (compound)
We stayed at home because it rained. (complex)

She was thrilled *to see* the result. (simple)
infinitive
She saw the result and was thrilled. (compound)
She was thrilled when she saw the result. (complex)

Running fast, she reached the stadium first. (simple)
participle
She ran fast and so she reached the stadium first. (compound)
She reached the stadium first because she ran fast. (complex)

EXERCISE A

Mark the following sentences as simple, compound or complex.

1. Australia, the largest island continent in the world, is almost two and a half times bigger than India but has only 22 million people.

2. It is believed that aborigines have lived in the country for at least 40,000 years, having travelled there from Southeast Asia, but it was colonised by the British only in the eighteenth century.
3. South Australia which is one of the seven states of Australia has many attractions like the rugged Flinders ranges, long stretches of golden beaches, picturesque vineyards, wildlife reserves, opal fields and the mysterious Blue Lake.
4. Adelaide, the capital of South Australia is an elegant, well designed city with extensive parklands, famous for its churches and cultural festivals.
5. Queensland state is home to the World Heritage site the Great Barrier Reef that stretches nearly 2000 km with more than two million species of underwater animal and plant life of astonishing variety.
6. Sydney, the capital of New South Wales is near a magnificent deep water harbour and its Opera House and Harbour Bridge, considered architectural feats, attract thousands of visitors.
7. Another unique natural feature of Australia is the rock monolith Uluru in Northern Territory. It is 348 m in height and 9 km in circumference and appears to change colour from fiery red to purple to blue to pink as the desert sun changes.
8. Victoria, the smallest state of Australia, offers a wide variety of landscapes, from sandstone cliffs along a dramatic coastline to snow in the Australian Alps whereas the largest state – Western Australia – is well known for its gold and diamond mines and profusion of native wild flowers.
9. The island state Tasmania has lavender farms, gorges, lakes and valleys, and World Heritage listed Cradle mountains, adding to the beauty of the Australian landscape.
10 To sum up, Australia is a land of contrasts with snow-capped mountains, volcanic and salt lakes, monoliths, scorching, trackless deserts, dense rainforests, long winding rivers and golden beaches.

EXERCISE B

Change sentences 1–5 to compound sentences, sentences 6–10 to complex sentences, and sentences 11–15 to simple sentences.

1. Being a kind person, Vasu cannot bear to see people suffer.

2. Prabha was absent because of her illness.
3. Sengupta, a hardworking man, is doing very well professionally.
4. Despite being busy, Ratna attended the conference.
5. Seeing Balu at a distance, I waved to him.
6. Daya was tired but she continued working.
7. Finishing her work for the day, Revati went home.
8. She went to Tiruvananthapuram and met Suresh.
9. Being ill, Madhu had to cancel his programme.
10. Because of Sam's excellent performance,we selected him to act in our play.
11. Vijay, who is my friend, works abroad.
12. I visited Ooty and took many photographs.
13. He behaves rudely because of which he is unpopular.
14. They hoped to meet some old friends and so went to Delhi.
15. Khadir has a beautiful house and we like to spend time there.

EXERCISE C

Rewrite the sentences as directed.

1. He could finish the work early because I helped him. (Change into a compound sentence.)
2. Finally, it would depend on what we decide. (Change into a simple sentence.)
3. Rekha was not well but she helped us a lot in organising the carnival. (Change into a complex sentence.)
4. I am sure he is capable. (Change into a simple sentence.)
5. He promised to do better next time. (Change into a complex sentence.)
6. In spite of our advice, he didn't join the basket ball team. (Change into a compound sentence.)
7. The teacher was sure that we would win. (Change into a simple sentence.)
8. He was late because he missed the bus. (Change into a compound sentence.)
9. When I saw Sarah, I invited her. (Change into a simple sentence.)
10. Salma was upset because of her marks. (Change into a complex sentence.)

Speaking

FORMAL TALKS AND PRESENTATIONS

A formal talk on academic as well as general topics of interest given to an informed audience is a form of spoken communication that has a specific purpose and plan. To give impressive talks, we need depth of knowledge and good presentation skills. Both these qualities, which contribute to career advancement, are common to essay writing as well. Hence, many of the points below are also listed in the essay writing section in unit 3. However, speaking to a live audience requires careful preparation in terms of both content and delivery.

You will find the following suggestions useful when preparing for a talk.

- ✦ Understand the purpose of your talk and your audience. That will give direction to your talk and help you decide on its content and language.
- ✦ Think carefully about the topic and collect as much information as possible.
- ✦ Do not depend only on a few books but refer to journals and websites to get the latest information on the subject and check for authenticity of facts. You may not use all the information in your talk, but having sound knowledge of the subject will give you confidence and also help you handle questions, if any, at the end of the session.
- ✦ Prepare an interesting and impressive introduction. It should define the subject and arouse the interest of the audience. Be creative wherever possible.
- ✦ Organise the content of your talk in a logical manner. Make sure the facts are accurate. Draw the attention of the audience to the latest facts. Illustrations should be supported by specific instances. Link ideas by using appropriate connecting words/ phrases such as 'to begin with', 'last of all', 'unless' and 'otherwise'. These signposts are very important as they help the listeners understand you better.

- If the subject of the talk happens to be controversial, you have to justify the stand you take with exact facts, clear examples and logical arguments. Quote the words of subject experts who hold the same opinion.
- You should have enough information on the opposite point of view in order to counter arguments that may come up at the end.
- Summarise what you said at the end of the talk. Do not be abrupt when you sum up but be brief. Try to be original and avoid stereotypes.
- Write a draft of your talk and then edit it. Revise and rewrite the talk till it is concise and fits the time slot.
- Be fluent when presenting the topic. Fluency is just as important as accuracy. Practise your speech by reading it aloud many times. Have teachers or friends assess your oral skills. Work on improving it. Practise until you are perfect.
- Talk naturally, varying the pitch of your voice and pausing at the right places to highlight important points. Try to be spontaneous and establish a rapport with the audience. Humour, when used appropriately, can enhance the effect of your talk, but do not overdo it.
- Keep to the allotted time. When you practise your talk, make sure you do not exceed it.
- Overcome stage fear. Acknowledge that stage fear is a common phenomenon that has to be gotten over. Work on it and find your own ways to overcome it. Use appropriate body language that shows confidence. Avoid gestures or other mannerisms that indicate nervousness. Make eye contact with the audience as often as possible.
- Use slides and other visual aids to reinforce your talk.
- Speaking on a topic involves much more than reading aloud a well-written essay. Memorising a talk and reproducing it does not always work very well. It may be a good idea to jot down the main points and important expressions on numbered cards (cue cards) and use them as an aid to memory. You

can also note down some pertinent data or information for your reference.

ORAL PRESENTATION

EXERCISE A

Work in groups of five. Brainstorm to assemble points for a talk. Note these down; support your statements with data. One of you should make a 5-minute presentation to the class. A few topics are given below. Collect data to support/ explain your topic and present it to the class after a week.

a. Inclusive education.
b. Community response to the homeless
c. Drug addiction and recovery.

EXERCISE B

Mark the following statements as True (T) or False (F).

1. Make notes before you make a presentation.
2. Links between various sections of the presentation need not be indicated using oral markers.
3. Research about the topic you will speak on only if you have time.
4. If you run out of time you do not need to conclude your talk.
5. If you are well prepared you are likely to be able to present without anxiety.
6. Visual aids may be used to entertain the audience.
7. Examples of signposts are 'As you may know' and 'The data shows'.
8. If the audience has not understood the point, repeat the sentence verbatim several times.
9. You may use quotations to support your argument.
10. Read out your presentation without a break.

Write the correct sentence for the sentences you marked False. Discuss your answers in class.

GROUP TEACHING

EXERCISE C

There has been an epidemic of viral gastroenteritis affecting hundreds of children in your town. In many cases, lack of proper, timely help has led to complications and death. Organise a group-teaching session for the people of the locality, highlighting the relevant aspects of the disease so that they would be able to cope with such situations when necessary. Use flash cards to make your lesson clearer. Refer to the format and pictures below for guidance.

Topic	:	Viral gastroenteritis
Objective	:	People should be able to identify the signs and complications of the disease, learn ways to prevent dehydration, learn to prepare oral hydration solution.
Teaching method	:	Discussion/question–answer method
Teaching aids	:	Flash cards/poster
Content	:	Introduction Causes of diarrhoea (poor hygiene/sanitation, contaminated food/water, etc.) What are the signs to look for? What are the complications? How can it be treated at home? Is hospitalisation necessary? Can the disease be prevented?

diarrhoea → loss of water and salt from body → dehydration → death

Medicines?

Local measures for making salt and sugar rehydration solution

8 level tsps sugar

+

1 level tsp salt

+

1 litre water

Boil and cool the above solution and administer to patient.

Signs of dehydration that parents need to watch out for

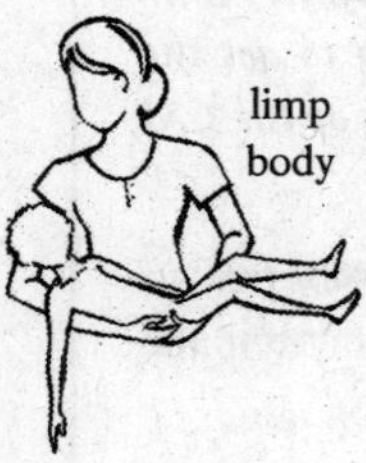

limp body

dry mouth

sunken, dry eyes

loose skin

hands and eyes still

sunken fontanelle

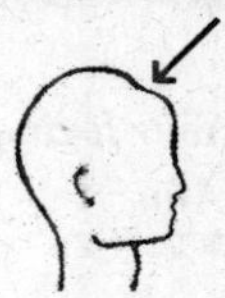

(based on illustrations in *My Name is Today* by D. Morley and H. Lowel, London: Macmillan, 1986)

Writing

ARTICLES FOR PROFESSIONAL JOURNALS

EXERCISE A

Using the material that you prepared for your group teaching, write an article for the journal of a primary health centre.

LETTERS

Read the two letters below, noting the similarities and differences in their formats and styles of writing.

Vellore *4 February 2014*

Dear Mother,

I have some exciting news for you. Guess what? Your dream has come true. Your daughter is going to get the Best Nurse of the Year award from the hands of the CM herself. Aren't you thrilled? I am so happy.

The function is on 11 March. Please keep yourself free on that day. You will receive a special invitation from the government.

What would I have done without your support all these years! My love to all at home.

Your loving,
Anu

4 February 2014

The Nursing Superintendent
CMC Hospital
Vellore

Dear Madam,

Sub: Request for two days leave

I am happy to inform you that I have been selected for the Best Nurse of the Year award by the Tamil Nadu government.

I request you to permit me to go to Chennai to receive the award on 11 March 2014. I would be grateful if you could grant me two days leave (10–11 March) for the purpose.

Thank you.

Yours faithfully,

Anu Rao
Staff Nurse, C ward
CMC Hospital, Vellore 632004

EXERCISE B

Write answers to the following questions and discuss them with your teacher.

1. What are the major differences between the letters?
2. Are there other forms of greeting and closing?
3. What are the other types of letters you have come across? Discuss your answers with your teacher.

EXERCISE C

You are a staff nurse. Your younger sister, on her way to school, has met with an accident and has been admitted in a hospital in your home town. You want to go and help her. Write two letters as directed below.

1. Write a letter requesting the nursing superintendent for leave.
2. Write a letter to your friend informing her or him about the accident.

EXERCISE D

Write a letter to the British Council, New Delhi, asking for the details about the International English Language Testing System (IELTS) test conducted by them.

Appreciating poetry

Laughter

A formed,
 formless
  sound of joy,
The ripple
 of a bubbling brook,
The sight of a child
 at play.
A task done...
 near perfectly.
A beautiful thought.
 A new idea.

Laughter
 is the clean freshness
  of pine trees...

The ghostly echoes
of invisible feet
touching
the quiet places
on the forest's floor.

Laughter
is a worldly life
accepted...
of an inner peace
given a quiet soul.

Howard G. Kirkman

EXERCISE

Write short answers to the following questions.

1. What is the author's concept of laughter?
2. What does the author mean by 'A formed, formless sound of joy'?

UNIT 7

My Friend Mike

> The purpose of human life is to serve, and show compassion and the will to help others.
>
> *Albert Schweitzer*

Empathy and efficiency are much valued attributes in health care settings. Read about the conflicting emotions of a doctor when a close friend with a life-threatening illness was admitted under her care.

1. As the new year begins, I reflect on all the patients I have met last year and set myself the somewhat difficult task of selecting one whose journey has inspired me. A doctor's role is a privileged one, to witness every day stories of immense suffering with courage and grace. It is impossible to grade these qualities for they are unique in the most memorable ways.
2. This year I lost a 90-year-old patient who, having endured the depravities of war considered her breast cancer to be fairly civilised battle where everyone fought on her side. I miss her smile, weary as it was towards the end. I said goodbye to a delightful young man. After many years it seems safe to say that he is cured of his cancer. He proposed to his fiancée when he walked out of my office for the last time.
3. But the person to whom I want to pay tribute to is my friend, and as such, was never expected to be a patient, naïve as it sounds.
4. Mike is one of my oldest friends. When I saw him two years ago, he brought crayons for my children. Watching their

pleasure we remarked on the passage of time. He reflected proudly that he has seen me grow from a medical student to doctor to wife and mother.

5. "See you soon," I waved to Mike little knowing that I would do so under dreadful circumstances.
6. A few weeks later I received a phone call telling me that Mike had suffered severe brain haemorrhage while driving and had been air lifted to the hospital. I rushed into Intensive Care Unit to find a lifeless looking man, hooked up to countless tubes and machines. My heart sank. In the ensuing days and weeks, tubes came out and went in, the doctors' expression of despair alternated with frustration, and there didn't seem to be one parameter that worked consistently in Mike's favour. He was either awake and agitated or worryingly unconscious. I was a stranger to him, as he to me.
7. Mike defied predictions and made it out of ICU. The tubes were out he was completely dependent on nursing care and devastatingly displayed minimal higher level brain function. I remember begging a nurse to help me change his soiled clothes. She was busy but I knew that because Mike couldn't move, press the bell or speak, I had to stay till she came. Sitting helplessly beside him, I recalled his intellect, global travels and his spirited independence. Unbelievably, he beat the odds and moved to rehabilitation.
8. It didn't need an expert to see that Mike's prospect of meaningful recovery was bleak. In those days, he was easily frustrated, could not obey commands and was physically weak. Depression crouched nearby. If it took you months to learn to manoeuvre a spoon over puréed food, it was sheer fantasy to conjure a different future. Sure enough my misgivings proved correct. Mike became acutely unwell, unfit for rehab and ended up ironically under my care. I had looked after hundreds of similar patients but each time my residents mentioned the delirious and febrile patient from the rehab, I was overcome with sadness. Who was the man burning with sweat, refusing to be calmed by any soothing presence, except when he fell into a deep exhausted sleep from which he awoke

as troubled as ever? I transferred his care, unable to function as a friend and physician. Mike survived this hospital ordeal too.

9. Next he went to transitional care bed in order to see whether his condition would improve enough to avoid a nursing home placement. Alas, the writing has always been on the wall. Mike's cognition and mobility were both poor and the day arrived that he was transferred to a nursing home and then, another.
10. Imagine yourself at the peak of your functions one day, then your entire life fractured before haphazard pieces were collected and cramped into a single room with no view. To call the initial months difficult is a vast understatement. Mike's total dependence and vulnerability were troubling to watch; I lack the words to describe how he must have felt. Our conversations were no longer about current affairs but the defective call-bell, the blocked catheter, the tasteless food and the aggressive demented patient next door. I often felt powerless against the system that he had become part of. Perhaps the most painful part was realising with Mike that all but a core group of friends had stopped visiting him, too occupied with their lives but also uncomfortable to confront a fate that could easily belong to any one of us.
11. But another year has passed since and here is the wonderful news. His doctors were right. Mike's brain has continued an initially slow but now a steady and promising recovery. Today, he can walk outdoors with his frame and breathe the summer air. He can catch a taxi to visit me so we can once again share sushi, meat pies and a cold drink. He can read, write and type again. He can email me his consent to write openly about his courage.
12. Mike's regeneration is as miraculous as it is a credit to his gritty perseverance, goodwill and grace in accepting his sudden turn of fate. I have never once heard him blame anyone although I am sure that the existential question of 'why' must always waft close to his now clear mind. He is a role model for all of us, ill and well.

13. Illness has its blessings – Mike has no memory of his worst days. As a witness, I assure him that they are days best forgotten. Today there is hope again. Hope that bounties of a more complete life will be slowly returned, among them his friends and greater independence.
14. Every year for as long as I have known him, Mike wrote me a card until the stroke stole his skill. As Christmas approached, I was thrilled to find a card in my letter box once again, in his familiar writing. It's going to be a good year.

Ranjana Srivastava

(Dr Ranjana Srivastava is an oncologist practising in Melbourne, Australia.)

Glossary

agitated	-	anxious
cognition	-	acquiring knowledge through senses or reasoning or intuition
confront	-	face something or somebody unpleasant
core group	-	the central or most important group
crouched	-	hid
defied predictions	-	did not happen as expected
depression	-	a state in which people may suffer from low spirits
delirious anxiety	-	a state of restlessness in which the person may also talk aimlessly
demented	-	mad
ensuing	-	following
frustration	-	annoyance due to disappointment
gritty	-	courageous and determined
haphazard	-	without plan or order
haemorrhage	-	bleeding
manoeuvre	-	move skilfully
misgivings	-	doubts
ordeal	-	difficult painful experience

privilege - advantage
prospect - chance of success
reflect - think deeply
regeneration - give fresh strength to life
sushi - a type of Japanese food usually consisting of raw fish
tribute - respect

UNDERSTANDING THE TEXT

EXERCISE A

Write brief answers to the questions based on the text.

1. What made the patient consider her cancer a lesser evil compared to the war?
2 Which sentence conveys the fact that Mike had known Dr Srivastava for some time?
3 Why were the doctors in the ICU looking after Mike immediately after his accident so frustrated?
4. How was Mike after he was transferred to the ward?
5. Describe Mike's condition at the Rehabilitation Centre.
6. Why did the author transfer Mike's case to another doctor?
7. List the conditions that made life difficult for Mike at the nursing home.
8. After his recovery, what were the activities he could engage in?
9. According to Dr. Ranjana Srivastava, which personality traits of Mike had enhanced his miraculous recovery.
10. What are the two things that the doctor considers essential for a "complete life"?

EXERCISE B

Have you ever taken care of someone in your family or a friend as a patient either at home or in the hospital? State your experience in

about 100 to 150 words. If you have not, imagine the thoughts and experiences of the patient, and write about these.

EXERCISE C

The author mentions some of the qualities that Mike exhibits that she admires. List any three of them.

1.
2.
3.

Pronunciation

LETTERS AND SOUNDS

EXERCISE A

Look up a dictionary and find out the pronunciation of the letters 'ough' in the following words.

1. plough
2. dough
3. cough
4. tough
5. hiccough
6. through
7. bought

EXERCISE B

Read the following poem aloud. How many times does the sound /z/ occur in it?

Buzz says the bee
As he flies to the daisy
I've been so busy

It's made me dizzy
So lazily he hums and goes
Drowsily home for a cozy doze.

EXERCISE C

Write down your full name in phonetic script.

Vocabulary

COLLOQUIALISM

The term *colloquialism* refers to the informal use of language and to linguistic forms that differ widely depending on the regional and social environment. Slang consists of words and expressions that are informal in nature, and it is usually used between people who know each other very well. Many slang words flourish for a time and then disappear and a few, in the course of time, gain social sanction. It is important to avoid colloquialism and slang in any writing of a formal nature.

EXERCISE A

Rewrite the following sentences to make them appropriate for written English.

1. He is ready to fix the cycle for you.
2. It is not advisable to bank on him.
3. I will inform my folks.
4. We spent the balance of the evening at the beach.
5. I was mighty irritated.
6. He had the cheek to insult his teacher.
7. She did not cotton on to the real meaning.
8. It was rotten luck that he fell ill just before the examination.
9. He has a lot of brass.
10. She was fed up with the whole affair.

EXERCISE B

Write down five slang expressions or colloquialisms which have risen to the level of standard language. Discuss them with your class.

WORD GAME

EXERCISE C

Think of three- to six-letter words that start with 'g' and that match the clues given below.

1. intestine ....
2. part of the mouth ....
3. a unit of weight ....
4. a person's way of walking ....
5. an interruption in continuity ....
6. to inhale and exhale with quick difficult breaths ....
7. a device used to keep the mouth wide open and allow oral treatment ....
8. the basic unit of heredity ....
9. look intently..........................
10. a microorganism ....
11. serious, severe ....
12. hold ....
13. furrow ....
14. a common term for esophagus ....
15. glaringly obvious ....
16. tube feeding..........................
17. a secretory organ or structure ....
18. a way of washing the throat ....
19. thin, loosely woven muslin used for bandaging ....
20. move in a smooth, virtually frictionless manner ....

Grammar

STYLE OF WRITING

A good style of writing and speaking can interest the readers or audience and draw them towards the writer's or speaker's point of view. Good style involves much more than grammatical correctness.

Clarity of thought and the ability to adapt the language to suit the topic and audience produce the best results. The right choice of vocabulary and grammatical structures which guarantee unambiguous, accurate statements play a vital role in developing a good style. A well-expressed thought in an appropriate style will have a striking effect. Compact expressions are clear and interesting to read, whereas wordy, long and complicated sentences usually result in confusion.

EXERCISE A

Read the following italicised sentences and see how you can improve on them.

1. From the play *Pygmalion* (Bernard Shaw, 1912):
   Mrs Higgins (at a party): Will it rain, do you think?
   Liza: *The shallow depression in the west of these islands is likely to move slowly in an easterly direction. There are no indications of any great change in the barometrical situation.*
2. From newspaper columns:
   a. *It will put the industry on a sound looting again.*
   b. *Boric acid as preservative could cause intestinal irrigation.*
   c. *The theatre has a sweating capacity of two thousand people.*
   d. *An employee of the hospital was suspended after death.*
3. Overheard:
   a. *He is so tired that he slept like a tree.*
   b. *She is well known for shedding alligator tears.*
   c. *That job at the bank was my bread and water.*
   d. *The poem is written on the backside of the paper.*

4. A story:
Everyone seemed to know Sudha well. She was as fair as a lily and as pretty as a picture. But there was an aching void in her life because she was an orphan. She fell in love with Ram, and his friends were green with envy. They considered it a feather in his cap, but Ram was as cool as cucumber. Sudha unfortunately was a clinging vine and demanded his attention all the time. Ram was blind as a bat to her faults and tried pleasing her to the bitter end.
5. A speech at a school-day function:
In conclusion I would like to say that a mass of concreted earthy material perennially rotating on its axis will not accumulate an accretion of bryophytic vegetation.
6. A plumber's correspondence with a company:
Plumber: I find hydrochloric acid very good for cleaning clogged drains.
Company: *The efficacy of hydrochloric acid is indisputable, but the corrosive residue is incompatible with metallic permanence.*
Plumber: Thank you for agreeing with me.
Company: *Stop using hydrochloric acid.*
7. A letter in reply to a request for more funds:
Further to your letter in connection with the allocation of funds, as already pointed out to you, all allocations for this period have been closed, and I therefore regret that it is not possible to add to the existing allocation which has been made to you and which covers your requirements for this period when originally received, by virtue of work on which you are engaged, a rather higher percentage has been given to you, namely 100% of the original requirements and at this stage I am afraid it is not practical for you to increase the requirement for the reasons already given.
8. From examination answer sheets:
   a. *If the baby refuses to drink milk, boil it for five more minutes.*
   b. *I saw a policeman carrying an umbrella and a man in khaki shorts.*
   c. *The boy likes the dog better than his mother.*
   d. *The motorist saw many buffaloes driving through Chennai.*
   e. *He took a photograph of the alligator sitting on his veranda.*

f. *She was running a high temperature and was delicious.*
g. *Soup water enema was administered to the patient last night.*
h. *Abraham Lincoln said, 'In onion is our strength.'*
i. *He is horizontally challenged.*

9. Part of a report:
The flow is so slow that we know it will be a blow to the oil company.
10. An announcement:
It is my painful duty to inform you that our dear friend Alok Das quit this vale of tears yesterday evening.

ACTIVE AND PASSIVE VERB FORMS

EXERCISE B

Fill in the blanks with the active or passive forms of the verbs in brackets.

The human brain (1) .... (make) up of hemispheres of approximately equal size. Before a person reaches the age of four, both the left and the right hemispheres (2) .... (involve) in all major activities. Thereafter the left hemisphere gradually (3) .... (gain) the upper hand and develops into a dominating one. By the age of thirteen, when the brain has considerably matured, the left hemisphere (4) .... (obtain) virtual control over speech and language. It also (5) .... (coordinate) reading, writing, scientific and analytical knowledge including logic and mathematics. On the other hand, the right hemisphere gains mastery over creativity, music, art appreciation etc. The left hemispheric domination in speech (6) .... (see) in 95% of right-handed people and 65% of left-handed people. However, there are people who (7) .... (believe) that both hemispheres work together to produce adaptive intelligent behaviour.

It is the corpus callosum lying between the two hemispheres that (8) .... (make) sharing of information possible. If the corpus callosum (9) .... (remove), information gets localised in each hemisphere. Amazingly each hemisphere begins to act as an independent brain, and the incompatibility between the two

(10) .... (demonstrate) explicitly on the two sides of the body. To cite just one case, an object out of sight (11) .... (hide) in the left hand of a person whose corpus callosum had been removed. He (12) .... (ask) to say what it is. Now this information from the left hand (13) .... (feed) into the right hemisphere, which cannot speak. Although the left hemisphere, does not possess the information, it makes guesses. Any wrong guess (14) .... (follow) by a frown because the right hemisphere also listens to the answer. If the left hemisphere gave the right answer, the result was a smile. Over the years, the domination of the right hemisphere in emotional behaviour (15) .... (prove) by many. That is why the subject's right hemisphere frowned and smiled.

(based on 'Human brain: Leftist or rightist?' by K. Joshua in the *Hindu*, 23 June 1996)

Speaking

GROUP DISCUSSION

EXERCISE

'Students can play an important role in protecting the environment'. Organise your class into groups and have a discussion on the topic.

SEMINARS, SYMPOSIUMS AND PANEL DISCUSSIONS

Seminars, symposiums and panel discussions are platforms for students and subject specialists to share information. The difference lies in the depth of knowledge shared and the level of formality during these sessions.

In seminars students specialising in a particular subject present papers on specific areas of their discipline and discuss the issues with classmates and subject specialists. It is a good learning experience and offers students an opportunity to present in front of an audience and communicate effectively.

A symposium is a more formal gathering where the host invites subject experts from other academic institutions also.

Presentations on a specific topic are followed by discussions and questions.

Panel discussion is a formal, prepared discussion on a topic by specialists. The topic and the speakers are chosen well in advance so that they have ample time to collect material and organise their presentation. There may be four to six panellists in a discussion and each one may present a specific aspect of the topic. The audience are students, teachers or the public; there is an opportunity to ask relevant, critical questions and express views. Questions related to their chosen area will be directed to the individual panellists, but they can react to or complement the views of their co-panellists. All panel discussions have a moderator who keeps track of the time and channels the discussion in the right direction. The success of a panel discussion to a large extent will depend on the moderator because it is s/he who introduces the topic, initiates the discussion and directs the questions to suitable panellists. At the end of the session the moderator integrates and synthesises the different points and presents the highlights to the audience.

Critical or complex issues (that people may have different views about) could be chosen as topics for a panel discussion. Panellists research and present the different dimensions of the topic. Panel discussions teach one to courteously differ, respectfully debate and develop critical thinking and presentation skills.

EXERCISE

CONDUCT A SEMINAR ON 'POLLUTION IN HOSPITALS'

Preparation time: One week

Divide the class into four groups. One student from each group will present and the others will help him/her to prepare by providing resources and ideas. The different dimensions of the topic that they could take up are:

1. definition and types of pollution
2. Causes of pollution
3. Impact of pollution

4. Solutions to overcome the problem

The teacher will help you with the following:

- Direct and guide the students in collecting, organising and presenting the data
- Discuss the presentation skills necessary to make an impact and how to handle the question–answer session
- Choose a suitable moderator.

At the end of it, you will be given time to question or clarify doubts.

Decide on other suitable topics for seminar so that everyone gets the chance to practise making oral presentations.

Writing

DOCUMENTATION IN NURSING

It is the nurse's responsibility to

- document details about the patients on admission,
- record the treatment plan and specific nursing procedures performed.
- register the reactions of patients to the treatment regime.
- maintain the patient's records on medication, vital signs, pain assessment, etc., which supplement the information about the patient and aid diagnosis and treatment plans.
- Clear, accurate and timely documentation ensures quality care. Documentation is used for quality assurance and also has legal implications.

All reports and records should be

- Objective (without personal interpretation)
- Precise (accurate)
- Unambiguous (clear without the possibility of two meanings)

- Without jargon (not too technical)
- Complete and comprehensive but not longwinded (not repetitive or wordy)
- Confidential and shared only with attending doctor, nurse in with specific members of the family (not to be discussed outside with friends or colleagues)
- Written without too much delay (when the details are fresh in mind)
- Signed with printed name, employment number and date and time.

In the wards, nurses fill in forms recording the personal, medical details about patients admitted for medical treatment. Most of the hospitals provide standardised forms for recording lab results, personal details, complications and treatment plan to suit the type of disease or mode of treatment. A few examples are given below.

- 'Initial assessment forms' with all details of the patients on admission.
- 'Pre- and post-operative check lists' before procedures or surgery
- 'Assessment, care and monitoring forms' for certain conditions like pressure sore.
- 'Comprehensive pain assessment and monitoring forms'
- 'GRBS (random blood sugar) and Insulin Chart' for diabetic patients
- 'Intake and Output Record'
- 'Transfusion Monitoring Record'
- 'Fall risk assessment forms'
- 'Pain Assessment and Management form'
- 'Discharge form'

Each hospital may have their own standardised forms. The important thing to remember is that you should record only after you assess or carry out the procedure.

Make sure reports and records have complete details such as:

1. Full name of the patient
2. Age
3. Sex
4. Hospital number
5. Ward and bed number
6. Date of admission
7. Unit
8. History of allergies ---- (food and medication)
9. Name and signature of the nurse
10. Date and time at the time of submission

Types of Records

1. VITAL SIGNS RECORDS

Blood pressure, pulse rate, temperature, respiratory rate are the vital signs and their values provide critical information about a person's health. These values are useful in detecting and monitoring and management of medical problems.

There is significant potential for measurement error so measure these carefully. Exertion, anxiety, pain, etc., can affect the values so take these into consideration while measuring the vital signs.

All recordings should mention the unit of measurement.

A. Blood pressure
B. Pulse rate
C. Temperature
D. Respiratory rate,
E. Pain assessment and management

A. **Blood Pressure (BP):** It is measured with a mercury based manometer. The reading is recorded in millimetres of mercury (mmHg). Digital apparatus are now available but many hospital personnel prefer the mercury based manometer.

B. **Pulse Rate:** While taking the pulse measurement one can check not only the heart rate but also heart rhythm and strength of the pulse.

Rate of the pulse should be 60 to100 beats per minute.

The best place to feel the pulse is by firmly pressing on the arteries located close to the surface of skin – inside of an elbow or wrist (the radial pulse is the most common site).

C. **Temperature:** Body temperature can range from 97.8 degrees F (or Fahrenheit, equivalent to 36.5 degrees C, or Celsius) to 98.4 degrees F (37.0 degrees C) for a healthy adult.

Temperature is measured in either Fahrenheit or Celsius.

A fever is indicated when body temperature rises about one degree or more over the normal temperature of 98.6 degrees Fahrenheit.

Hypothermia (low body temperature) is defined as a drop in body temperature below 95 degrees Fahrenheit.

D. **Respiratory Rate:** It refers to the number of breaths one takes in a minute. Normal value is 12 to 16 breaths for an adult. The rate is usually measured by counting how many times the chest rises when a person is resting. Respiration rates may increase with fever, other medical conditions. This value is very important in cardiopulmonary illnesses.

2. MEDICATION RECORDS

Record the type of medication, dosage and time it was administered.

Type	*Name*	*Dosage*	*Time*	*Reaction*	*Duration*
Tablet (Tab)		q.i.d			
Capsule (Cap)		BD			
Syrup (Syr)		p.r.n			
Injection (IM)		BD			
Intravenous injection (IV)		q.4h			
		q.6h over half an hour			

3. INTAKE–OUTPUT CHART

Type of Intake	*Type*	*Quantity*
Oral	Tea	100 ml
Intravenous	Inj.Dextrose Saline	4 pints
Miscellaneous	Candida mouth paint	q.2h

Type of Output

This should also be recorded: urine, stool, vomitus, gastric juice by suction, others such as wound drainage, chest drainage, etc.

4. NURSING CARE PLANS

Nursing care plans provide direction for the individualised care of patients and their specific needs. They can be made for treatment of illness, prevention of illness or promotion of health. They ensure continuity of care when a new set of nurses take over. These plans are diagnosis specific. Goals are assessed in terms of observable patient responses.

Nursing care plans have both subjective and objective details. The nursing process includes assessment of patient, formulation of nursing diagnosis with the expected outcome, and implementation of the planned interventions and evaluation.

Nursing care plans include the

- patient's personal and family details, socioeconomic status, past and present medical histories with hospital number, and the details of their allergies
- reason for admission and date of admission with details of the presenting complaints
- present treatment plans and the outcome expected by the physician
- present restrictions if any (non-weight bearing, nil by mouth, etc.)
- nursing interventions to implement the plans will include all the basic and therapeutic needs such as airway, breathing, circulatory, nutritional, sleep and comfort, safety, fluid and electrolyte balance, social, psychological needs etc.

Good nursing interventions are measureable, patient specific, prioritised and correlate with the outcome. Keep the outcome in mind while planning the intervention. Then provide therapeutic action and coordinate the care process.

In case the intervention has an adverse effect, immediately stop the procedure and report it to the doctor or nurse in charge and carry out the recommended orders immediately.

- Set a time frame for progress
- Identify observable goals at the end of the process

A few examples of nursing interventions are monitoring health status, health education, ambulation therapy, breast feeding support, assistance in daily care, pressure sore care, pain control, bowel ostomy care, bladder care.

Sample Nursing Care Plan

1. Subjective and Objective Data
   - Three-year-old Master Subhash looks malnourished
   - Weight 10 kg; Height 89 cm
   - Mid-arm circumference 12 cm
   - Mild edema in the feet and abdomen
   - Intake 1000 Kcal, 25 g protein per day
   - Serum albumin 2.5 mg%
   - Is on nasogastric feeds
   - Has anorexia and chronic diarrhoea
2. Nursing Diagnosis
   - Imbalance in nutrition and less intake than required due to loss of appetite and parental lack of awareness
   - Loss of protein due to malabsorption
3. Expected Outcome in 2 weeks
   - Master Subhash's optimal nutrition will be maintained
   - Oral feeding pattern will be restored
   - Parents will be advised about how to enhance a balanced intake for Subhash
4. Nursing Intervention
   - Assess nutrition status
   - Check weight daily
   - Maintain intake-output chart daily
   - Provide protein rich milk powder supplement via nasogastric tubes
   - Administer IV fluids as per order

- Health teaching for parents on diet for the child

5. Rationale
   - To plan the diet for Master Subhash
   - Change in weight is an important indicator of nutritional status
   - To estimate nutrient loss
   - To meet the calorie and protein demands
   - To supplement the fluid requirement
   - To offer the right nutritious food requirement at home in hygienic conditions.
6. Final Outcome after 2 weeks
   - Master Subhash showed improvement in appetite
   - Started to demonstrate adequate weight gain
   - His nasogastric tube was removed and he was discharged from the hospital
   - Parents were aware of the importance of giving Subhash balanced high calorie diet at home in hygienic conditions.

Summary of the nursing care plan

Three-year-old Master Subhash was extremely thin with a body weight of 10 kg, height 89 cm and 12 cm mid-arm circumference. He had no desire for food and his intake per day was 1000 KCal with 25 g protein. Had anorexia and chronic diarrhoea and was fed through nasogastric tube. His condition was attributed to his imbalanced and insufficient intake of food and loss of protein. His parents were not aware about the concept of a balanced diet or the impact of hygiene on one's health. Plans were made for him to receive and maintain optimal level of nutrition and also increase the parents' awareness of the importance hygiene and balanced diet.

To achieve this goal, a number of nursing interventions were carried out. His nutritional status was assessed regularly so that a suitable diet could be planned. His weight was checked daily to monitor his improvement. His intake and output were monitored to estimate the nutrient loss. Based on the findings, he was given rich milk powder supplement to meet the protein demands. He was also given IV fluids to supplement the required calories and fluid requirements. His parents were given health education on hygiene and nutritious diet and the importance of sustaining it.

By the end of a fortnight Master Subhash started gaining weight. He tolerated oral feeding and started eating normally. His parents became aware of the importance of a balanced diet for Subhash.

5. ANECDOTAL RECORDS

Anecdotal records are written by the senior staff in the ward about the performance of staff and students which will enable the staff nurse in charge of the ward or the supervisors to evaluate the staff or student. It can be positive or negative. Anecdotes should have details such as date, time of the event, corrective or complimentary action taken, staff or student's response etc, with the exact narration of the incident.

These records help identify the merits or difficulties of the students and staff and guide them accordingly. Also, they are referred to when the staff nurses are due for promotion.

6. INCIDENT REPORT

Errors related to administering medication, recording of lab test results or adverse events like extravasation of intravenous fluids, etc. impact heavily on patient care. Such incidents are recorded by the sister in charge of the ward and forwarded to higher authorities so that corrective measures can be put in place. Also disciplinary action is taken against those responsible for these so that in future these errors do not occur.

Incident reports also include events such as 'fall in the bathroom' which are unexpected but impact significantly on patient care. Based on these events subsequent patient care plans may have to be modified.

A patient rolling off the bed could be an example of an incident report. This event implies that the bed side rails which are meant to be used are not being used diligently. The patient care plan should be modified to include reiterating the importance of using this facility with the patient's attendant and also include periodic checks by the nurses to ensure implementation of the same. Any incident report should be intimated to the nursing administrative office within 24 hours through the proper channel.

7. DIARY

A diary records one's daily activity in the ward. Student nurses are expected to record their daily activities in the ward in their diaries. It is a handy tool for nurses at all stages of their career. It improves one's understanding of medical information. It enhances continuity of information and aids memory. It helps a lot while one hands over information. Make the entries as soon as possible so that you do not miss important details. Record the date and the timing of action or intervention.

Avoid judgemental comments. Be clear and specific. Accuracy and objectivity are absolutely essential while you write the diary.

8. HANDOVER REPORTS

These reports can be oral or written; it is the exchange of information between nurses who have finished their shifts and those who take over the patients from them. Give specific information on what has already been done and then state what has to be done.

The major facts to be conveyed are

1. Name of the patient with bed number
2. Reason for admission and date of admission
3. Present restrictions (diabetic diet, no weight bearing)
4. Nursing interventions carried out (breathing exercises completed, BP monitored till 2 pm)

5. What is to be done in that shift (take BP at 6 pm, give sponge bath)

EXERCISE A

Answer the following questions.

1. What are the units of measurement for BP and temperature?
2. Why is accuracy important in recording data? Explain briefly with an example.
3. Why are allergies recorded in the records of the patients?
4. How will you assess the 'success' of any intervention? Explain briefly with an example.
5. What are the advantages of writing a diary?

EXERCISE B

Record an eventful experience (in about 150 words) related to patient care in your ward.

Appreciating poetry

A Psalm of Life

Tell me not, in mournful numbers,
Life is but an empty dream!
For the soul is dead that slumbers,
And things are not what they seem.
Life is real! Life is earnest!
And the grave is not its goal;
Dust thou art, to dust returnest,
Was not spoken of the soul.
Not enjoyment, and not sorrow,
Is our destined end or way;
But to act, that each to-morrow

Find us farther than to-day.
Art is long, and Time is fleeting,
And our hearts, though stout and brave,
Still, like muffled drums, are beating
Funeral marches to the grave.
In the world's broad field of battle,
In the bivouac of Life,
Be not like dumb, driven cattle!
Be a hero in the strife!
Trust no Future, howe'er pleasant!
Let the dead Past bury its dead!
Act,—act in the living Present!
Heart within, and God o'erhead!
Lives of great men all remind us
We can make our lives sublime,
And, departing, leave behind us
Footprints on the sands of time;
Footprints, that perhaps another,
Sailing o'er life's solemn main,
A forlorn and shipwrecked brother,
Seeing, shall take heart again.
Let us, then, be up and doing,
With a heart for any fate;
Still achieving, still pursuing,
Learn to labor and to wait.

Henry Wadsworth Longfellow

EXERCISE

Write short answers to the following questions.

1. What, according to you, is the main message that the poet has tried to get across to the readers?
2. What is the tone of the poem? Tick the words that describe it best: hopeful, pessimistic, encouraging, fatalistic, sad, humorous.

UNIT 8

The Circle of Life

> How far that little candle throws its beams!
> So shines a good deed in a naughty world.
>
> —*Shakespeare*

Sharing what you have with others and giving to people in need is an expression of love and goodwill. Read a real-life story of what a family gave at their moment of great loss.

1. Two years ago, my nursing career began at our tertiary-care centre as a graduate nurse, which led eventually to my attaining a level-1 registered nurse (RN) status. During that time, I cared for many patients who left a lasting impression on me, but none as much as a recent patient on the labour and delivery floor. There was simply no way to anticipate the impact our introduction and that night would have on my life and nursing career. It was through this experience that I came to fully understand and appreciate the full meaning of the 'circle of life'.

2. Looking back, it was a typical night shift for me, beginning like many others. I received a report from the RN who had been caring for a woman I will call Megan—a 27-year-old, morbidly obese (weighing more than 500 pounds), 24-week-pregnant woman who had not previously had prenatal care. The explanation Megan gave was that she was too busy caring for her other children—of ages eighteen months and three years—to be able to attend prenatal care. The crisis

that precipitated her arrival for health care that particular evening was a severe headache, described by Megan as 'the worst headache I have ever had.'

3. At the end of the change-of-shift report, the nurse commented, 'So we will probably give her the million-dollar workup and finally get her out of here.' In our health-care setting, many of our unregistered, pregnant patients often seek primary care at our labour and delivery unit after outpatient health-care offices have closed. Therefore, this nurse's comment was based on past experiences with other patients in our setting. To provide the safest care for our pregnant women, our practice requires that we eliminate all chances of a pregnant woman's complaint being related to her condition before we transfer her to an outpatient setting. Consequently, Megan's complaint was viewed the same as that of other pregnant women who presented with headaches that were often alleviated with over-the-counter medications. This nurse truly believed that Megan's complaint was minor and that she was occupying a bed that was desperately needed for our already overcrowded labour and delivery floor.

4. When I first walked into Megan's room, she was alone and crying, saying how much her head still hurt, even after receiving both Tylenol and Percocet, neither of which had any effect on her pain. I tried several comfort measures that seemed to have no positive effect on her headache, and she appeared to be getting more anxious. In an attempt to allay her anxiety, I offered to call family or friends to come to be with her, but she declined, saying that her cousin was taking care of her children while she was here at the hospital. Megan's headache persisted despite the interventions implemented.

5. I consulted with the obstetrics resident, and it was decided that the most likely cause of her headache was pre-eclampsia. Therefore, we implemented a pre-eclampsia screen that included intravenous infusions, lab assays and a head computed-tomography (CT) scan to rule out any other structural abnormalities. All these procedures, except for

the CT scan, were performed at the patient's bedside. Since Megan was alone, I made it a priority to accompany her to the CT scan. Luckily, the scan was completed in ten minutes, and then we just needed to await the results, which arrived approximately two hours later.

6. The laboratory values appeared within normal limits, but the neurology resident stated that the CT scan appeared abnormal, without providing further details. Upon entering her room to inform her of the results, I found her sitting on the side of the bed, diaphoretic and covered in emesis. She informed me her headache was worse and she was now having trouble breathing. Her vital signs were stable, but repeat laboratory work was done. The Department of Respiratory Medicine was called for a nebuliser treatment. Remaining with Megan, I encouraged her to relax and take slow, deep breaths, while modelling appropriate breathing techniques and providing positive reinforcement. This intervention appeared to be successful as she was much calmer without further complaints of shortness of breath. During this time I also bathed Megan and changed her bedding and gown. She was sincerely appreciative of my efforts and continually said, 'Thank you!' for everything that I did for her. As I had other duties, I made her as comfortable as possible so that she could get some rest. Before I left her room, she again said, 'Thank you so much for taking care of me.'

7. Throughout the night, I continued to check on Megan to see if her headache had subsided as the residents continued to evaluate her CT scan. At quarter past six in the morning, she said that her headache was 'a little better' and I encouraged her to continue to rest.

8. Before being relieved of my shift at quarter past seven, I assessed Megan one last time. I noticed that she had finally fallen asleep and was breathing heavily with audible secretions. Her vital signs continued to be stable, including her pulse oximetry. Knowing from her medical report that she used a continuous positive air pressure (CPAP) machine at night

for treatment of sleep apnea, my first thought was that her change in breathing was due to the absence of her CPAP and that she may need a respiratory treatment. I called Megan's name hoping she would wake up and be able to clear her secretions on her own. Megan did not respond. I repeated her name louder, resulting in no response. I performed a sternal rub. Megan still did not respond. The obstetrics resident was notified immediately that the patient was unresponsive, and I directed another nurse to call respiratory and anaesthesia to the room—stat.

9. Megan continued to lie unresponsive. Within moments, the room began to fill with additional hospital personnel including obstetrics residents and attending anaesthesiologists and nurses. Although many of them seemed confused at the change in Megan's status, everyone worked collaboratively, starting additional intravenous lines, inserting an A-line and an endo-tracheal tube for airway maintenance, drawing more blood for laboratory assays, and performing portable chest X-rays. Once emergency measures were instituted, we transferred Megan to the intensive care unit, repeating the CT scan prior to transfer. Following her transfer, I completed my shift and departed for the day.

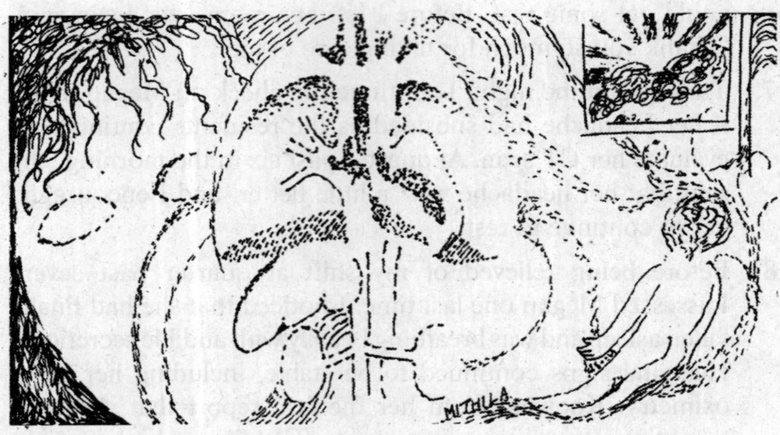

10. Later that evening, I called from home to follow up on Megan's status. I was informed that she had been diagnosed with a cerebral aneurysm and within the next few hours, the health-care-provider team would probably declare Megan brain dead. In the meantime, she was receiving betamethasone steroids to stimulate the development of her unborn baby's lungs to enhance the baby's chance for survival after delivery.

11. I do not recall, before or after meeting Megan, ever having been so personally upset. I cried because it was so unfair that Megan was only twenty-seven years old and because she had two small children who would never see her again. I cried because Megan would never hold her unborn child, and I cried because she had no family or friends with her that night. I was the one at her bedside, and I could not help but question if I had done everything I could have done for her. Yet, I was somehow consoled remembering how appreciative she was of my care. In some way, I realised how blessed I was to have been the last one with her while she was conscious, treating her with compassion, respect and all the skill gleaned as a registered nurse.

12. Two days after I had found her unresponsive, Megan, having been declared brain dead, delivered a baby girl through caesarean section. During this crucial 48-hour period, the betamethasone medication had an opportunity to stimulate the development of Megan's baby girl's lungs. The baby was doing well despite her extreme prematurity. In addition, during the same forty-eight hours, plans were made for donating Megan's organs to multiple receivers identified as being compatible. The Gift of Life Donor Programme helped facilitate the family's end-of-life decision for donation of her organs to five transplant recipients.

13. Following the delivery of Megan's baby, another group of surgeons harvested organs that would become life-saving gifts for some very sick patients. Her right kidney was transplanted into a 17-year-old boy who was suffering from kidney disease since birth, and the left kidney was received by

a 15-year-old girl. Megan's heart was donated to a 43-year-old teacher who was married and a mother of three children, while a 56-year-old man received her liver. The pancreas was donated to a 38-year-old woman with insulin-controlled diabetes. Also recovered for possible future transplant were Megan's corneas.

14. Since caring for her, I often find myself thinking of Megan and her family. I wonder how her family is coping and am distraught to think that her children, especially her baby girl, will never know their mother. On the other hand, words cannot express my gratitude at the thought of the remarkable good that resulted from such a tragic circumstance. Megan's baby is alive and doing well along with the other patients who have been given a second chance at life due to organs received from Megan. I think it goes without saying just how important and meaningful it is to learn from our experiences with our patients and realise how precious life truly is. I feel we are remarkably blessed to have had these life-changing experiences, doing what we love to do as nurses in a profession where it is our duty to care for others and a privilege to play a part in their circle of life.

Kathleen M. Blong

Glossary

allay - to make a strong emotion such as fear or worry felt by someone less

alleviate - to make less severe

assay - here, a test for measuring biochemical or immunological activity

collaboratively - doing something together

compatible - well suited

crucial - very important

diaphoretic - perspiring heavily

distraught - very upset

decline	-	to refuse
eclampsia	-	convulsive seizures in a pregnant woman suffering from high blood pressure, often followed by coma
emesis	-	vomiting
enhance	-	to improve
glean	-	to gather information
implement	-	to carry out; to as planned
intervention	-	here, action taken to improve a medical disorder
morbidly obese	-	fat to a degree indicative of disease
oximetry	-	a procedure to determine the amount of oxygen in blood
precipitate	-	to cause to happen suddenly or sooner than due or expected
prematurity	-	here, the state of a baby born prior to completion of thirty-seven weeks
priority	-	the condition of being regarded as more important
subside	-	to become less intense

Understanding the text

EXERCISE A

Answer the following questions in one or two sentences each.

1. In which department was Kathleen, the author, working at the time of the incident?
2. Why had Megan not gone for prenatal care earlier?
3. What finally made Megan go to the hospital?
4. Why did Megan not let the nurse call her family?
5. When Megan was having trouble breathing, how did Kathleen help her?
6. What is CPAP and what is it used for?
7. What were the emergency measures taken by the hospital team when they found Megan unresponsive?

8. What was the diagnosis for Megan's condition?

EXERCISE B

Answer the following questions in about 50 words each.

1. What was the 'end-of-life' decision taken by Megan's family? What is your reaction to their decision?
2. What do you think would have been the reaction of the recipients of Megan's organs and of their families?
3. What does 'patients who have been given a second chance at life' in the last paragraph mean?
4. Suggest five ways to encourage the concept of organ donation.

Pronunciation

LEARNING THROUGH PHONETICS

EXERCISE A

Given below are a few commonly mispronounced words. Refer to the dictionary and transcribe them. Also, mark the stressed syllables.

1. allergy	2. café
3. convalescence	4. extempore
5. gauze	6. injury
7. menu	8. mercury
9. midwifery	10. pamphlet
11. viva voce	12. vice versa

EXERCISE B

Rewrite the transcribed sentences below in the Roman script, which is used to write English.

Subhash: /aɪ ˈlʌv fəˈnetɪks./
Sushma: /ˈɑː juː ˈkreɪzi?/

Vocabulary

MEDICAL TERMINOLOGY

EXERCISE A

The meanings of some medical terms are given below. Write one word substitutes for them. For example:

- **process of listening for sounds within the body with the aid of a stethoscope: auscultation**
- **collection of fluid below or within the epidermis: blister**

1. mental or physical deterioration associated with old age s_ n_ _ _ _ y
2. a device consisting of a tube and optical system for observing the inside of a hollow organ or cavity en_ _ s _ _ _e
3. spoon-shaped scraping instrument for removing unwanted tissue or tissue for examination c_ _ _tt_
4. death of a tissue caused by inadequate blood supply g _ _ g _e_ _
5. instrument for holding back the incisions open or for keeping the tissue out of the way of the operating surgeon r _ t _ _ _ _ _ _
6. temporary or permanent loss of sensation or loss of ability to move or to control movement p _ _ _ _ y _ _ s
7. excision of the breast m _ _ _ _ _ _ _ _ y
8. to examine by touch p _ _ p _ _ _
9. persistent and irrational fear of something p _ _ b _ _
10. to tap parts of the body to aid diagnosis p _ _ _ _ s
11. disease commonly transmitted by a mad dog r _ _ _ _ s
12. the process of identifying the disease causing a particular set of clinical signs and symptoms d _ _ _ _o _ _ _

13. replacing one's organ with that of a healthy person t _ a _ _ _ l _ _ _
14. unpleasant sensation usually preceding vomiting n _ _ s _ _
15. an acquired hypersensitivity to a substance that does not commonly cause a reaction a _ _ _ r _ _

EXERCISE B

Depending on their origin, placement and function, muscles are grouped under general headings. (For example, an 'extensor muscle' is a muscle that extends a part and an 'articular muscle' is one that is attached to the capsule of a joint.) Match the terms in column A with their meanings in column B.

A	B
1. abductor	a. muscles whose action is controlled by will
2. flexor	b. muscles that counteract the action of another muscle
3. evertor	c. muscles that bend a part
4. adductor	d. muscles that turn an organ outward
5. sphincter	e. muscles that lower the jaw
6. voluntary	f. muscles that draw towards the midline
7. cardiac	g. muscles that encircle a duct
8. synergistic	h. muscles that help one another in function
9. digastric	i. muscles that pull against the force of gravity to maintain posture
10. antagonistic	j. muscles of the heart
	k. muscles of a limb
	l. muscles encircling and controlling an opening
	m. muscles that draw away from the midline

WORD GAMES

EXERCISE C

Do the crossword on the next page with the help of the given clues.

Across

1. the iron-containing pigment of the RBCs
6. completely filled
7. a substance that is used to colour another material
8. pain
10. space between two lines that meet or a point of view
12. of or on the back of an animal or plant
15. too fat
17. appearing to have less haemoglobin than usual
18. period in history
19. amount of medicine to be taken at a time or over a period

Down

2. severe
3. not adjusted well
4. from/of/at/towards the sides
5. a pointed instrument for stitching
7. substance used as medicine
9. cushion of soft material used to apply pressure, relieve pressure or support a part/organ (starts with p)
11. A .... of dust covered the furniture.
13. of/by/for the mouth
14. process of losing
16. discern with eyes

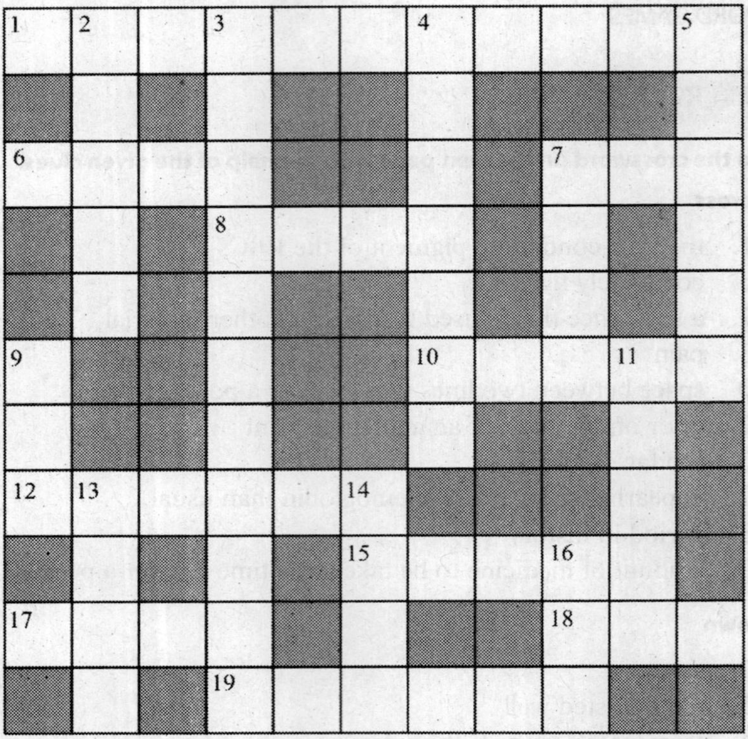

EXERCISE D

Fill in the blanks below with words that match the meanings given alongside. In each pair, strike out the first two letters of the first word to get the second word. Here is an example you could follow.

a. become visible: appear

b. a fruit: pear

1. a. a secretory organ ....
   b. also ....
2. a. a tremulous movement; move lightly and quickly ....
   b. speak ....
3. a. mankind ....
   b. male member of the human species ....

4. a. state the meaning precisely ....
   b. good; enjoyable ....
5. a. expand ....
   b. after the proper or usual time ....
6. a. a membranous sac or receptacle for secretion ....
   b. small poisonous snake ....
7. a. mammary gland ....
   b. opposite of west ....
8. a. complete; total ....
   b. the substance that is dissolved in a solution ....
9. a. pain ....
   b. a pronoun ....
10. a. to stick ....
    b. in this place ....
11. a. adapt ....
    b. reasonable; exactly ....
12. a. pamphlet ....
    b. deed; to perform ....
13. a. obvious ....
    b. father or mother ....
14. a. quality; caused by ....
    b. compliment ....
15. a. smell ....
    b. belonging to us ....
16. a. the beginning, especially of something bad ....
    b. group of similar things; scenery used for a play, film, etc. ....
17. a. exhausted ....
    b. a colour ....
18. a. an involuntary response to a stimulus ....
    b. to bend upon itself ....
19. a. containing salt ....
    b. long, narrow marks traced on a surface; row of people or things ....
20. a. make the greatest possible effort; pass food, etc. through a sieve ....
    b. condensed moisture in the atmosphere falling as separate drops ....

21. a. a secretion of the glands in the skin ....
    b. take into mouth and swallow for nourishment ....
22. a. to gulp down ....
    b. to let ....
23. a. that part of the heart cycle in which the heart is in contraction ....
    b. took dishonestly ....
24. a. bring back to former condition ....
    b. a shop; accumulate ....
25. a. severe; very strong ....
    b. unable to relax ....

Grammar

MODAL VERBS

Modal auxiliaries ('can', 'may', 'will', 'shall', etc.) are used to perform language functions, such as requesting, advising, inviting, suggesting and permitting. They also indicate possibility, willingness, ability, obligation, etc. For example, the auxiliary verb in the sentence 'You must do it' suggests that it is obligatory to do something. Substituting one modal for another can change the meaning or affect the degree of formality or probability in the statement.

EXERCISE A

Spot the difference in each of the following pairs of sentences. Discuss the differences in your class. How would change in intonation patterns affect the meanings of the sentences in these pairs?

1. a. You can have one cup of water after meals.
   b. You may have one cup of water after meals.
2. a. He could be awake now.
   b. He will be awake now.
3. a. She could not have walked that long yesterday.
   b. She might not have walked that long yesterday.

4. a. You must take these tablets regularly.
   b. You should take these tablets regularly.
5. a. Will you help me?
   b. Would you help me?

WORD ORDER

Correct positioning of adjectives and adjuncts in a sentence contributes to its clarity. In general, exact and specific adjuncts precede the general ones. When there are many adjuncts, the following order is usually accepted though variations are possible. Adverbs of manner usually precede those of place and time. For example:

> He worked *steadily* (manner) *in the garden* (place) the *whole day* (time).

In adjectives of quality, the order is size, age, shape, colour, origin and purpose. For example:

> The buttons are in *a small, round, blue* tin.

On many occasions, the position of these adjuncts decides the meaning of the utterance. For example:

> *Only* I saw his sister. (The others did not see her.)
>
> I *only* saw his sister. (I did not speak to her.)
>
> I saw *only* his sister. (And not his brother, parents, etc.)
>
> I saw his *only* sister. (He has only one sister.)

EXERCISE B

Arrange the groups of words below to form meaningful sentences. If a group of words could have different meanings with change in word order, give all the sentences and discuss their meanings.

1. met / concerned / I / the / clerk
2. can't / understand / this / I / just
3. of / you / what / it / do / make
4. Mary / phoned / also / me
5. decided / leave / they / city / secretly / to / the / yesterday

6. foolishly / the / answered / he / questions
7. afraid / am / not / I
8. sign / here / just
9. scientist's / met / famous / I / son / the / British
10. get / money / didn't / honestly / he / the

ADVERBS

EXERCISE C

Fill in the blanks with suitable adverbs chosen from those given below.

totally	ever	always	greatly	absolutely
carefully	mainly	regularly	fortunately	well

I have (1) .... wanted to visit the Lake District in the UK, (2) .... because Wordsworth, my favourite poet, had lived there for many years. (3) ...., I was sponsored for a field trip to England and planned my itinerary (4) .... so that I could spend a week in the Lake District. When I reached the place, I was (5) .... fascinated by the picturesque scenery. The blue lakes, cascading waterfalls, daffodil-strewn meadows, mountains and valleys (6) .... held my attention. I (7) .... enjoyed visiting the Dove cottage and Rydal Mount, which were Wordsworth's home for nearly forty years. The Lake District was also home to John Ruskin, the famous art critic and writer. Boat races, hill climbing competitions, parades, recitals, etc., are held (8)........................., and the participants as well the visitors are looked after (9) .... The district, with its historical and scenic highlights, is considered one of the popular holiday destinations in England, so if you (10) .... go there, do not miss the opportunity of visiting it.

TENSE

EXERCISE D

Fill in the blanks in the following sentences with the most appropriate options chosen from those below each of them.

1. I .... a book when the telephone rang.
   a. read b. was reading
   c. are reading d. have read
2. She .... lunch by the time I arrived.
   a. finished b. have finished
   c. finishing d. had finished
3. My sister .... yoga for three years now.
   a. has been teaching b. is teaching
   c. teaches d. taught
4. .... you ever .... to Scotland?
   a. did . . . gone b. have . . . go
   c. have . . . gone d. has . . . gone
5. If I .... you, I would not go to Agra in summer.
   a. was b. were
   c. am d. will be
6. Ramya will give you a call when she ....
   a. will arrive b. would arrive
   c. arrives d. arrived
7. If Karuna .... he was coming, she would have got the room ready.
   a. has known b. had known
   c. knew d. knows
8. She .... she wanted to come.
   a. said b. says
   c. told d. has said
9. The Ahmeds .... to Kolkata recently.
   a. have moved b. will move
   c. had moved d. moved

10. I wonder why the appointment letter .... yet.
    a. has not arrived b. did not arrive
    c. is not arriving d. had not arrived

Speaking

PSYCHOSOCIAL ASPECTS OF COMMUNICATION

EXERCISE A

In unit 4, we discussed the importance of combining proficiency in language with sound psychosocial attributes that facilitate communication. Study the situations described below. Comment on the effectiveness of the utterances. Point out the communication barriers, if any. Suggest modifications where necessary. Remember that it is often possible to have more than one alternative. (Non-verbal communication, though not mentioned here, will always supplement verbal messages and, in fact, on certain occasions can be a substitute for them.)

1. Mathai, aged fifty, is admitted with cancer of the liver. He is on four-hourly, pain-relieving medication but keeps asking for his shot well ahead of time.
   Nurse: How many times do I have to explain that there should be a gap of four hours between the shots? You men are always fussy. Ask the doctor if you want a change.
2. After his synovectomy, Pavan is suffering from a nagging pain in his joint. He has had a particularly bad night.
   Nurse: How are you this morning?
   Pavan: Not too good. The operated joint is very painful. Couldn't sleep well.
   Nurse: Oh, here is your diet sheet. There are slight changes in the intake of sugar. Follow them carefully.
3. Fifteen-year-old Nargis has been paralysed hip downwards after a road accident a month ago. Unable to accept her condition, she cries a lot.
   Nurse: Come on Nargis, you are lucky to be alive. Look at the positive side of things. There are so many who are denied even this.

4. Pushpa has been admitted for a week for a routine check up and is tired of the food from the hospital's kitchen.
   Pushpa: The food here is monotonous. Is it possible to order something different?
   Nurse: It is far better than it is in other hospitals. When you cook for such a large number, you can't expect more than this.
5. A doctor is on his morning rounds.
   Doctor to nurse: Sister, take blood samples to test Mr Ahmed's blood sugar every half an hour. Call me if necessary.
6. Sandhya has been posted for a cystoscopy. Her only son who is at college has not visited her for the last two days. She is restless and keeps complaining of nausea and abdominal pain.
   Nurse: You are depressed and that's why you are imagining these problems. They will disappear the moment your son visits you.
7. After a bad attack of arthritis, 50-year-old Ravinder Kaur has difficulty in walking. As an in-patient, she goes for regular physiotherapy sessions.
   Ravinder: Sister, today I could walk a few steps without support!
   Nurse: Only a few steps? You have been attending this clinic for so many days. You must do better than that!
8. Vasu, admitted for a bone biopsy, is about to be discharged after a week's stay in the hospital.
   Ward sister: So you are going home today. The nurses took good care of you, didn't they?
9. Afried, aged sixty, admitted in the rehabilitation unit is friendly by nature. But in the presence of Sister Saramma, she is withdrawn and answers her questions mechanically.
   Sr Saramma: What's the matter with you? Can't you respond to my greeting with a little more enthusiasm?
10. Mr David, aged seventy-five, is in the fourth stage of carcinoma of the pancreas. He is on morphine and is barely conscious. Mrs David, seventy, is sitting by his side looking desperate.
    Nurse: It's such a lovely day, Mrs David. I don't understand why you look so gloomy.

ROLE PLAY

EXERCISE B

Work in small groups. Prepare and enact a skit of about fifteen-minute duration on one of the following topics.

1. The ill-effects of overpopulation
2. Bridging the generation gap

Writing

INSTRUCTIONS

Instructions are statements used to tell somebody what to do or how to do it. They are most effective if they are concise and clear. For example, look at the instructions given by a doctor on how to avoid problems caused by working for a long time on a computer.

- Keep the wrist straight while typing.
- Do not cradle the phone on the shoulder while typing.
- Sit up straight while working. Do not slouch.
- Blink frequently to prevent dryness in the eyes.
- Look away from the screen as often as possible.
- Close your eyes for at least five minutes every hour.

(based on 'Boot up your health' by Dr Rajeev K. Sharma in the Hindu, 24 March 2013)

EXERCISE A

Study the picture on the next page, which illustrates how blood pressure is measured, and identify the errors in it. Write down instructions on how to take a person's blood pressure correctly using the auscultatory method.

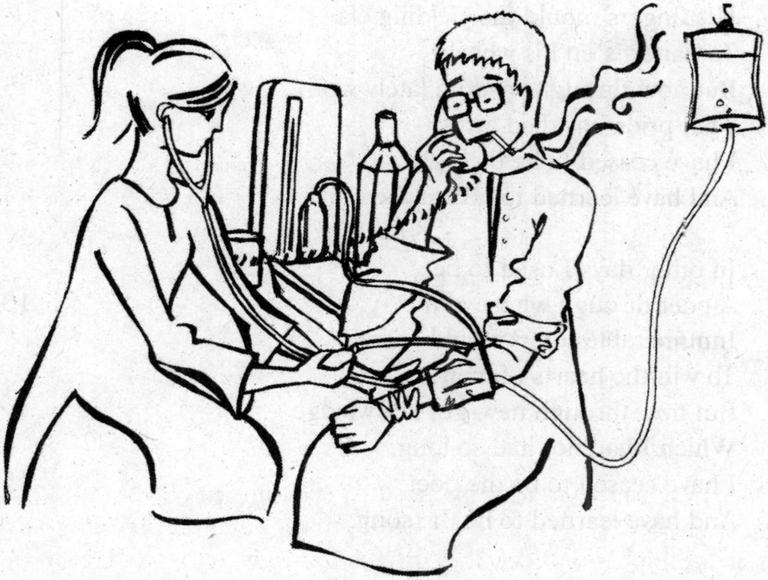

ARTICLES FOR NEWSPAPERS / MAGAZINES

EXERCISE

You are a paediatric nurse. Ten children are admitted to your hospital following an explosion at a fireworks factory where they are employed. Collect information about the families of children who are made to work instead of being sent to school and also on the kind of work they do (working in factories, quarries and agricultural fields, taking care of poultry and livestock, caring for younger children, etc). Use this as well as your own observations to write an article to be published in the newspaper, appealing against child labour.

Appreciating poetry

Shaper Shaped

In days gone by I used to be
A potter who would feel

His fingers mould the yielding clay
To patterns on his wheel;
But now through wisdom lately won,
That pride has died away;
I have ceased to be the potter
And have learned to be the clay.

In other days I used to be
A poet through whose pen
Innumerable songs would come
To win the hearts of men;
But now through new-got knowledge
Which I had not had so long,
I have ceased to be the poet
And have learned to be the song.

I was a fashioner of swords
In days that now are gone
Which on a hundred battlefields,

Glittered and gleamed and shone;
But now that I am brimming with
The silence of the Lord,
I have ceased to be sword-maker
And have learned to be the sword.

In bygone times I used to be
A dreamer who would hurl
On every side an insolence
Of emerald and pearl;
But now that I am kneeling
At the feet of the Supreme
I have ceased to be the dreamer
And have learned to be the dream.

Harindranath Chattopadhyaya

EXERCISE

Write short answers to the following questions.

1. Who are the various 'shapers' that the poem speaks of? How were they 'shaped'?
2. Comment on the spiritual significance of the title 'Shaper Shaped'.

UNIT 9

Young at Heart

> Pleasure in the job puts perfection in the work.
>
> —*Aristotle*

Read the following report about a group of remarkable women.

1. Everything about them is extraordinary, be it their photographic memory, passion for medicine or zest for life. Age is a number for these lady doctors. In their 70s, 80s and 90s, they see patients, perform surgeries, pursue research and write books. Ask them about the source of their boundless energy, they will tell you it is their passion for medicine.

2. The person who epitomises this is 99-year-old Dr S. Padmavati, India's first woman cardiologist and Padma Vibhushan recipient. "I have not retired; it is just that I work a little less now," she says.

3. We met six doctors, who took up medicine at a time when it was not common for women to do so. Not only did they manage to break the glass ceiling, these doctors also proved their mettle by having several firsts to their credit. They all have been witness to radical transformation in medicine, be it technological advancements or medical ethics.

Dr T. S. Kanaka (72), Neurosurgeon

4. As a neurosurgeon, Dr T. S. Kanaka's life has always revolved around her patients. "Those days, it was unusual for a women to get admission to general surgery, leave alone neurosurgery.

Along with me two other women got admission to general surgery because they had won the Johnson Medal, the highest recognition for a student at Madras Medical College (MMC). But they didn't pursue it." Kanaka persevered and finished the course and got the opportunity to work as assistant surgeon at MMC. Her supervisor Dr B. Ramamurthy, a neurosurgeon, helped her hone her skills. "That was when I became interested in neuro-surgery," says Kanaka.

5. Kanaka further specialised in stereotaxic surgery, a relatively new branch in which doctors used manual calculations to reach a particular part of the brain. The age of equipment was yet to dawn in India at that time. "I have always tried to find Indian solutions for Indian problems. I am still working on a low-cost deep brain stimulation kit." She also runs a holistic wellness centre in Chennai.

Dr Sneh Bhargava (85), Radiologist

6. Dr Sneh Bhargava is as passionate about her profession now as she was in 1955 when she passed out of Lady Hardinge Medical College in Delhi and decided specialise in Radiology. Her parents managed to send her to UK to the Westminster Medical School in London; she returned to India in 1959 and joined All India Institute of Medical Sciences (AIIMS) in Delhi.

7. When she was on a WHO Fellowship in UK in 1972, she was sent to New York to attend a neuroradiology workshop where Godfrey Hounsfield, who discovered computerised tomography (CT), showed them a CT scan of the brain. "It was astounding." On her return she showed a few of these images to the Director of AIIMS and insisted they get a CT scan machine. In 1977, AIIMS got India's first CT scan machine. "It dramatically changed the way we were treating neuro problems," says Sneh Bhargava. "It enabled us to diagnose tumours at an early stage. Surgeries too got refined."

8. Dr Bhargava is senior consultant and head of Radio Imaging services at the Dharamshila Cancer Institute in Delhi. So

what keeps her going? "Yoga, I believe, and a good set of genes," she says.

Dr Ramesh Sarin (78), Oncosurgeon

9. It is 5 pm when Dr Ramesh Sarin finally steps out of the operation theatre at Indraprastha Apollo Hospitals in New Delhi, after a long day of surgeries. "When I went to England to study surgery, I was the only woman in a group of 20. Initially nobody took me seriously. I started reaching the hospital half an hour in advance. I would see the patients, their reports, make notes and prepare notes to every possible question my consultant could ask while examining the patients. It worked eventually."
10. Sarin's passion for work and her liveliness are contagious. Though dealing with cancer patients can be emotionally draining, Sarin gives adequate time for her patients to share their fears and anxieties. "Thankfully with so many advancements in reconstructive surgery, plastic surgeons can reconstruct the breasts soon after I finish my surgery." Cracking jokes is a stress buster for Sarin.

Dr V. Shantha (88), Oncosurgeon

11. Right from school days Shantha wanted to be a doctor. Her first posting after MBBS was in the cancer unit in a general hospital. In 1954, when her colleague Dr Krishnamurthy set up the Adyar Cancer Institute, she joined the 12-bed hospital for a salary of Rs 200. His sister had died of cancer and the family wanted to do something for cancer patients.
12. Cancer treatment in the 1950s was about surgery and high voltage radiation. People were afraid of it as it used to burn the skin too. Medical oncology was unheard of. The cobalt unit was the first advancement that came in the mid-50s, but the hospital didn't have the resources to buy it. However, the Atomic Energy Centre in Canada donated a unit to the hospital, probably impressed with the service rendered.
13. The major problem then was patients coming very late to the hospital with untreatable stages of cancer. So Shantha started

a preventive oncology programme to educate and encourage patients to come the hospital for routine check-ups. It helped many and today the system is in place in all hospitals.

Dr Sarada Menon (92), Psychiatrist

14. Sarada loves reading detective novels by Agatha Christie and Sherlock Holmes. Not surprising, considering that her job as a psychiatrist entails decoding the myriad mysteries of the mind. Born in a family that did not encourage career ambition in girls, Sarada managed to do medicine. She did Psychiatry at the National Institute of Mental Health and Neuro Sciences in Bengaluru and was posted in a mental hospital at Chennai.

15. The hospital appointed social workers to coordinate between patients, families and the doctors. Sarada played an important role in starting rehabilitation programmes like spinning, weaving and mattress making for patients who recovered from the illness. "It gave them the opportunity to socialise and interact, something very important for their inclusion in society," says Sarada.

16. "If you invest in life, you get the returns," says Sarada. She also believes that keeping some time aside for oneself is the key to a long professional life because it prevents early burnout.

Dr S. Padmavati (99), Cardiologist

17. Born in 1917 in Burma, Padmavathy moved to Coimbatore in 1941 during World War II, after completing her MBBS at the Rangoon Medical College. She did her post-graduation in the UK and won a scholarship to study Paediatric Cardiology at John Hopkins University. She returned to India in 1952 and started the first cardiac clinic and cath lab in Lady Hardinge Medical College in Delhi. The department became so popular that even men with cardiac problems started visiting the hospital which treats only women.

18. "Technology, no doubt has revolutionised the way we diagnose a problem, but I feel it has claimed clinical skills of a physician", says Padmavathy. She feels that this has

increased the cost of health care. Padmavathy still meets her patients and visits the Indian Heart Institute in Delhi which she founded in 1977.

19. "Swimming is my favourite activity. But now the walk to the pool is a bit tiring," says Padmavathy.

Gunjan Sharma

(Source: Excerpted from "Young at Heart " by Gunjan Sharma in *The Week Supplement*, 28 February 2016)
<http://www.theweek.in/health/cover/medicines-super-women.html>

Glossary

adequate	-	enough
astounding	-	amazing
contagious	-	spreading by contact
epitomise	-	represent
eventually	-	finally
hone one's skill	-	sharpen/develop one's skill
mettle	-	courage
myriad	-	many
pursue	-	follow
stereotaxic surgery	-	a minimally invasive form of surgery, using a three-dimensional coordinate system to locate small organs in the body
zeal	-	enthusiasm
zest	-	excitement

Understanding the text

EXERCISE A

Write short answers to the following questions based on the text.

1. What are the qualities that all the doctors mentioned in the text share?

2. What is the meaning of the phrase "they have several firsts to their credit"?
3. Why didn't the two ladies who got admission to general surgery at MMC join the programme?
4. In what way did stereotaxic surgery help Dr Kanaka?
5. What difference did the purchase of a CT scan make to the doctors at AIIMS?
6. What did Dr Ramesh Sarin do to be taken seriously when she went for higher studies to the UK?
7. Why did Dr Krishnamoorthy set up the Adyar Cancer Institute?
8. What were the challenges faced by cancer patients in the early 1950s?
9. Why did Dr Sarada Menon start a rehabilitation programme for her patients?
10. Why does Dr Padmavathy feel that too much dependence on technology is not a good thing?

EXERCISE B

Mark the following sentences as True or False based on your understanding of the text. Discuss the reasons with the class.

1. Dr S. Padmavathy was awarded the Padma Shree award.
2. These doctors were forced by their parents to take up medicine as their profession.
3. Dr Kanaka doesn't believe in using modern equipment.
4. Dr V. Shantha began her career in a cancer hospital.
5. Dr Sneh Bhargava first saw the CT scan images when she was in the UK.
6. Dr Ramesh Sarin is too busy to share the anxieties of her patients.
7. The Adyar Institute bought the Cobalt unit from the Atomic Energy Centre in the USA.
8. Dr Sarada is good at writing detective novels.
9. Dr Sarada believed that day care facility is better for psychiatric patients than admission into the ward.
10. Even male patients preferred to come to the women's hospital where Dr. Padmavathy was the Cardiologist.

EXERCISE C

In paragraph 10, it is said "cracking jokes is a stress buster". What does the term stress buster mean?

What is your stress buster? Describe it in 3–4 lines, explaining why it is effective.

Pronunciation

LEARNING THROUGH PHONETICS

EXERCISE A

Work in pairs. Using a dictionary if you need to write down the phonetic symbols for the sounds of the underlined letters and take turns to say the words aloud.

1. abdomen
2. atmosphere
3. circuit
4. clerk
5. colleague
6. eleven
7. odour
8. official
9. onion
10. professor

EXERCISE B

Fill in the blanks in the following sentences with the transcribed words given below. Rewrite the words in the Roman script before using them.

/ɪkspreʃən/ /ɪntrəst/ /wɜːd/
/æksɪdənt/ /drɒp/ /læŋgwɪdʒ/
/pəsɪstəns/ /ætɪtjuːd/ /fənetɪks/
/pəzɪʃən/

1. Why isn't .... spelt phonetically?
2. It is .... that helps develop reason and complexity of thought.
3. Of all the things you wear, your .... is the most important.

4. Success is more .... than aptitude.
5. Don't learn safety rules by ....
6. A smile doesn't cost a cent but it gains a lot of ....
7. Failure is the path of least ....
8. Life is not so much a matter of .... as disposition.
9. To break a bad habit, ... it.
10. One thing you can give and still keep is your ....

Vocabulary

WORDS WITH MULTIPLE MEANINGS

Addition of an 's' to a noun usually indicates its plural. But in some cases the plural form can have an additional meaning too. For example:

arm - hand
arms - hands; weapons

The same pattern is seen in some adjective/adverb/verb inflections. For example:

look - see (verb)
looks - sees (simple present tense verb form in the case of third person singular); appearance (noun)

EXERCISE A

In the following pairs of words, the meaning of the first word is given. Write the meaning of the other word in each pair.

1. a. air - atmosphere
   b. airs - ....
2. a. brain - part of human body
   b. brains - ....
3. a. comfort - console
   b. comforts - ....
4. a. custom - habit of a community
   b. customs - ....

5. a. green - colour
   b. greens - ....
6. a. gut - bowel
   b. guts - ....
7. a. pain - discomfort
   b. pains - ....
8. a. regard - consider
   b. regards - ....
9. a. remain - be in the same place
   b. remains - ....
10. a. work - job
    b. works - ....

EXERCISE B

Many words in the English language have more than one meaning. Write down the different meanings of the words in their specific contexts.

1. disc
   a. I have copied all the grammar exercises on a *disc*.
   b. He fell and had a slipped *disc*.
2. culture
   a. We must accept the good things in other *cultures*.
   b. The *culture* results show she has typhoid.
3. tender
   a. She spoke to him in a *tender* manner.
   b. Her abdomen is *tender*.
4. rash
   a. He is a *rash* driver.
   b. The doctor prescribed an ointment for the *rash*.
5. bear
   a. The injection will help you *bear* the pain.
   b. The mango trees in grandmother's garden *bear* sweet fruit.
6. stiff
   a. It was a *stiff* climb.
   b. He has a *stiff* neck.

7. sore
   a. He is *sore* about the turn of events.
   b. His leg is very *sore* after the accident.
8. stool
   a. She stood on a *stool* and reached for a book.
   b. The baby passed many *stools* today.
9. motion
   a. The train is no longer in *motion*.
   b. He is taking tablets to have regular *motions*.
10. pulse
   a. Include more *pulses* in your diet.
   b. The doctor felt for his *pulse*.
11. discharge
   a. The doctors have decided to *discharge* you in a day or two.
   b. There is a heavy *discharge* from the infected wound.
12. contract
   a. Wood *contracts* in summer.
   b. The child has *contracted* measles.
13. fume
   a. She *fumes* at the way matters are delayed.
   b. It is not healthy to be in this room thick with *fumes*.
14. host
   a. He has won the Best *Host* award for this year.
   b. The definite *host* for the malarial parasite is the female anopheles mosquito.
15. fit
   a. Farid is not *fit* to travel.
   b. Whenever Sheila's temperature rises, she is prone to *fits*.
16. boil
   a. *Boil* the milk for five minutes.
   b. Don't let him scratch the *boil*.
17. chill
   a. As forecast, there is quite a *chill* in the air today.
   b. He was admitted with *chills*.

18. drip
    a. The tap is *dripping* and needs repair.
    b. Mr Narang is still unconscious and on a saline *drip*.
19. invalid
    a. This document is *invalid* because the signature is not clear.
    b. Kusum is afraid she will be an *invalid* all her life if the operation is not successful.
20. gravity
    a. The *gravity* of the situation hit him hard.
    b. The specific *gravity* of water is 1.

WORD GAME

EXERCISE C

Write a single-word substitute for each of these definitions. (*Hint*: Every word begins with the last two letters of the previous word. For example, the word for the second definition will begin with 'en'.)

1. part of the trunk below the chest <u>*abdomen*</u>
2. hard, white, dense substance forming a covering for the crown of the teeth ....
3. capable of being stretched and of then returning to its original state ....
4. the solid form of water ....
5. edible seed or grain ....
6. a group of simple proteins widely distributed in plant and animal tissues ....
7. a hormone secreted by the islets of Langerhans of the pancreas ....
8. one of the cutting teeth ....
9. a part of the body having a special function ....
10. feeling of apprehension or worry ....
11. a disease ....
12. a thought, a concept ....
13. land ....

14. any treatment designed to improve health ....
15. a very small person ....
16. study of fungus ....
17. a person who performs physical exercise as a sport ....
18. to almost fall ....
19. clearly written ....
20. smallest in number, size ....

Grammar

DIRECT AND INDIRECT SPEECH

Indirect speech is used to convey messages or report the words of other speakers. On being converted from direct speech to indirect speech, sentences undergo certain changes depending on whether they are statements, requests or questions. Here are some rules that govern the changes that take place.

- While changing statements into indirect speech, the word 'that' is added next to the reporting verb.
- If the reporting verb is in present tense, the verbs in the reported sentence in indirect speech can be in either present or past tense. For example:

  He *says*, 'Johar *is* a spirit, an expression of welcome.'
  He *says* that Johar *is* a spirit, an expression of welcome.

  Reema *says*, 'The student nurses in the 2004–2005 batch in my college *were* all very committed to their work.'
  Reema *says* that the student nurses in the 2004–2005 batch in her college *were* all very committed to their work.

- If the reporting verb in a sentence in direct speech is in past tense, the tenses of the verbs in the reported clause are usually moved back. Thus, verbs in present tense (simple/continuous/perfect) are changed to their corresponding past tense forms unless the reported clause refers to some universal truths/scientific facts. For example:

He *said*, 'I *am* very happy to see Jaya.'
He *said* that he *was* very happy to see Jaya.

but The nursing tutor *told* her students, 'Diabetic patients *have* to eat at regular intervals'.
The nursing tutor *told* her students that diabetic patients *have* to eat at regular intervals.

- If the verb in the sentence being changed into indirect speech is already in the past tense, there is, normally, a further backshift of tense and in such a case the verb appears in the past perfect form. For example:

  He *said*, 'I *gave* the photographs to her.'
  He *said* that he *had given* the photographs to her.

  Vijay *said*, 'Khadir *ate* sandwiches for breakfast.'
  Vijay *said* that Khadir *had eaten* sandwiches for breakfast.

  It is to be noted, though, that if the verb in the reported sentence is in simple past tense, it is not always changed to the past perfect tense in actual practice (unless, of course, we wish to emphasise that the event concerned occurred before another). For example:

  Kalpana said, 'I *made* vegetable curry for lunch.'
  Kalpana said that she *(had) made* vegetable curry for lunch. (both the simple past and past perfect forms are acceptable)

- A verb in past perfect tense always remains unchanged in reported speech because it is not possible to move back any further. For example:

  They *said*, 'We *had decorated* the room before Afifa entered.'
  They *said* that they *had decorated* the room before Afifa entered.

- While converting questions that seek information of some kind, the word order of verb + noun in direct speech sometimes changes to noun + verb in indirect speech. For example:

Leela said to Benny, 'Where *are the sketches*?'
Leela asked Benny where *the sketches were*.

He asked me, 'Where *were you* yesterday?'
He asked me where *I was* the previous day.

However, when questions of this kind have an auxiliary verb that indicates tense appearing before the main verb, then in indirect speech, the auxiliary verb is dropped, the main verb carries the tense marker and the word order remains unchanged. For example:

The children asked us, 'Why *does (aux. vb-simple present tense) it rain (vb)*?'
The children asked us why *it rained (vb-past tense)*.

- 'If' or 'whether' is added when changing Yes–No questions from direct to indirect speech. For example:

  He asked her, 'Do you want to visit Jharkhand?'
  He asked her *whether* she wanted to visit Jharkhand.

  He asked her, 'Are you coming tomorrow?'
  He asked her *if* she was coming the following day.

- While converting direct speech into reported speech, the pronouns/adverbs in all types of sentences should be changed accordingly as seen in the examples given above.
- When orders and requests are changed from direct speech into indirect speech, the reporting verb is followed by a noun or pronoun and the infinitive form of the verb (e.g. 'to give', 'to work', etc). For example:

  The officer said to the cadets, '*Walk* in single file!'
  The officer ordered the cadets *to walk* in single file.

  Kiran said to her friend, 'Please *help* me with the essay.'
  Kiran requested her friend *to help* her with the essay.

- Exclamations, like interrogatives, appear in indirect speech as declarative sentences. For example:

  Chandini said, 'A fantastic performance!'

Chandini *exclaimed* that it was a fantastic performance.

✦ When offers and suggestions, even if they are in the form of questions, appear in indirect speech, they are introduced by reporting verbs 'suggest' and 'offer'. For example:

Pankaj asked, 'Can I help you with the cooking?'
Pankaj *offered* to help with the cooking.

Shobha said, 'Gita, let's meet next week.'
Shobha *suggested* to Gita that they meet the following week.

EXERCISE A

Rewrite the following sentences in indirect speech. Remember the rules relating to tense, word order, reporting verbs, pronouns and adverbs.

1. Radha says, 'I have been selected to act in the English play.'
2. Sunder said, 'I always come first in the 100 metre race.'
3. Raju told me, 'I will help you to organise the talent show.'
4. Our teacher tells me, 'If you work hard, you can get the first rank.'
5. The captain said to the players, 'You should be on time for the practice sessions tomorrow.'
6. Father told me, 'I will come to your school next Monday.'
7. I told my friend, 'I will support you on this issue.'
8. My friends told me, 'We are coming to your house today.'
9. I asked him, 'Are you ready?'
10. He asked her, 'Are you taking part in the music competition?'
11. They said to us, 'Did you like our piano recital?'
12. He said to the girl, 'Can you help me?'
13. Ravi asked Prabha, 'Where is your house?'
14. We asked the teacher, 'When can we have the rehearsal?'
15. She asked Varun, 'Do you want me to help?'
16. Karim said to the children, 'Don't talk!'
17. The motorcyclist told us, 'Keep out of my way!'

18. Mr Thomas said to his friend, 'Please don't drive so fast.'
19. I told Mohit, 'Sharpen your pencil!'
20. The customer said to the waiter, 'Could I have a glass of ice water, please.'
21. Smita said at the end of her colleague's presentation, 'Well done!'
22. Tara said, 'What a beautiful painting!'
23. Sukhvinder said, 'How late I am going to be today!'
24. Grandmother said, 'Hope Naveen gets the job he has applied for!'
25. Catherine said to me, 'I am sorry about the delay.'

EXERCISE B

Fill in the blanks in the following sentences with the correct forms of the verbs *is, are, has* or *have*.

1. Every one of the girls .... promised to help us win the election.
2. The majority of the students .... agreed to sign the petition.
3. Either Rekha or her brothers .... to take on the responsibility of managing the family business.
4. Whatever you say .... acceptable to us.
5. Our principal, along with his colleagues, ... published a book on research methodology.

EXERCISE C

Fill in the blanks in the following sentences with the active or passive forms of the verbs 'swell', 'drive', 'cling', 'shake' or 'sting'. Do not use the verbs with modals ('can'/'could'/'may'/'might'/'must'/'should', etc.) or in the continuous tense ('is reading'/'was swimming', etc.).

1. When the car hit the lamp post, the passengers ....
2. A scorpion .... Balu while he was playing in the backyard.
3. It is true that peer pressure .... him to take up engineering instead of fine arts.

4. He had to see a dentist because his gums ....
5. When her friends criticised her, Lekha .... to me.

EXERCISE D

Fill in the blanks in the following pairs of sentences with appropriate linkers, such as 'so' and 'subsequently'.

1. Sindhu was always a good student. ...., we were not surprised when she topped the final exam.
2. I love watching Tamil films. ...., my friends prefer Hindi films.
3. We will receive some funding for the project. ...., I am not sure if it will be enough.
4. The village is green and beautiful. ...., the people there are friendly.
5. Guavas and mangoes are rich in vitamin A. ...., spinach and carrots contain a significant amount of the vitamin.

EXERCISE E

Fill in the blanks in the following sentences with suitable prepositions.

1. The boys ran .... the house when it started raining.
2. She bought the old edition of the book .... mistake.
3. The house is .... fire! Call the fire service and an ambulance.
4. The hotel has a play area .... children.
5. The book shop does not accept payment .... cheque.

Speaking

NARRATION/GROUP DISCUSSION/TALK

EXERCISE A

Work in groups of four. Think of interesting anecdotes or jokes of about ten to fifteen lines. Taking turns, present them to the class. The effectiveness of your presentations will depend on how well you are able to hold the attention of your classmates. Capture the interest of your audience by speaking clearly and by making use of changes in pitch, tone and volume.

EXERCISE B

Here is a picture with a message. What do you think are the implications of the message? From the point of view of health, how will you interpret it? Discuss.

Give a person a fish, and you feed the person for a day.

Tomorrow, the person may be a beggar.

Teach a person to fish, and you feed the person for life.

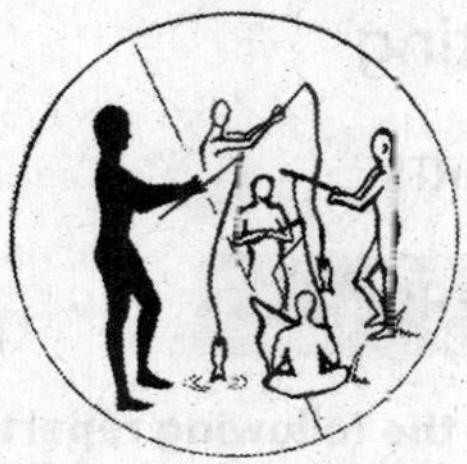

Tomorrow, if well taught, the person will teach others.

EXERCISE C

Based on the picture below, give a brief talk on removing ignorance and creating awareness among people about how to take care of themselves.

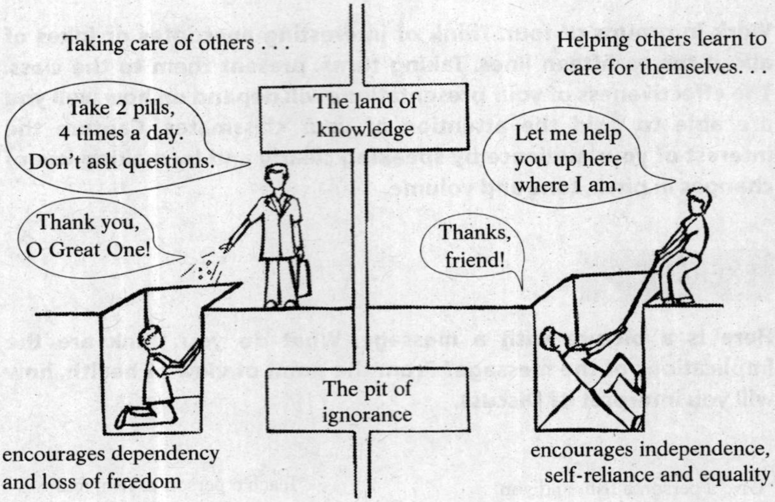

Writing

REPORTS

EXERCISE

Read the following report on the health problems that result from a traditional diet being replaced by a less healthy new one. Then write two brief reports on similar dietary changes in India which affect the well-being of people.

For hundreds of years, millet was the main food in many parts of Africa. As a whole grain it provided most of the vitamins and protein people needed. But today in many parts of Africa, people mainly grow and eat cassava. This new food, introduced from Latin America, is easier to grow but less nutritious than millet. It fills children with water and fibre before they get enough calories.

So in areas where cassava is now grown instead of millet, more children are malnourished.

You can start the first report this way:

Bottle feeding and the use of artificial powdered milk have become popular, replacing the old tradition of breast feeding . . .

Appreciating poetry

Give Me Strength

This is my prayer to thee, my lord—strike,
strike at the root of penury in my heart.

Give me the strength lightly to bear my joys and sorrows.
Give me the strength to make my love fruitful in service.

Give me the strength never to disown the poor or
bend my knees before insolent might.

Give me the strength to raise my mind high above daily trifles.
And give me the strength to surrender my strength to thy will with love.

Rabindranath Tagore

EXERCISE

Write short answers to the following questions.

1. What does the poet mean by the words 'penury in my heart'?
2. List three wishes expressed by Tagore in the poem.

UNIT 10

Palliative Care for Cancer Patients

> True compassion means not only feeling another's pain but also being moved to help relieve it .
>
> —*Daniel Goleman*

Among the most important functions you will perform as a nurse are providing relief and offering comfort. Read this article by a doctor who runs a palliative care centre.

1. Palliative care, also called comfort care, is aimed at providing relief to a terminally-ill person through symptom and pain management. Its goal is to maintain the highest quality of life possible. But in our present-day health care situation, the emphasis is still more on curing diseases, and if that does not happen, patients are often left to fend for themselves with whatever support their families and friends are able to give them. In the majority of cases, patients who are terminally ill and in pain suffer terribly and have a poor quality of life.

2. Let us consider the case of Radha, a 65-year-old woman, who had cancer of the breast. She underwent surgery followed by radiotherapy and chemotherapy. A year later, Radha developed ulceration of the chest and experienced acute pain. Added to this, there was the emotional pain of disfigurement, which was just as traumatic. All Radha wanted was relief from the pain and the care of her family. Unfortunately, as it

often happens, when she became weak and was unable to eat, her family admitted her to hospital. The disease had taken its toll, and the woman died in terrible pain—much against her wishes, away from her family and home.

3. Looking back, regular assessment and frank communication between Radha and her family could have prevented her from suffering alone in the terminal stage and dying in a strange environment. The pain could have been controlled, and the anxieties of the patient and her family relieved. However, neither her doctors nor her family can be blamed because the management of patients in an advanced stage of cancer is not yet well-developed in our country.

4. Cancer is a classic example of a terminal disease, almost every patient of which has the need for relief from distressing symptoms and comfort from anxieties during the course of its treatment. The physical and emotional burdens on patients and their families affect their quality of life drastically. The worst thing a person can be told at this stage is that there is nothing more that can be done. That is directly contrary to the philosophy of palliative care, which focuses on the patient as a person rather than on the disease. When a cure is not possible, there is still so much that can be done for these patients to provide them relief and improve their quality of life—by offering palliative care. There is thus no need for anyone to suffer terrible pain simply because there is no hope of a cure for their illness.

5. Palliative medicine is a medical specialty, which deals with the management of patients who are in the advanced stage of a disease, when cure is almost impossible. The word 'palliate' means 'to reduce the bad effects of something or to reduce pain and suffering'. When patients feel helpless and insecure, they go to a palliative care unit wondering if anything can be done at all to relieve their pain and other symptoms, which cause them acute distress. The specialists there do not do anything extraordinary for them straight away. They make them comfortable in a home or hospital environment,

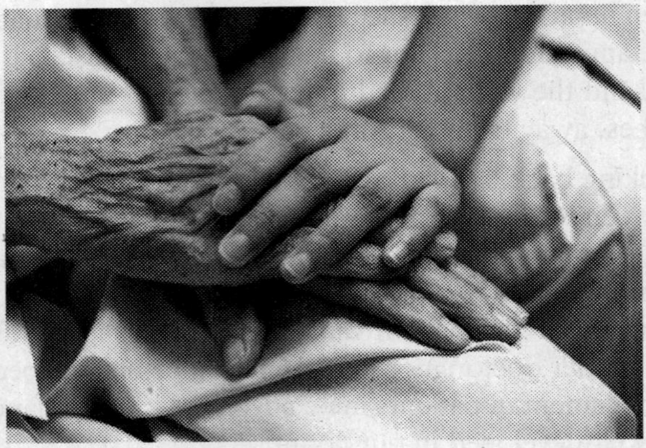

and after listening attentively to all they have to say, show empathy and provide appropriate care. Palliative care doctors combine compassion with science and give expert medical care to relieve the distressing symptoms of an advanced stage of disease.

6. Palliative care specialists go through their patient's medical history to understand his or her physical, emotional, psychological, social, spiritual and financial problems. Unless each one of these issues is addressed, the patient's quality of life cannot be improved. The doctors examine the patients, look specifically for the cause of pain and explain it to them, discuss treatment plans and options, and give them hope that something can be done to alleviate their symptoms.

7. To understand the importance of the role that palliative care can play in managing the terminally ill, let us see what problems patients of cancer at an advanced stage of the disease face. Pain, which has an emotional component too, is the most common symptom a patient experiences at that stage. Cancer pain can be treated with inexpensive medication, following World Health Organization (WHO) guidelines. Most patients experience relief with oral medication. For severe pain, oral morphine is the drug of choice, and it should never be denied to patients who need it. Oral morphine is not addictive and should not be reserved for the end stage, making the patient

suffer misery unnecessarily. The WHO recommends it for cancer pain, and it is used by millions of patients all over the world.

8. Other symptoms that end-stage cancer patients may experience are vomiting, insomnia and breathlessness, which can be corrected by appropriate medications or procedures. For example, breathlessness may be due to fluid collection in the lungs. Once it is drained, there is immediate, noticeable relief. In the case of wounds and ulcers, the family can be taught appropriate first-aid and even their long-term management effectively and inexpensively in a home environment. For example, a patient with a large open wound on his face continued to work, watch television and take liquid food almost to the very end of his life. That is what good pain relief medication, effective communication, educating the family and regular follow-up can do to keep up a patient's morale.

9. Swelling of the arm or leg can be painful and demoralising for patients with certain cancers. This can be tackled to some extent by massaging the skin, bandaging the limb and encouraging activity. Counselling is also very important. Sometimes, even in an advanced stage of cancer, depending on the physical condition of the patient, a surgical procedure can make a difference to the quality of his or her life. For example, a cancerous tumour in the stomach can result in acute vomiting. A bypass surgery can help in such cases. Similarly, fractures due to bone cancer, can be fixed by an orthopaedic surgeon.

10. Pain is only a part of the total suffering of a terminally ill cancer patient. Therefore, unless other issues—emotional, psychosocial and spiritual—which also contribute to the patient's suffering are dealt with, his or her quality of life will continue to be poor. For this, effective communication and counselling are necessary. Palliative physicians often come across patients who do not know they have the disease and have anxious family members who do not want their loved

ones to learn about it. Very often, patients are completely in the dark about what is happening to them. In such situations, there are specialised ways of communicating with them and counselling them to bring them comfort and peace of mind. Lastly, cancer is also known as a 'family illness', as the families of patients experience as much emotional distress as they do. Therefore, their feelings too have to be dealt with.

11. Patients must always be offered hope, but it must be appropriate to the stage of the illness. It is better to avoid giving false assurances like 'Everything will be all right,' when the patient is at a terminal stage. A better way of comforting the patient in such a situation may be, 'We will do all that we can to help you.' In cancer, there can be hope of a cure at an early stage, but only hope of control of the spread of the disease or hope of palliation of distress causing symptoms at a more advanced stage. Palliative care physicians maintain continuity of care, assessing the patients at regular intervals throughout their illness, till the very end. Patients either visit a palliative care centre or they are provided with home care.

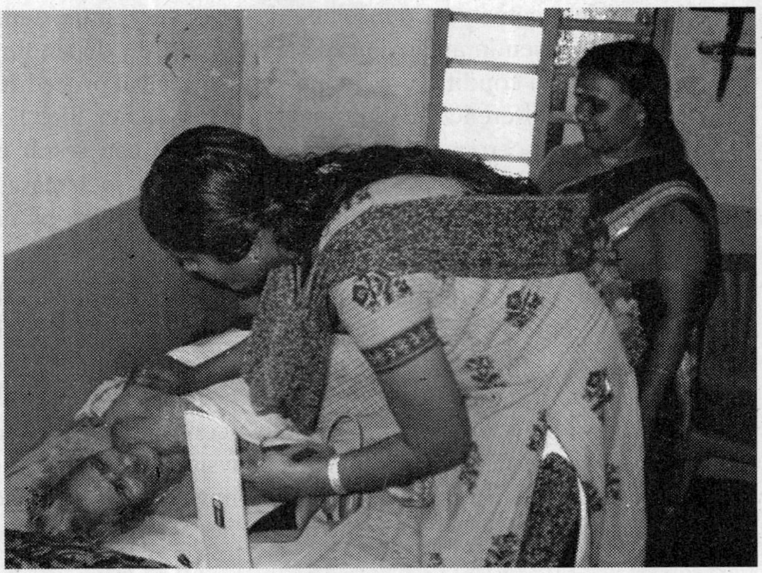

12. It is necessary to have a multidisciplinary team to meet the needs of terminally ill cancer patients. The team must consist of trained doctors, nurses, social workers, volunteers and families, who are the main caregivers. The team also interacts with doctors of other specialties, such as surgeons, oncologists, physiotherapists, psychiatrists and occupational therapists. The three essentials of palliative care are:
    - symptom relief
    - psychosocial support
    - teamwork and doctor-patient partnership
13. Palliative care, based on a philosophy of care giving, can be practised in a place of the patient's choice. It can be provided in a hospital, in a hospice or at home. A hospice combines the love of a home and the facilities of a hospital. Active treatment is given, and patients go back home whenever they want to. All hospitals involved in cancer treatment must have facilities for providing palliative care. Some facts that highlight the urgent need for palliative care for cancer patients in India are:
    - A million patients are diagnosed with cancer every year in the country.
    - About 70 per cent still present themselves for treatment at an advanced stage.
    - More than 80 per cent suffer with unbearable pain.
14. Something has to be done for these suffering millions.

    'To cure sometimes, to relieve often, to comfort always!' is widely accepted as the duty of a doctor. The philosophy of palliative care is well brought out in the words of Dame Cicely Saunders, a nurse-turned-palliative care physician and founder of the first hospice run according to the findings of scientific research on pain and symptom control combined with compassionate care—St Christopher's Hospice, London. 'You matter because you are you. You matter to the last moment of your life, and we will do all that we can, not only to help you die peacefully but also to live until you die.'

Mallika Tiruvadanan

Glossary

acute	-	severe
alleviate	-	to make pain and problems less severe
appropriate	-	suitable
assurance	-	a promise
be in the dark	-	to know about something that other people know about
chemotherapy	-	a form of treatment using chemicals
classic	-	typical
compassion	-	a feeling of sympathy and kindness for those who suffer
demoralising	-	making someone lose their confidence, enthusiasm and hope
disfigurement	-	something that spoils the appearance of someone or something
empathy	-	the ability to understand and share the feelings of others
fend for yourself	-	to look after yourself, without any help from others
hospice	-	a hospital for people who are dying
insomnia	-	sleeplessness
morale	-	the confidence felt by someone, especially in a difficult situation
palliative care	-	medical treatment that reduces pain, discomfort, etc., caused by an incurable disease
radiotherapy	-	a form of treatment using radiation
tackle	-	to try to deal with something or someone
take its toll	-	to cause great damage
terminal	-	here, leading to or close to death
traumatic	-	causing severe emotional shock and pain
ulceration	-	formation of ulcers, breaks in the skin or on the surface of an organ

Understanding the text

EXERCISE A

Based on paragraphs 1 to 5, mark the following statements true (T) or false (F).

1. Palliative care is the best treatment for many serious illnesses.
2. Terminally ill patients in India usually receive more support from their families than the country's health care system.
3. Radha had a relapse of cancer a year after she was treated for the disease.
4. When her condition became so bad that her family could not manage, she was completely neglected.
5. In the case of patients like Radha, families and doctors cannot be blamed because we do not have facilities in India to look after them.
6. End-stage cancer patients need relief only from painful physical symptoms.
7. Palliative care aims to make the dying comfortable and make sure they have a good quality of life until the end.
8. Palliative medicine helps oncologists take care of patients for whom there is still some hope of being cured.
9. Terminal cancer patients who go to a palliative care centre receive immediate alternative treatment for their illness.
10. Palliative care doctors must be good listeners.

EXERCISE B

Write short answers to the following questions based on paragraphs 6 to 14.

1. What do doctors in palliative care centres do when an end-stage cancer patient comes to them?
2. How can cancer patients get relief from the acute pain that many of them experience?

3. Besides pain, what are the other distress causing symptoms commonly experienced in the last stage of cancer?
4. How can simple procedures be used to relieve some symptoms caused by specific kinds of cancer?
5. In what way can the family be trained to manage ulcers and swelling of the limbs at home?
6. Dying cancer patients often face problems other than physical distress. How can palliative care deal with them?
7. Why do the family members of some cancer patients hide the fact of the disease from them and what is the role palliative care doctors must play to help both patients and their families?
8. According to you, which of the places where patients can choose to receive palliative care seems the best option? Why?

Pronunciation

QUIZ

EXERCISE

Conduct a quiz on pronunciation in your class. Each group of five students can prepare a set of ten questions to test the other groups. You can base your questions on the different areas covered in the book—minimal pairs, words with silent letters, homonyms, homographs, homophones, stress shifts and one letter–many sounds.

Vocabulary

IDIOMS AND COLLOCATIONS

Idioms are phrases or expressions which are peculiar to a language and rarely make sense if translated literally. They are difficult to understand for a person learning English as a second language. For example:

Give it to me *in black and white* (in writing).

The only way to master idioms is to consciously try to remember these word collocations and use them in appropriate settings. If we are not sure of them, it is better to replace them with words conveying the same meaning. For example:

He came in *at the eleventh hour* (the last minute).

Many of these phrases have lost their power to make an effect because of overuse. When this happens, an idiomatic phrase becomes a 'cliché' (pronounced /kli:ʃeɪ/). A few such expressions are 'pearls of wisdom', 'pull some strings', 'get the ball rolling', 'think outside the box', 'you can't judge a book by its cover', and 'fish out of water'. Avoid using these tired old expressions often if you want to be creative in academic and professional contexts.

EXERCISE A

Replace the idioms in the following sentences with suitable words that convey the same meaning.

1. She is *the apple of my eye*.
2. I meet him *once in a blue moon*.
3. He was struck by *a bolt from the blue*.
4. He could easily *break the ice*.
5. Don't let them *burn the midnight oil*.
6. This will be *a feather in his cap*.
7. He is sure to come off *with flying colours*.
8. She is capable of *facing the music*.
9. She was *on tenterhooks* till the results were published.
10. We are *in the same boat*.

EXERCISE B

Write the meanings of the italicised expressions in the following sentences.

1. Ravi *broke the news* to me.
2. Our teacher organised a few games to *break the ice.*
3. Please *take a seat*.

4. Let us *take turns* to sit by grandmother's bed at night.
5. *Make yourselves at home*. I will be back in a moment.
6. After the exams, Reena decided to *take a break*.
7. Please *drop me a line* when you reach Hyderabad.
8. Raja is good at *paying compliments*.
9. Joy's actions *speak volumes* for her honesty.
10. He was arrested because he *broke the law*.

EXERCISE C

Match the phrases in column A with the words in column B. In some cases, more than one combination is possible.

A	B
1. a bed of	a. coal
2. a board of	b. sunlight
3. a cluster of	c. sugar
4. a cloud of	d. soldiers
5. a school of	e. insects
6. a lump of	f. smoke
7. a shaft of	g. houses
8. a suite of	h. fish
9. a troupe of	i. children
10. a wisp of	j. roses
	k. rooms
	l. interviewers
	m. artistes

EXERCISE D

Fill in the blanks in the noun collocations below with suitable words.

1. .... of news
2. .... of grass
3. .... of conversation
4. .... of sand
5. .... of musicians
6. .... of people

7. .... of good weather
8. .... of anxiety
9. .... of enthusiasm
10. .... of scenery

WORD GAME

EXERCISE E

Supply a word for each of the meanings given. All words start with the letter 'a'. The second letter in the first word will be 'b' and it will be 'c', 'd', 'e', and so on in consecutive words. For example, above, account, admonish, aegis, etc.

1. part of the body below the chest and diaphragm containing the stomach, bowels and digestive organs ....
2. pertaining to sound or sense of hearing ....
3. sticky, holding together ....
4. use of air in the treatment of diseases ....
5. without fever ....
6. make worse or more serious ....
7. further forward in space or time ....
8. minor illness ....
9. door slightly open ....
10. similar or related ....
11. an acquired hypersensitivity to a substance that normally does not cause a reaction ....
12. able to walk ....
13. an agent that neutralises acidity, especially in the digestive tract ....
14. the main trunk of the arterial system of the body ....
15. strong desire, especially for food ....
16. of water ....
17. speak clearly ....
18. absorb digested food ....
19. deviating from the normal ....

20. postmortem examination of the organs and tissues of the body to determine the cause of death or pathological conditions ....
21. strong dislike ....
22. having knowledge of ....
23. the armpit ....
24. yes ....
25. bright blue ....

Grammar

PREPOSITIONS AND PHRASAL VERBS

Prepositions express the relation between two words in a sentence. They usually come before a noun or a pronoun. For example:

The book is *on /inside/ under /near /beside* the box.

Simple prepositions consist of one word. For example:

about, above, across, after, against, along, among, around, at, before, behind, below, beneath, beside, besides, between, by, despite

Complex prepositions consist of two or more words. For example:

along with, away from, because of, due to, except for, together with, instead of, in comparison to

There are other words that look like adjectives or verbs but they are used as prepositions. For example:

barring, concerning, excepting, following, including, like, minus, near, plus, unlike

Prepositions can have different functions—to indicate time, place, purpose, direction, movement, means/instrumentality, concession, comparison, source and manner. Look at the following sentences in which the prepositions have these functions.

Sudha sits between *Saroj and Usman.* (position)

Vijay went from *Kanpur* to *Ahmedabad.* (movement and direction)

Father returned at *6 o'clock.* (time)

The road is blocked because *of the wedding procession.* (reason)

We went to the market for *vegetables.* (purpose)

Jaya cut the lemon with *a knife.* (instrument)

Let's go to Mumbai by *bus.* (means)

In spite of *the heat, the children are playing outdoors.* (concession)

She sings like *a koel.* (comparison)

Leela does all her work with *great care.* (manner)

They fetched water from *the river.* (source)

Prepositions and adverbs combine with verbs to from phrasal verbs. Some of these phrasal verbs preserve the individual meanings of the constituent verb and particle. But in others, the meaning of the combination cannot be predicted from the meanings of the verb and particle in isolation. The figure on the next page will give you the meanings of thirteen phrasal verbs consisting of the verb 'look' in combination with different prepositions and adverbs.

Avoid using phrasal verbs if you are not sure of their meanings. There are three types of errors that occur commonly when we use these verbs.

- inserting the wrong particle
- inserting a particle where it is not needed
- not inserting the particle where it is needed

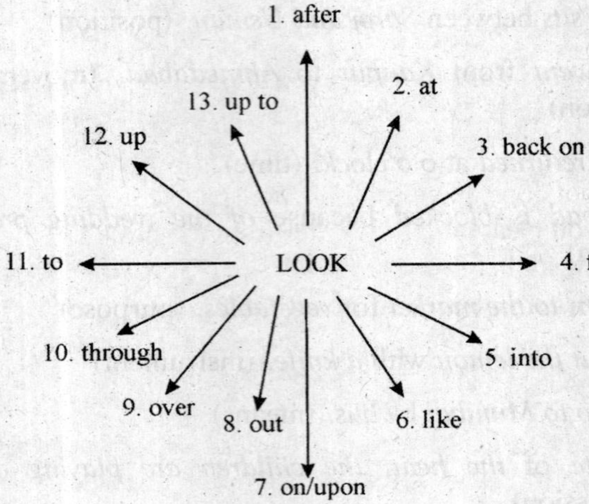

1.	look after	-	take care of
2.	look at	-	consider
3.	look back on	-	recall
4.	look for	-	search
5.	look into	-	investigate
6.	look like	-	resemble
7.	look on/upon	-	regard
8.	look out	-	watch
9.	look over	-	inspect
10.	look through	-	a. read superficially
			b. look at without appearing to recognise
11.	look to	-	a. turn for help
			b. expect
12.	look up	-	a. search for
			b. get in touch with
			c. improve
13.	look up to	-	admire

EXERCISE A

The following sentences (except one) have errors related to the use of prepositions. Write down the corrected sentences in your notebook.

1. He cannot cope up with this responsibility.
2. Would you please refer the letter from the press?
3. I agreed with her suggestions.
4. The teacher discussed about our performance with the headmaster.
5. The course comprises of English, physics, chemistry and biology.
6. She is good in mathematics and will surely win the prize.
7. Their venture succeeded and now they are well of.
8. He took a long time to reply my letter.
9. I consider him my best friend.
10. I am sorry of what she has done.

EXERCISE B

Point out the difference in the meanings of the sentences in each pair given below.

1. a. He is engaged to her.
   b. He is engaged with her
2. a. I don't think much of our new class representative.
   b. I don't think much about our new class representative.
3. a. He speaks as a lawyer.
   b. He speaks like a lawyer.
4. a. I will be there at 10 a.m.
   b. I will be there by 10 a.m.
5. a. He turned to me.
   b. He turned against me.
6. a. She laughed at him.
   b. She laughed with him.
7. a. I apologised to Mary.
   b. I apologised for Mary

8. a. She divided it between them.
   b. She divided it among them.
9. a. He passed out on the way to the hospital.
   b. He passed away on the way to the hospital.
10. a. She will definitely back out.
    b. She will definitely back up.
11. a. I believe him.
    b. I believe in him.
12. a. I approve it.
    b. I approve of it.
13. a. I am well.
    b. I am well off.
14. a) I was glad I could beat him.
    b. I was glad I could beat him up.
15. a. He picked it.
    b. He picked it up.
16. a. I will see you sometime.
    b. I will see you for some time.
17. a. She swept out the room.
    b. She swept out of the room.
18. a. My village is to the northeast of Bihar.
    b. My village is in the northeast of Bihar.
19. a. He sat up when he saw me.
    b. He sat down when he saw me.
20. a. He shouted to me.
    b. He shouted at me.
21. a. I waited for him.
    b. I waited on him.
22. a. I asked for him.
    b. I asked after him.
23. a. He sat at the table.
    b. He sat on the table.
24. a. He wanted to buy them off.
    b. He wanted to buy them out.
25. a. His song was in the beginning.
    b. His song was at the beginning.

26. a. You will profit by it.
    b. You will profit from it.
27. a. He spoke to himself.
    b. He spoke of himself.
28. a. He tried many times and finally gave in.
    b. He tried many times and finally gave up.
29. a. You must get along with him.
    b. You must get across to him.
30. a. He couldn't catch up on the reading.
    b. He couldn't catch on to the reading.

ACTIVE AND PASSIVE VERB FORMS

EXERCISE C

Fill in the verbs with suitable forms of the verbs given in the brackets.

Mrs. Linda Jones is the most amazing patient I (1) --------(treat). When she first came to our clinic, she had heart related and immune problems. In 2000 she (2) ------ (diagnose) to have small cell carcinoma of the lung. The survival rate for this type of cancer (3) ---------- (be) usually 18 months. She (4) ---------- (treat) with chemotherapy and radiotherapy. After two years she (5) ------(develop) non–small cell carcinoma for which she (6) --------- (undergo) lobectomy.

Eleven years later Linda (7) ------------- (come) for a routine bronchoscopy and her samples (8) ---------------(review) by pathologists. The diagnosis of recurrent non–small cell carcinoma (9) --------- (confirm). When I (10) ----------- (explain) the condition, Linda did not want further intervention. She was 80 and (11) ------------- (want) only comfort care and so she (12) ------- (refer) to the Palliative Care Unit.

Linda's subsequent scans after 6 months (13) ----------- (show) a reduction in the size of the lump in the lung. It was a surprise to me as well as the family that the cancer (14) -------------- (regress) without treatment. I remembered other anecdotal case reports that had suggested this possibility.

Linda was overjoyed but aware that she would need monitoring. Linda's main symptom then (15) ------------ (be) fatigue, related to her underlying immune disorders, for which she (16) ----------- (treat) by immunologists.

Recently I spotted her in a park, happily engaging her grandchildren. She introduced me to them and assured me she is coping well.

EXERCISE D

Some of the following sentences have errors in them. Rewrite them correctly.

1. Though he belonged to the rival team, I paid Tony a complement.
2. Nitya asked me whether her camera was in the dining table.
3. The final exams start tomorrow, but Rohan is whiling away his time with friends.
4. A number of problems were highlighted at the conference.
5. Seenu has more problems than us, but he is always cheerful.
6. They were trapped inside of a multistorey building on fire.
7. Where I can find a supermarket?
8. Every year I am going to Delhi to visit my grandparents.
9. At the conference I did not hardly know any of the delegates.
10. The lecture was interesting, but it did not convince nobody.
11. I am surprised that he does not know to swim.
12. The doctor wants to examine you. Take out your shirt.
13. They refused to give us blankets to cover us.
14. After reaching the concert hall, we spent half an hour looking for the parking slot.
15. This new book is like the prize winning book on tropical flowers published last year.
16. Our editor was more acquainted with the manager than the lawyer.
17. He ordered for fried rice because it is my favourite dish.
18. She has not gone to Chennai already, but I am sure she will go.
19. They have been learning French from 1995.
20. However much I tried, I could not get an employment that matched my qualifications.

Speaking

ROLE PLAY

EXERCISE A

Read the situation described below and do as directed.

Mrs Rafia Rana, aged 30, is posted for lumpectomy next week. She is withdrawn and refuses to cooperate with the medical team in following their instructions. The staff nurse in charge of her ward tries to draw her out and help her.

In pairs, assume the role of the nurse and Mrs Rana and enact the situation in two different ways where the conversation

1. facilitates healing;
2. further widens the gap between Mrs Rana and the health team.

At the end of the presentations, discuss the communication facilitators and barriers with the rest of the class.

EXTEMPORE TALK

EXERCISE B

Work in groups and prepare a speech of about three minutes duration on any of the topics suggested by your teacher. You may take five minutes to prepare.

Writing

ARTICLES FOR NEWSPAPERS / MAGAZINES

EXERCISE

Write an article in about 200 words on the topic 'My most unforgettable patient'.

CURRICULUM VITAE (CV) AND RESUMÉ

A curriculum vitae (CV) is the record of your personal profile and educational and professional achievements. It is also known as a resumé (pronounced rey-zhu-may). It is usually prepared to give a prospective employer an overview of your work. A detailed CV includes career objectives, academic background, work experience, publications, papers presented, awards received, participation in workshops and in service programmes and memberships in professional organisations. Awards in areas not directly related to your profession, but reflecting your personality can be included. Names of two professionals should be included as referees.

When preparing a CV make sure they are not look too long despite the number of items to be covered. The facts presented in your CV should be up to date and authentic, highlighting your abilities and achievements without exaggeration. Update the CV at regular intervals and send the latest one when you apply for a job or course.

When you apply for higher education or training or a job, you are expected to submit your CV. You must match your CV to the position you are applying for, highlighting your skills in those specific areas. Highlight relevant and pertinent facts.

Your publications in journals have great value and have to presented in a particular style in the CV. The Vancouver style may be followed and the following details should be included: Name(s) of authors, Title of the article. Journal name, Year, Month, Vol (issue number) and page numbers. The format is as in the given example: Jenitha C, Richards RH and Deakins WM. Postoperative pain management after abdominal surgery in infants: A case series. *Ind J Nursing*. 2010 Sept; 23(4):45–6.

A good CV should be well designed with pleasing format. Do not fill it with details. Be precise and avoid long sentences. Use adequate space between lines; the font size should be readable but not too large. People looking at the CV should be able to gather relevant details at a glance.

CVs are sent with a formal covering letter. In the letter, briefly state the specific skills and knowledge you have to do well in the course or job you are applying for. Key words from the job description can be discreetly included in the covering letter. For maximum impact draw attention to the skills that match the requirements of the job.

If there are noticeable gaps in your career, explain it, mainly to prevent unnecessary speculation. Make sure that you check the spellings in the document before you send it.

Given below is a model CV.

Curriculum Vitae

Name	Sahaya Mary A
Date of birth	10 June 1980
Gender	Female
Permanent Address	12B, Second floor, Renu Apartments, Third Cross Street, Kuravalangad, Kottayam 686 003, Kerala
Email:	mary4sahaya1980@gmail.com

Career Objective:

Committed to paediatric care, I am keen to work in a setting which offers high quality health care for children.

I hope to be able to put to use my knowledge and skills to enhance care and innovate techniques and strategies relevant to our setting which will impact on patient outcome.

I would also like to be part of the academic training of nursing students in this specialty and focus on novel methods of interactive and problem based learning.

Educational Qualifications:

Course	Year	Institution	University	Marks/ Grade
Postgraduate Diploma in Critical Care Nursing	2013–14	Children's Speciality Hospital	Singapore	A
MSc Child Health Nursing	2002–2004	Kasthuribha College of Nursing and Multi-Specialty Hospital, Coimbatore	Dr MGR Medical University	78% (Distinction)
BSc Nursing	1997–2000 St Mary's College of Nursing, Kottayam	Kerala University		85% (Gold Medallist)

Current Employment and Teaching Experience:

2013 till date

Currently working at the Children's Speciality Hospital (CSH) in Singapore and from Jan 2015 have been in charge of the paediatric and neonatal intensive care units, which are 30-bedded and 100-bedded facilities respectively. Since this is a referral centre I have been involved in the care of extremely sick children with complicated medical conditions. I have gained insight and expertise in planning and organising the Paediatric Intensive Care Units (PICU). I have also been involved in the teaching and training of nursing interns.

Work Experience

2005 to 2012

Worked at the Kasthuribha College of Nursing and Coimbatore Multi Speciality Hospital in various capacities holding both teaching and clinical responsibilities

Reader in Nursing 2011–2012

- Was in charge of a section of the Paediatric ward
- Supervised the nursing staff and students posted in the ward
- Organised workshops for departmental sisters. Was responsible for quality assurance of nursing activities in the ward
- Took classes for MSc in Child Health Nursing programme
- Taught Paediatric Nursing for students of both basic and post basic BSc Nursing programmes. Was the class advisor for the third year BSc Nursing
- Was examiner in Paediatric Nursing for BSc Nursing

Lecturer in Nursing 2008 to 2010

- Took care of patients in the Paediatric wards.
- Taught Paediatrics for BSc and Diploma Nursing courses. Supervised clinical experience in paediatric ward
- Conducted seminars and clinical presentations

Junior Lecturer in Nursing 2005 to 2007

- Taught Paediatrics for BSc and Diplcma Nursing. Supervised learning; evaluated student performance
- Was staff advisor for first year Diploma Nursing
- Worked in the paediatric ward and was responsible for patient care

Publications:

Sahaya Mary A. Leukaemia in children – A Nurse's perspective. *Ped Nursing J Ind*. 2010 Apr; 12(2):21–2.

Rachel J and Sahaya Mary A. Wilson's Disease – A Nursing perspective. *Nursing J Ind* 2013 Aug; 25(3):43–4.

Papers presented:

Artificial Nutrition and Hydration at the conference on Paediatric Advanced Life Support, 20 to 24 Jan 2015, Rainbow Paediatric Hospital, Bengaluru.

Family Communication in PICU at the Paediatric Oncology Conference, 5 to 9 March 2014, Children's Hospital, New Delhi.

Workshops and Conferences attended:

Traumatic Brain Injury Assessment: 15–20 Nov 2013, Pediatric Academy, Chennai

Critical Care Management: 15–19 August 2011, College of Nursing, Trivandrum

In Service Programmes attended

Controlling Infections in ICU

Biomedical Equipment Handling

Research in Nursing

Teaching Methodology for Nursing Colleges

Syllabus of Diploma Programme in Nursing

Competencies and Skills:

- "Best Teacher Award" in 2011
- "Best Outgoing Student Award" in 2004 for MSc Nursing
- "Gold Medallist "in 2000 for BSc Nursing
- "Student President" in 1999 during BSc Nursing
- Was the "Student Editor" for college magazine Pulse in 1998
- Have won prizes in oratory competitions

- Have done a course in Counselling
- Good at establishing rapport with colleagues, students, patients and patient relatives
- Can communicate fluently in English, Tamil, Malayalam and Hindi
- Have passed IELTS with 8 point score
- Competent in the use of computers

Membership in Professional Organizations

Life member of Christian Medical Association of India

Life member of Trained Nurses Association of India

Referees:

1. **Prof. Ching Lee MSc(N), PhD**
   Head of Paediatric Nursing ICU
   Children's Speciality Hospital
   120 Bukit Timah Road,
   Singapore 229 899
   Phone: +65 6334 2343
   Email: leeching@gmail.com
2. **Dr. Mekhala Manivannan MSc(N), PhD**
   Dean
   Kasthuribha College of Nursing,
   Coimbatore, Tamil Nadu 641 003
   Phone : +91 -422 -3211 235
   Email : mekhalam@gmail.com

Covering Letter

From
Sahaya Mary A
12B, Second floor, Renu Apartments, Third Cross Street,
Kuravalangad, Kottayam 686 003, Kerala
0-93421-26000
mary4sahaya1980@gmail.com

11 Jan 2016

To
The Director
Rainbow Paediatric Hospital
Bengaluru 560035

Dear Madam/Sir

In response to your advertisement in *The Hindu* dated 15 April 2016, I would like to apply for the post of Associate Nursing Superintendent in charge of the Paediatric and Neonatal ICUs in Rainbow Paediatric Hospital at Bengaluru.

Attached please find a copy of my CV that provides details of my qualifications and work experience.

Since January 2013, I have been working at the Children's Speciality Hospital (CSH), in Singapore. I am currently in charge of the Paediatric and Neonatal ICUs of the CSH. My other interests are counselling and mentoring co-workers and students. I have eight publications in peer-reviewed journals.

In January 2015, I presented a paper "Artificial Nutrition and Hydration" at the conference on Advanced Life Support organised by your hospital at Bengaluru. I was impressed by the quality of health care in your institution and would consider it a privilege if given an opportunity to be part of your nursing team.

I hope you will consider my application favourably. I look forward to hearing from you at your earliest convenience.

Thank you.

Yours sincerely

[Signature]

Sahaya Mary A

INTERVIEWS

After you have applied for a job you may be invited by the prospective employers for an interview. This may be either face-to-face or over telephone or videocall. Success at interviews depends on how you project yourself at the meeting. Some of the basic tips for preparation are:

- Find out something about your employers, their specialisation and their profile.
- Be clear why you are applying for this job.
- Dress appropriately and if there is a dress code, follow it. Have your credentials ready at hand (or send them in advance in case of a long-distance video interview) if they want to check them out.
- Be on time for interview.
- Be confident, natural and relaxed. If you are tense you may not be able to give your best.
- Greet the interviewers as you enter.
- Don't be too loud or too soft.
- Make eye contact with the interviewers when they are talking to you and answer questions directly. Do not be vague or ambiguous.
- Ask for clarification if you do not understand the question.

- If you don't know the answer to some of the questions, say so; do not attempt to bluff or lie.
- Most interviewers also note what soft skills you possess, since these are important in the work place. Highlight your strengths in these areas during the interview.
- Prepare a few questions that you may wish to ask the interviewers.
- Thank the interviewers before you leave.

Some sample questions are given below.

- Tell us about yourself. (Focus mainly on previous career highlights and be brief.)
- Where would you like to see yourself in five years?
- What is your greatest strength?
- What skills do you have to lead a team?
- What is your approach for getting along with difficult staff members?
- How do you handle problem patients and/or families? Why have you applied for this particular job?
- Why are you leaving your present position?
- Give us two reasons why we should hire you.
- What do you know about our hospital?
- What salary do you expect?
- Do you have any questions that you would like to ask us? (You could ask: How soon could you let me know about the outcome of this interview? What are the duties in this job? What is the career path for this job?)

EXERCISE A

Simran is a BSc nurse with 3 years experience in a 100-bed hospital. She wants to apply for a nursing position in a 500-bed Government hospital in the nearby town.

Write a letter of application in response to an advertisement for a nursing position in that Government hospital. Prepare a brief CV;

prepare 5–6 questions you would like to ask the hospital before you decide to join.

Some of the details/phrases you could use are:
I look forward to more responsibilities ...
I hope to gain more experience by ...
If selected, when would I be expected to join?
What are our duty hours?

EXERCISE B

You have been invited for an interview next month. Identify two areas of weakness in soft skills that you may have. How will you address these before the interview so that you can suitably impress the interviewers?

	Area of Weakness	Redressal
1.		a. b.
2.		

EXERCISE C

This is a role play exercise. One student will volunteer to be the interviewee and three students will play the role of interviewers (Nursing Superintendent, Head of Medical Surgical Ward and Head of Nursing College). Enact the interview in the classroom.

Preparation time: One week

The student should prepare a CV and prepare for the interview. The interviewers have to ask relevant questions about the interviewee's qualifications and soft skills. Use some of the questions given above.

After the interview, the class gives feedback on the enactment. What was done well? What could have been done better? How? List specific phrases that could have been used in the communication to make it proceed smoothly.

Appreciating poetry

Song of a Dream

Once in the dream of a night I stood
Lone in the light of a magical wood,
Soul-deep in visions that poppy-like sprang;
And spirits of Truth were the birds that sang,
And spirits of Love were the stars that glowed,
And spirits of Peace were the streams that flowed
In that magical wood in the land of sleep.

Lone in the light of that magical grove,
I felt the stars of the spirits of Love
Gather and gleam round my delicate youth,
And I heard the song of the spirits of Truth;
To quench my longing I bent me low
By the streams of the spirits of Peace that flow
In that magical wood in the land of sleep.

Sarojini Naidu

EXERCISE

Write short answers to the following questions.

1. What is the tone of the poem?
2. What makes the wood magical?

Appendix

Additional Vocabulary Exercises

GENERAL QUIZ

Differentiate between the meanings of the sentences in each of the following pairs.

1. a. I gave him an example.
   b. I set him an example.
2. a. Our team leader is far-sighted.
   b. Our team leader is long-sighted.
3. a. Ajit overheard a conversation.
   b. Ajit eavesdropped on a conversation.
4. a. We decided to make the best of it.
   b. We decided to make the most of it.
5. a. Neelam was uninterested in taking up the project.
   b. Neelam was disinterested in taking up the project.
6. a. Dr Saha wrote the preface to the book.
   b. Dr Saha wrote the foreword to the book.
7. a. They left him deeply wounded.
   b. They left him seriously wounded.
8. a. This is a scarce item.
   b. This is a rare item.
9. a. He gave me a reference.
   b. He gave me a testimonial.
10. a. The men worked hard all day.
    b. The men hardly worked all day.
11. a. He worked hard all day.
    b. He worked hard every day.
12. a. The woman complemented the painting.
    b. The woman complimented the painting.
13. a. Sneha is childish.

b. Sneha is child-like.

14. a. I convinced him.
    b. I persuaded him.
15. a. Shirley is gracious.
    b. Shirley is graceful.
16. a. In accord with your instructions, we arranged it.
    b. In accordance with your instructions, we arranged it.
17. a. It is their habit to drink wine at every meal.
    b. It is their custom to drink wine at every meal.
18. a. He is famous for his deeds.
    b. He is notorious for his deeds.
19. a. Bala is alone.
    b. Bala is lonely.
20. a. It was an exhausting study.
    b. It was an exhaustive study.
21. a. The boy made a superficial remark.
    b. The boy made a superfluous remark.
22. a. It is delightful.
    b. It is delicious.
23. a. The children watched the troops.
    b. The children watched the troupes.
24. a. This is your suit.
    b. This is your suite.
25. a. What is the price of this?
    b. What is the cost of this?
26. a. The book is valueless.
    b. The book is invaluable.
27. a. I am attending the biannual conference.
    b. I am attending the biennial conference.
28. a. Buy the cloth from the shop on M. G. Road.
    b. Buy the clothes from the shop on M. G. Road.
29. a. Tony bought a pair of reading glasses.
    b. Tony bought a couple of reading glasses.
30. a. Ahmed's character is good.
    b. Ahmed's conduct is good.

31. a. I stood in the middle of the room.
    b. I stood in the centre of the room.
32. a. Gagan is an industrious worker.
    b. Gagan is an industrial worker.
33. a. He received his wages.
    b. He received his salary.
34. a. This is a classic play.
    b. This is a classical play.
35. a. Nursing is her profession.
    b. Nursing is her vocation.
36. a. Professor Ray waived the assignment paper.
    b. Professor Ray waved the assignment paper.
37. a. Prema is talented.
    b. Prema is skilled.
38. a. I admire his antics.
    b. I admire his antiques.
39. a. Lal Bagh is a popular area.
    b. Lal Bagh is a populous area.
40. a. We saw the reminder you left for us.
    b. We saw the remainder you left for us.
41. a. I admire his morale.
    b. I admire his morals.
42. a. Vipin is devoted to it.
    b. Vipin is addicted to it.
43. a. He likes her more than I.
    b. He likes her more than me.
44. a. Did anyone phone yesterday?
    b. Did someone phone yesterday?
45. a. The people belong to an urban community.
    b. The people belong to an urbane community.
46. a. Madhu avoided the rally.
    b. Madhu prevented the rally.
47. a. It was a terrific sight.
    b. It was a terrible sight.

48. a. Suman's mother is a good councillor.
    b. Suman's mother is a good counsellor.
49. a. Shanti found the road easy.
    b. Shanti found the road easily.
50. a. He worked hard all day.
    b. He worked hard every day.

MEDICAL QUIZ A

Complete the following sentences by choosing the correct option.

1. A grazed knee refers to a wound with
   a. superficial scraping of skin.
   b. only bruises.
   c. severe bleeding.
   d. deep cuts.
2. Before transfusion, the samples of the donor and the recipient are
   a. cross-checked.
   b. cross-matched.
   c. cross-examined.
   d. cross-grained.
3. Body movement is explained by the word
   a. squint.
   b. squirm.
   c. squad.
   d. squirt.
4. Sleeping soundly means
   a. sleeping well.
   b. talking in sleep.
   c. snoring.
   d. being restless.
5. A thready pulse is
   a. weak pulse, difficult to feel.
   b. slower than usual.

c. strong but irregular.
d. faster than usual.

6. If a wound is oozing blood, it is
a. bleeding a lot.
b. bleeding a little.
c. becoming infected.
d. not bleeding.

7. When an artery is cut, the blood
a. spurts.
b. oozes.
c. bursts.
d. shoots.

8. Using heavy weights to pull broken ends of bones into correct positions is called
a. transfixing.
b. traction.
c. transmission.
d. tackling.

9. When once-repaired hernia comes back after surgery, it is called a .... hernia.
a. reformed
b. recurrent
c. remitting
d. renewed

10. .... is not used for patients to lie on.
a. bed cradle
b. trolley
c. stretcher
d. couch

11. .... does not describe a patient's position in bed.
a. prone
b. ambulant
c. recumbent
d. supine

12. When a broken bone is put back into its normal position, the doctor has .... it.
    a. reduced
    b. realigned
    c. related
    d. renewed
13. A store of blood voluntarily given by people and kept in hospitals for use in emergencies is called a blood
    a. donation.
    b. collection.
    c. bank.
    d. deposit.
14. The word .... means mentally abnormal.
    a. mentally deficient
    b. mentally deranged
    c. mentally retarded
    d. mentally subnormal
15. A human being's .... is about 70 years.
    a. life cycle
    b. life history
    c. life span
    d. life story
16. Temperature, pulse, respiration rate and blood pressure are known as the .... signs.
    a. varying
    b. vigorous
    c. visual
    d. vital
17. A bland diet does not include
    a. boiled potatoes.
    b. fried meat.
    c. poached fish.
    d. scrambled eggs.

18. In case of an emergency situation, a doctor and a nurse must always be
    a. on demand.
    b. on the phone.
    c. on call.
    d. on receipt.
19. The phrase .... means to die during an operation.
    a. to die in harness
    b. to die of one's wounds
    c. to die on the table
    d. to die because of the knife
20. The ratio between the amount of carbon dioxide breathed out and oxygen breathed in during a specified time is called the respiratory
    a. quota.
    b. quantum.
    c. quotient.
    d. quantity.
21. Radiotherapy is
    a. treatment by radio.
    b. radiobiology.
    c. treatment by radiation.
    d. radial treatment.
22. To rehabilitate patients means
    a. to re-educate them to help them adjust after serious illness.
    b. to change their mode of treatment.
    c. to send them home.
    d. to make them more comfortable in another room.
23. The electronic instrument which is used to correct weak or irregular heartbeat is called a
    a. pace setter.
    b. pacemaker.
    c. pace regulator.
    d. pace keeper.

24. Many items of equipment in hospitals are used only once and thrown away. These are
    a. dispensable items.
    b. disposable items.
    c. discarded items.
    d. destructive items.
25. When blood from a wound soaks through the dressing and shows on the outside, we say that the blood is .... through it.
    a. gushing
    b. spilling
    c. running
    d. seeping
26. When we put a patient with a contagious disease in a room by himself we are
    a. extricating him.
    b. insulating him.
    c. isolating him.
    d. segregating him.
27. Which of the completed sentences does not have the same meaning as others? 'His condition showed .... improvement.'
    a. considerable
    b. marked
    c. marginal
    d. noticeable
28. The prognosis of the disease is concerned with its
    a. cause.
    b. outcome.
    c. source.
    d. type.
29. If Uma is being brave in a situation, she is ....
    a. making a face about it.
    b. facing it.
    c. trying to save face.

d. setting her face against it.

30. A person with a slipped disc has pain in his
 a. back.
 b. eye.
 c. knee.
 d. shoulder.

(based on *Know Your Nursing English* by Pauletta Edwards, London: Hutchinson and Co., 1979)

MEDICAL QUIZ B

1. Give one-word equivalents for the following phrases.

a. persistent fear of high places
b. persistent fear of closed places
c. persistent fear of blood
d. persistent fear of being alone
e. persistent fear of disease
f. the study of cells
g. the study of muscles
h. the study of bones
i. the study of fermentation
j. the study of blood

2. Match the following.

a. coccyx	i. bone in the foot
b. pepsin	ii. stomach
c. sternum	iii. cortisol
d. suture	iv. liver
e. cuboid	v. blood
f. malleus	vi. vertebrae
g. adrenal cortex	vii. psychiatry
h. coccus	viii. pancreatic juice
i. hepatitis	ix. virus
j. erythrocyte	x. maltose
	xi. surgery

xii. bacteria
xiii. stapes
xiv. manubrium
xv. sporadic

3. Write the meanings of the following words.

a. kleptomaniac
b. paranoid
c. megalomaniac
d. photophobia
e. hydrophobia

4. Write the antonyms of the following words.

a. ventral
b. digestion
c. hygienic
d. interior
e. toxic
f. perforated
g. vertical
h. antenatal
i. extrovert
j. benign tumour

MEDICAL QUIZ C

Complete the following sentences by choosing the correct option.

1. A substance which inhibits the growth of or destroys harmful microorganisms is called an
   a. antibody.
   b. antigen.
   c. antibiotic.
   d. antidote.
2. Toxicity is connected to
   a. tonics.
   b. tonsils.

c. diet.
d. poison.

3. A 'terminal case' is where the
   a. patient has been discharged.
   b. disease will result in death.
   c. patient has to wait till the end of the term to be examined.
   d. disease is of technical interest.
4. If a person is 'stone deaf' he or she
   a. cannot differentiate the tones.
   b. is slightly deaf.
   c. is completely deaf.
   d. is deaf as well as dumb.
5. An agent which relieves or lessens pain is called an
   a. analogy.
   b. analgesic.
   c. amnesia.
   d. enzyme.
6. Auscultation is the process of
   a. listening for sounds produced in body cavities.
   b. making the patient breathe heavily while examining.
   c. checking the blood flow.
   d. assessing the rate of natural immunity.
7. The apparatus that sterilises by steam pressure is known as a/an
   a. autopsy.
   b. automachine.
   c. autoclave.
   d. stabiliser.
8. The blue-baby syndrome refers to a/an
   a. male baby.
   b. baby born dead.
   c. baby with a defect in the heart.
   d. orphan.

9. Bedsores occur mainly
   a. because of bedbugs.
   b. because of bad hygienic conditions.
   c. if one is bedridden for a long period.
   d. if the same beds are used by many people.
10. Temporary loss of consciousness is called a
    a. blackhead.
    b. coma.
    c. block up.
    d. blackout.
11. A drop of blood spread on a slide for the purpose of microscopic examination is called a
    a. blood sample.
    b. blood smear.
    c. blood slide.
    d. blood stain.
12. Transplanting a healthy bone to replace a missing or defective bone is known as
    a. bone reflex.
    b. bone grafting.
    c. booster.
    d. bone replacement.
13. Braille is meant to help those who are
    a. deaf.
    b. dumb.
    c. blind.
    d. lame.
14. .... is known as insomnia.
    a. loss of memory
    b. sleeplessness
    c. fear of darkness
    d. hysterical behaviour
15. To cater to individual idiosyncrasies means
    a. to serve food according to individual tastes.

b. to accept the religious beliefs of different persons and act accordingly.
c. to give special care to people with a low IQ.
d. to take into consideration the behaviour or way of thought peculiar to an individual and act accordingly.

16. A bandage used for the head or the stump of an amputated limb is called a
    a. cap.
    b. capillary.
    c. capeline.
    d. capsular.
17. Capillus is a
    a. minute blood vessel.
    b. hair.
    c. small lymphatic duct.
    d. thin ligament.
18. When a person is prone to respiratory infections, he or she
    a. never gets respiratory infections.
    b. is susceptible to respiratory infections.
    c. fears respiratory infections.
    d. fights respiratory infections.
19. Acoustics is connected to
    a. sight.
    b. hearing.
    c. smell.
    d. feeling.
20. When doctors manage to arrest a disease, it means they
    a. find the cause of the disease.
    b. stop the progress of the disease.
    c. eradicate the disease.
    d. contract the disease.
21. Reflex action is a/an
    a. involuntary action.
    b. voluntary action.
    c. planned action.

d. mild action.

22. Enslavement to a bad habit is known as
    a. adduction.
    b. addiction.
    c. abduction.
    d. devotion.
23. A benign tumour is
    a. nonmalignant.
    b. hereditary.
    c. malignant.
    d. infectious.
24. Adiposity results in
    a. losing weight.
    b. gaining weight.
    c. taking more rest.
    d. being active.
25. A drug having adverse effects is a drug that has
    a. unexpected effects.
    b. additional benefits.
    c. favourable effects.
    d. bad effects.

MEDICAL QUIZ D

Complete the following sentences by choosing the correct option.

1. An air bed is used for patients with
    a. bedsores.
    b. breathing difficulty.
    c. head injury.
    d. lung infection.
2. A teetotaller is one who
    a. takes only tea.
    b. does not take tea.
    c. does not take any alcoholic drinks.
    d. sells tea and alcohol.

3. Introduction of a foreign substance into the body is called
   a. allenthesis.
   b. allergy.
   c. alma mater.
   d. alienation.
4. Allophasis is the technical term for
   a. forgetfulness.
   b. delirium.
   c. pain.
   d. treatment by medicine.
5. When a person is allergic to a drug,
   a. he will get well soon.
   b. he must continue to take the drug regularly.
   c. he must change the dosage.
   d. he must stop taking the drug.
6. Denture is associated with
   a. density.
   b. dentistry.
   c. duodenum.
   d. a paste or powder for cleaning the teeth.
7. The science of the use of foods in health and disease is known as
   a. diary.
   b. dietetics.
   c. dietitian.
   d. calorie.
8. The difference between nausea and vomiting is as follows:
   a. the words both mean the same.
   b. nausea is the inclination to vomit.
   c. severe vomiting is nausea.
   d. vomiting because of hunger is called nausea.
9. A person acting as a potential distributor of an infection without clinically manifesting the disease is called a
   a. career.
   b. carrier.

c. transmitter.
d. transporter.

10. The process of determining the possible diseases producing different symptoms is referred to as
    a. physical diagnosis.
    b. clinical diagnosis.
    c. comparative diagnosis.
    d. differential diagnosis.
11. A lethal dose of medicine refers to a/the
    a. fatal dose.
    b. small quantity given at intervals.
    c. smallest dose that will be effective.
    d. largest dose safe to administer.
12. Dosimeter measures specify
    a. the dose of medicine given at a time.
    b. booster doses.
    c. absorbed dose of radiation.
    d. the dorsal pressure.
13. Migraine is characterised by .... pain.
    a. burning
    b. shooting
    c. stabbing
    d. throbbing
14. When one is immune to an infection, one
    a. gets it easily.
    b. will not get it.
    c. will spread the infection.
    d. cannot be cured of the infection.
15. A duct conveying secretion from a gland is known as a/an .... duct.
    a. biliary
    b. efferent
    c. lacrimal
    d. lymphatic

16. When there is pus in the stools during diarrhoea, it is called .... diarrhoea.
   a. infantile
   b. lienteric
   c. chronic
   d. purulent
17. Buffy coat is connected to
   a. blood.
   b. dress.
   c. muscles.
   d. skin.
18. Loss of memory relating to isolated events is known as .... amnesia.
   a. retrograde
   b. periodic
   c. tactile
   d. transient
19. When only one small part of the body is anaesthetised, we say that the patient is given .... anaesthesia.
   a. spinal
   b. local
   c. general
   d. neural
20. In the list below, ... is the odd one out.
   a. iris
   b. ossicles
   c. retina
   d. sclera

Verb forms: Irregular Verbs

	present	past	past participle
1.	beat	beat	beaten
2.	become	became	become
3.	begin	began	begun
4.	bend	bent	bent
5.	bind	bound	bound
6.	bleed	bled	bled
7.	blow	blew	blown/blowed
8.	bring	brought	brought
9.	broadcast	broadcast	broadcast
10.	burn	burnt/burned	burnt/burned
11.	burst	burst	burst
12.	buy	bought	bought
13.	catch	caught	caught
14.	choose	chose	chosen
15.	cling	clung	clung
16.	come	came	come
17.	cost	cost	cost
18.	cut	cut	cut
19.	deal	dealt	dealt
20.	do	did	done
21.	draw	drew	drawn
22.	dream	dreamt/dreamed	dreamt/dreamed
23.	drink	drank	drunk
24.	drive	drove	driven
25.	eat	ate	eaten
26.	fall	fell	fallen
27.	feed	fed	fed
28.	feel	felt	felt
29.	fight	fought	fought
30.	find	found	found
31.	fling	flung	flung
32.	forget	forgot	forgotten

33.	freeze	froze	frozen
34.	get	got	got
35.	give	gave	given
36.	go	went	gone
37.	grind	ground	ground
38.	grow	grew	grown
39.	hang	hanged/hung*	hanged/hung*
	(*depending on the meaning of the verb 'hang')		
40.	have	had	had
41.	hear	heard	heard
42.	hide	hid	hidden
43.	hit	hit	hit
44.	hold	held	held
45.	hurt	hurt	hurt
46.	keep	kept	kept
47.	kneel	knelt/kneeled	knelt/kneeled
48.	know	knew	known
49.	lay	laid	laid
50.	lead	led	led
51.	learn	learnt/learned	learnt/learned
52.	leave	left	left
53.	lend	lent	lent
54.	let	let	let
55.	lie	lied/lay*	lied/lain*
	(*depending on the meaning of the verb 'lie')		
56.	lose	lost	lost
57.	make	made	made
58.	meet	met	met
59.	pay	paid	paid
60.	put	put	put
61.	read	read	read
62.	ring	rang	rung
63.	run	ran	run
64.	say	said	said
65.	see	saw	seen

66. shake	shook	shaken
67. show	showed	showed/shown
68. shrink	shrunk/shrank	shrunk
69. sing	sang	sung
70. sink	sank	sunk
71. sit	sat	sat
72. sleep	slept	slept
73. slide	slid	slid
74. slit	slit	slit
75. smell	smelt/smelled	smelt/smelled
76. speak	spoke	spoken
77. spend	spent	spent
78. split	split	split
79. spoil	spoilt/spoiled	spoilt/spoiled
80. spread	spread	spread
81. stand	stood	stood
82. steal	stole	stolen
83. stick	stuck	stuck
84. sting	stung	stung
85. strike	struck	struck
86. swell	swelled	swelled/swollen
87. swim	swam	swum
88. take	took	taken
89. teach	taught	taught
90. tear	tore	torn
91. tell	told	told
92. think	thought	thought
93. throw	threw	thrown
94. thrust	thrust	thrust
95. undertake	undertook	undertaken
96. wake	woke	woken
97. wear	wore	worn
98. weep	wept	wept
99. win	won	won
100. write	wrote	written

Pronunciation Key

VOWELS AND DIPHTHONGS

	symbol	word	pronunciation
1.	/iː/	seat	/siːt/
2.	/ɪ/	sit	/sɪt/
3.	/e/	set	/set/
4.	/æ/	sat	/sæt/
5.	/ɑː/	card	/kɑːd/
6.	/ɔː/	born	/bɔːn/
7.	/ɒ/	box	/bɒks/
8.	/ʊ/	book	/bʊk/
9.	/uː/	boon	/buːn/
10.	/ʌ/	bus	/bʌs/
11.	/ɜː/	bird	/bɜːd/
12.	/ə/	bigger	/bigə/
13.	/eɪ/	play	/pleɪ/
14.	/aɪ/	buy	/baɪ/
15.	/ɔɪ/	boy	/bɔɪ/
16.	/aʊ/	out	/aʊt/
17.	/əʊ/	go	/gəʊ/
18.	/ɪə/	here	/hɪə/
19.	/eə/	there	/ðeə/
20.	/ʊə/	poor	/pʊə/

CONSONANTS

	symbol	word	pronunciation
1.	/p/	pin	/pɪn/
2.	/b/	bin	/bɪn/
3.	/t/	tin	/tɪn/
4.	/d/	din	/dɪn/
5.	/k/	kin	/kɪn/
6.	/g/	gun	/gʌn/
7.	/tʃ/	church	/tʃɜːtʃ/

8.	/dʒ/	jug	/dʒʌg/
9.	/θ/	thin	/θɪn/
10.	/ð/	that	/ðæt/
11.	/f/	fine	/faɪn/
12.	/v/	van	/væn/
13.	/s/	soon	/su:n/
14.	/z/	zoo	/zu:/
15.	/ʃ/	shine	/ʃaɪn/
16.	/ʒ/	pleasure	/pleʒə/
17.	/h/	help	/help/
18.	/m/	man	/mæn/
19.	/n/	neat	/ni:t/
20.	/ŋ/	sing	/siŋ/
21.	/l/	live	/lɪv/
22.	/w/	win	/wɪn/
23.	/r/	run	/rʌn/
24.	/j/	young	/jʌŋ/